Patterns of Software

Tales from the Software Community

Richard P. Gabriel

OXFORD UNIVERSITY PRESS
New York   Oxford

Oxford University Press

Oxford   New York
Athens   Auckland   Bangkok   Bogotá   Bombay
Buenos Aires   Calcutta   Cape Town   Dar es Salaam
Delhi   Florence   Hong Kong   Istanbul   Karachi
Kuala Lumpur   Madras   Madrid   Melbourne
Mexico City   Nairobi   Paris   Singapore
Taipei   Tokyo   Toronto   Warsaw

and associated companies in
Berlin   Ibadan

First published by Oxford University Press, Inc., 1996

First issued as an Oxford University Press paperback, 1998

Oxford is a registered trademark of Oxford University Press

Library of Congress Cataloging-in-Publication Data
Gabriel, Richard P.
Patterns of software: tales from the software community.
p. cm. Includes Bibliographical references
ISBN 0-19-5100269-X
ISBN 0-19-512123-6 (Pbk.)
1. Computer software—Development. 2. Object-oriented
programming (Computer science) I. Title.
QA76.76D47G33 1996
005. 1—dc 2095-41883

1 3 5 7 9 10 8 6 4 2

Printed in the United States of America
on acid-free paper

To Jo Lawless, who led me away from the lion

Midway on our life's journey, I found myself
In dark woods, the right road lost. To tell
About those woods is hard—so tangled and rough

And savage that thinking of it now, I feel
the old fear stirring: death is hardly more bitter.

Dante, *Inferno*

Foreword

A year or two ago, I was astonished to get several letters from different people in the computer science field, telling me that my name was a household word in the software engineering community: specifically in the field of object-oriented technology. I had never even heard of object-oriented programming, and I had absolutely no idea that computer scientists knew my work, or found it useful or interesting; all this was a revelation to me. It was a pleasant revelation, but one that I did not really grasp at first; nor did I think much about it. I assumed the people who wrote to me were exaggerating anyway, out of politeness.

Then, one of these people, Marc Sewell from IBM in Atlanta, came to see me and told me much the same, to my face, in a discussion over coffee. Naturally, I assumed he too was exaggerating. When I expressed my surprise and doubts about the depth of this "alexandrian patterns movement," he told me that in any given issue of *The Journal of Object-Oriented Programming*, there was almost certain to be some mention of my name. To prove it the next day he came with the current issue of The Journal of Object-Oriented Programming. There was in it, an article by Richard Gabriel, the essay that appears in this book as the chapter entitled "The Bead Game, Rugs, and Beauty."

I sat down to read the article; and for the first time, became truly interested in this connection. What was fascinating to me, indeed quite astonishing, was that in his essay I found out that a computer scientist, not known to me, and whom I had never met, seemed to understand more about what I had done and was trying to do in my own field than my own colleagues who are architects.

Indeed, a cool factual appraisal or summary of my lifelong struggle with the problems of what to do in the field of architecture, has rarely been written objectively in the architectural literature. Architects, many of them agonizingly tied to a field which does not work, are mentally and emotionally tied up in the problems of the discipline, are often shocked by what I have said (either because it makes them angry or because it makes them ecstatic), and have therefore rarely given large-scale cool appraisals of what I have written. Principally, I think this is because what I have to say, once taken seriously, has such enormous basement-shaking results for architecture that it irrevocably changes the field.

Yet here in Richard Gabriel's essay, far away from the internecine struggles of architecture, and without the sense of panic that so often accompanies reviews of my work in the architectural press, was sober stuff, written by a person who clearly understood it profoundly, and had taken the trouble to make himself familiar with a great deal of what I have done and written.

I found that the scientific and artistic problems I have described in my work, are being assessed, reported, without bias or prejudice, just as a matter of fact, with failures and successes given equal weight, and with the same feelings that I myself have about the task in hand, the experiments, the attempts, what works, what doesn't work—with discussion of what works and what doesn't written in rather plain English. It was tremendously refreshing, and stimulating. I was by now astonished and delighted.

That was about a year ago. Then, out of the blue, Bill Zobrist, an editor at Oxford University Press, sent me this book and asked me to read it and comment on it.

Now, I am on different ground. Suddenly the tables are turned, and I have to struggle to make out what is actually being *said* in the field of object technology and software engineering. Can I understand it? Within my limited understanding, does it make sense? Is the analogy, metaphor, or extension, from architecture to programming legitimate? Suddenly, from being reviewed, I became the reviewer.

In architecture, the question, the question I have been asking is very simple: "Can we do better? Does all this talk help to make better buildings?"

Are the questions being raised by Richard Gabriel equally straightforward? I think they are not. His questions, though in simple words, are not only about this kind of programming. He seems, to me, to be trying to jolt the software engineering community into an entirely new state of awareness, trying to create the possibility of a new field, more elevated, more marvelous, without knowing whether this is possible, because it has never been done before.

In this sense, as he describes himself, he is a Dr. Johnson, a "critick," not necessarily a practical man, but a goad, a spiritual leader, a man who sees possibilities and the glimpse of some distant promised land in software engineering.

But still a fundamental question of practicality must lie at the forefront. Does all this thought, philosophy, help people to write better programs? For the instigators of this approach to programming too, as in architecture, I suppose a critical question is simply this: Do the people who write these programs, using alexandrian patterns, or any other methods, *do they do better work?* Are the programs better? Do they get better results, more efficiently, more speedily, more profoundly? Do people actually feel more alive when using them? Is what is accomplished by these programs, and by the people who run these programs and by the people who are affected by them, better, more elevated, more insightful, better by ordinary spiritual standards?

Here I am at a grave disadvantage. I am not a programmer, and I do not know how to judge programs. But, speaking only about what appears in this book, I must confess to a slight— reluctant—skepticism. I have not yet seen evidence of this improvement in an actual program. Of course my ignorance is such that I would not have good instincts, at first anyway, about a given bit of code, not even enough to be able to say "This is a beautiful program, this one less so." I do not therefore ask these probing questions in a negative or hostile spirit at all. I ask them, because I hope, and believe it may propel readers of this book, programmers themselves, into trying to do better. But I cannot tell, as yet, whether the probing questions asked in this book, will actually lead to better programs, nor even what a better program *is*.

In my life as an architect, I find that the single thing which inhibits young professionals, new students most severely, *is their acceptance of standards that are too low*. If I ask a student whether her design is as good as Chartres, she often smiles tolerantly at me as if to say, "Of course not, that isn't what I am trying to do. . . . I could never do that."

Then, I express my disagreement, and tell her: "That standard *must* be our standard. If you are going to be a builder, no other standard is worthwhile. That is what I expect of myself in my own buildings, and it is what I expect of my students." Gradually, I show the students that they have a *right* to ask this of themselves, and *must* ask this of themselves. Once that level of standard is in their minds, they will be able to figure out, for themselves, how to do better, how to make something that is as profound as that.

Two things emanate from this changed standard. First, the work becomes more fun. It is deeper, it never gets tiresome or boring, because one can never really attain this standard. One's work becomes a lifelong work, and one keeps trying and trying. So it becomes very fulfilling, to live in the light of a goal like this.

But secondly, it does change what people are trying to do. It takes away from them the everyday, lower-level aspiration that is purely technical in nature, (and which we have come to accept) and replaces it with something deep, which will make a real difference to all of us that inhabit the earth.

I would like, in the spirit of Richard Gabriel's searching questions, to ask the same of the software people who read this book. But at once I run into a problem. For a programmer, what is a comparable goal? What is the Chartres of programming? What task is at a high enough level to inspire people writing programs, to reach for the stars? Can you write a computer program on the same level as Fermat's last theorem? Can you write a program which has the enabling power of Dr. Johnson's dictionary? Can you write a program which has the productive power of Watt's steam engine? Can you write a program which overcomes the gulf between the technical culture of our civilization, and which inserts itself into our human life as deeply as Eliot's poems of the wasteland or Virginia Woolf's *The Waves*?

I know Richard Gabriel opens these kinds of doors. I feel, blowing through these pages, a breeze, an inspiration which could begin to make a programmer ask herself these kinds of questions, ones that reach for the stars.

But so far, I do not yet see the programs themselves to fulfill this promise. So far, there is still the danger that all this paraphernalia, all this beautiful work, thought, and inspiration is only marginal comment on an activity which is still static, still not actually, *as a program*, really better.

In Richard Gabriel's next book, I would hope to see examples of programs which make you gasp because of their beauty. And I would hope for a growing knowledge, in the field of software engineering, of what this means.

Perhaps too, a knowledge more widespread in our culture, so that people outside the field, lay people like me, could also begin to grasp the beauty of programs, could have some idea of what it might mean . . . and would above all, feel helped in their lives, on the same level that they are helped by horses, and roses, and a crackling fire.

That—I think—has not happened yet.

Will this book make it happen? This is the critical issue above all, our ability to make real improvement in the geometry of buildings, in the geometry of code, in the quality of buildings, and in the quality of programs.

As I reached the end of *Patterns of Software*, I realized that my story as told by Richard Gabriel—was incomplete in a number of important ways, which may have direct bearing on the computer scientists struggling with just these questions.

Richard Gabriel focuses, very much, on *unsolved* problems, on the struggle and the path to almost ineluctable difficulties in architecture. He does not comment, perhaps enough, on the fact that these problems are solvable in practice, in fact are *being* solved right now. The geometry of life, in buildings, which I wrote about for 25 years, in order to attain it, is finally being attained, just now.

That is of crucial importance, because if the analogy, or parallel, between architecture and software engineering that he has drawn in this book, has validity, then the fact that it is solvable, must have a parallel too. If the parallel exists, then the questions are not only inspiring, but there really are programs, code, etc., which have these nearly magical qualities that breath life. And programs and code with these qualities are attainable, *now*, in our lifetime, as a practical matter in the world of programming. This is a stunning conclusion, one which Richard Gabriel has not sufficiently emphasized.

In order to better understand how these problems might be solved in software engineering, we might look at where Richard Gabriel's examination of my work stops short and at the remainder of my work, particularly, the progress my colleagues and I have made since 1985. It is in this time period that the goal of our thirty-year program has been achieved for the first time. We have begun to make buildings which really do have the quality I sought for all those years. It may seem immodest, to presuppose such success, but I have been accurate, painfully accurate in my criticism of my own work, for thirty years, so I must also be accurate about our success. This has come about in large part because, since 1983, our group has worked as architects and general contractors. Combining these two aspects of construction in a single office, we have achieved what was impossible when one accepts the split between design and construction. But it has come about, too, because theoretical discoveries, considerably more potent than the pattern language have supplemented the power of the patterns, and the way they work, and their effectiveness.

In 1992 a pair of articles appeared that show, in short summary form, what can be achieved by these ideas when you bring together the roles of architect and builder, within the framework of the ideas of *A Pattern Language* and *The Timeless Way of Building*.*

The articles describe a number of my building projects that have indeed succeeded; they are both large and small, and include both private and public buildings. The first article gives concrete glimpses of material beauty, achieved in our time. Here the life, dreamed about, experienced in ancient buildings, has been arrived at by powerful new ways of unfolding space. These methods have their origin in pattern languages, but rely on new ways of creating order, in space, by methods that are more similar to biological models, than they are to extant theories of construction. Above all, they reach the life of buildings, by a continuous unfolding process in which structure evolves almost continuously, under the criterion of emerging life, and does not stop until life is actually achieved. The trick is, that this is accomplished with finite means, and without back-tracking. The second article describes the nature of the social process I believe is needed in the design-construction business to get these results; it is a kind of Hippocratic oath for the future. The second shows what kind of social and professional program may be needed to change things effectively in the world. If anything similar is

* Ziva Freiman and Thomas Fisher, "The Real Meaning of Architecture," *Progressive Architecture*, July 1991, pp. 100–107, and Christopher Alexander, "Manifesto 1991," *Progressive Architecture*, July 1991, pp. 108–112.

needed for computer programmers, it would be fascinating. Both these articles may have a bearing on the way software people understand this material.

A full description of all these new developments, together with a radical new theoretical underpinning, will appear shortly in *The Nature of Order*, the book on geometry and process which has taken more than 20 years to write, and is just now being published. The book, being published by Oxford, will appear in three volumes: *Book 1: The Phenomenon of Life, Book 2: The Process of Creating Life*, and *Book 3: The Luminous Ground*. These three books show in copious detail, with illustrations from many recently-built projects all over the world, how, precisely how, these profound results can be achieved. What is perhaps surprising, is that in these books I have shown, too, that a radical new cosmology is needed to achieve the right results. In architecture, at least, the ideas of *A Pattern Language* cannot be applied mechanically. Instead, these ideas—patterns—are hardly more than glimpses of a much deeper level of structure, and is ultimately within this deeper level of structure, that the origin of life occurs. The quality without a name, first mentioned in *The Timeless Way of Building*, finally appears explicitly, at this level of structure.

With the publication of *The Nature of Order* and with the mature development of my work in construction and design, the problems that I began to pose 35 years ago are finally being solved. There are immense difficulties, naturally, in implementing this program throughout the field of architecture and building. But the feasibility of the whole matter, and the extent to which it is well-defined, can, I think, no longer be in doubt. What is most important is that all this can actually be *done*. Buildings with these qualities, can be made, in our time, within the context of the modern age, using modern and hypermodern techniques. That is the prototype fact, which must, perhaps, appeal to those in software engineering, who hope to arrive at similar results within their field.

I am very sorry that Richard Gabriel and I did not meet, and that this material was not available to him, because I believe that he wants our quest to have succeeded, at least succeeded better than it seemed to him it had as of 1985 when we were just beginning to see the last part of the way. Because I get the impression that road seems harder to software people than maybe it did to me, that the quality software engineers might want to strive for is more elusive because the artifacts—the programs, the code—are more abstract, more intellectual, more soulless than the places we live in every day.

Once again, for the readers of *this* book, the question remains, whether this— the solution of the architectural problem—like anything else in architecture, has a true parallel in the field of software engineering.

I do find the vision which Gabriel summons up, the possibility of a world of computer programs which really do meet the Zen-like conditions that I have brought to light, quite fascinating in their implications for the world.

Although, by now, we all experience computer programs—indirectly at the very least— and benefit from them, the vision of a technical world out of control, soulless, in which we are merely digits, still looms large, and for some is getting larger. It has frightened the core of modern man. Thoughtful people wonder, no doubt, whether humanity can be regained or maintained.

If the heart of human existence, what matters most deeply to man, woman, child, really can find its way into computer programming, and into the programs, and into the meanings of those programs, and into the actual code and substance of those programs, and into their effects—then the future world will be changed immeasurably.

And if that happens, Richard Gabriel must take enormous credit for his courage in writing such a crazy and inspiring book, based on the work of a visionary drunk in God, outside his field and outside the field of his readers. I should like to take my leave of him, and you, and salute my friend, whom I have never met, and hope that his wish is fulfilled, and that looking back from the year 2100 he may be known, in some new fashion, as a Dr. Johnson of the twenty-first century.

Berkeley, Calif.   Christopher Alexander
May 1996

Preface

The essays in this book started out as a series of columns for the *Journal of Object-Oriented Programming*. I was trying to model myself somewhat after Samuel Johnson, and the series was aimed at being the digital age's equivalent of *The Rambler*. I'm certain I didn't succeed in matching Johnson's wit and style, but I matched at least two of his characteristics—procrastination and laziness. Johnson was well known for writing his essays right up to the deadline, often keeping the publisher's runner waiting for the manuscript as Johnson completed it. In fact, you can notice the effect in many of his essays: An essay starts to make an argument in one direction (corresponding to the first sheets Johnson handed the runner) and then the argument shifts radically or even to the opposite pole as Johnson continued writing and thinking—but revision of the earlier parts was impossible, as it was being typeset for final copy as Johnson pondered.

For my essays I chose the stance of *critic at large*. In this role I attempted to examine topics of interest to the object-oriented programming community from the point of view of someone whose experience has always had a sour component—this will be the subject of some of the essays. I had been working in the object-oriented field for seven years when I started writing them.

Object-oriented programming has a very long history, which the newly initiated sometimes finds surprising. First designed primarily as a means of simulation, later as programming languages for children, object-oriented languages have become nearly mainstream, largely as a means of achieving reuse and productivity.

You see, the history of computing is replete with attempts at making programming easier and, more important, cheaper. Current software makes machines of a sort previously unknown and with capabilities unheard of, partly because there can be built into them some small portion of reason and consideration and intelligent—rather than merely mechanical—reaction. Automobiles can run for dozens of thousands of miles without tuning because their internal operation is governed by software—it's almost more likely that your car can be fixed by a Ph.D. in computer science than by your grandfather's auto mechanic.

When we start cataloging the gains in tools sitting on a computer, the benefits of software are amazing. But, if the benefits of software are so great, why do we worry about making it easier—don't the ends pay for the means? We worry because making such software is extraordinarily hard and almost no one can do it—the detail is exhausting, the creativity required is extreme, the hours of failure upon failure requiring patience and persistence would tax anyone claiming to be sane. Yet we require that people with such characteristics be found and employed and employed cheaply.

We've tried to make programming easier, with abstraction as a tool, with higher-level programming languages, faster computers, design methodologies, with rules of thumb and courses and apprenticeships and mentoring, with automatic programming and artificial intelligence. Compilers, debuggers, editors, programming environments. With structured programming and architectural innovations.

With object-oriented programming.

But programming still requires people to work both alone and in teams, and when people are required to think in order to achieve, inherent limitations rule. Object-oriented programming—which is merely a set of concepts and programming languages to support those concepts—cannot remove the need to think hard and to plan things, to be creative and to overcome failures and obstacles, to find a way to work together when the ego says not to, that the failures are too many and too pervasive.

Reuse, productivity, reliability—these are values prized by managers and moneymakers.

Software creators are usually called *engineers*, a connotation that usually brings to mind a person who applies well-known principles and methods to create variations on known themes. For example, a bridge builder is an engineer who uses a long list of known techniques to erect a structure to traverse rivers, chasms, and rough terrain while supporting a certain load while withstanding natural forces like wind and earthquakes.

Even though the word engineer comes from the same basic root as ingenuity does, the feeling one gets when hearing the word is of careful, detailed, nearly plodding predictability of work. This makes sense to a degree because engineering disciplines frequently have handbooks from which they work that prescribe a series of rules and principles and ways of solving problems according to a long tradition and experience. For instance, bridge builders have centuries of experience bridge building to draw upon.

Building software—some call it *software engineering*—is only 30 or 40 years old, and it shares with other engineering disciplines virtually nothing. Engineering teams for bridge building are composed of well-known roles whereas in software we are still experimenting. While building bridges, known solutions are adapted to the situation at hand whereas in software we frequently need to invent new techniques and technology. What's easy and hard is not known, and there are very few physical principles to guide and constrain us.

To emphasize this, consider that not only is there a large set of principles for bridge building but there are hundreds of known examples of bridges and even we, as laypeople, know of some of the best examples and even one of the worst— the Tacoma Narrows Bridge, which catastrophically collapsed 50 years ago. But in software, there isn't even a literature of programs that programmers know and can talk about.

The Tacoma Narrows Bridge—let's think about it for a minute. This was a bridge built in Washington State across a strait in the 1940s. Because of the gorge it spanned, it was subject to strong winds. The engineers who built it adapted a design used on the East Coast that was known to be able to withstand strong wind. However, the designers added a feature for pedestrians, a low windbreak about the height of a guardrail that would protect people and cars from the wind. But as soon as this fence was built, the bridge started oscillating from the wind, which flowed over it like an airfoil.

After a few months on a day when the wind was particularly strong and at a particular speed, the airfoil started to oscillate wildly, and the bridge collapsed. The incident was captured on newsreels. The only casualty was a dog who would not get out of a car when its master tried to coax him out to safety.

Even though it was a disaster, the methodology was to modify an existing solution, and when it failed its failure was analyzed. How often does that happen in software? Almost never, because such failures are simply locked away and forgotten—perhaps the folks who participated learn something, but the project is rarely viewed by people outside the project, and there is little interest in the failure itself except perhaps because of its effects on the organization that sponsored it.

So yes, we are engineers in the sense of using cleverness and inventiveness to create an artful engine that is itself clever. But we don't have—perhaps yet—the inherent predictability of schedules and results to be engineers in the sense most people, especially businessfolk, expect.

One of my goals in writing these essays was to bring out the reality of commercial software development and to help people realize that right now software development—except when a project essentially is creating a near variant of an existing program—is in a state where the artifact desired is brand new and its construction is unknown, and therefore the means to approach its construction is unknown and possibly difficult to ascertain; and, furthermore, a group of people is trying to work together—maybe for the first time—to accomplish it. An image I like to use is that every large software project is similar to the first attempt to build a flying-buttress construction cathedral. Imagine how many of them collapsed before we figured out how to build them.

Software development is done by people with human concerns; although someday this component will be a smaller part of the total picture, today it is the high-order bit. The software community approaches these issues with high hopes and a pride in the term engineer. I approach it as a critic.

Let me turn to what I hoped to accomplish as a critic at large. I start with a quote from Samuel Johnson's *The Idler*:

> *Criticism is a study by which men grow important and formidable at a very small expence. The power of invention has been conferred by nature upon few, and the labour of learning those sciences which may by mere labour be obtained is too great to be willingly endured; but every man can exert such judgement as he has upon the works of others; and he whom nature has made weak, and idleness keeps ignorant, may yet support his vanity by the name of a Critick.* (Number 60, Saturday, June 9, 1759)

A critic, at his best, aims at raising questions that otherwise might remain hidden. The role of a critic is to look at things in new ways, to present a perspective that others with less time on their hands can use as the basis for real progress, to ask the question that turns the course of inquiry from a backwater whirlpool toward rapids of exciting new work.

So don't look to these essays for answers—I planned not to, and yet dare not, claim new insight or wisdom: You have to find that for yourself or within yourself. I claim only to be able to expand the playing field to include new considerations and maybe new perspectives.

However, be warned: Nothing is off limits for me. There are no dead ends I won't go down, no agreements I'll honor about what's on or off limits. Every idea out there is fair game—yours included.

But don't worry that your pet idea will be abused or harmed—again Johnson:

> *This profession has one recommendation peculiar to itself, that it gives vent to malignity without real mischief. No genius was ever blasted by the breath of criticks. The poison which, if confined, would have burst the heart, fumes away in empty hisses, and malice is set at ease with very little danger to merit. The Critick is the only man whose triumph is without another's pain, and whose greatness does not rise upon another's ruin.*

The bias I started with in these essays was this:

The promise of object-oriented programming—and of programming languages themselves—has yet to be fulfilled. That promise is to make plain to computers and to other programmers the communication of the computational intentions of a programmer or a team of programmers, throughout the long and change-plagued life of the program. The failure of programming languages to do this is the result of a variety of failures of some of us as researchers and the rest of us as practitioners to take seriously the needs of people in programming rather than the needs of the computer and the compiler writer. To some degree, this failure can be attributed to a failure of the design methodologies we have used to guide our design of languages, and to larger degree it is due to our failure to take seriously the needs of the programmer and maintainer in caretaking the code for a large system over its life cycle.

ৡ৹   ৡ৹   ৡ৹

This book is broken into five parts:

- Patterns of Software

- Languages

- What We Do

- Life of the Critic

- Into the Ground

"Patterns of Software" explores the work of the architect Christopher Alexander as it relates to the creation of software. Christopher Alexander has spent the bulk of his professional life—from around 1960 through the mid-1990s—trying to find the way that those who build buildings, cities, and towns also create beauty and what Alexander calls the *quality without a name*.

Over the last decade, the computer software community discovered Alexander and his concept of *pattern languages* and has tried to incorporate those ideas into software design. The essays in this part examine Alexander's quest for the quality without a name and for beauty and try to see what connections to software, especially object-oriented software, are appropriate.

"Languages" looks at programming languages and how software developers use and react to them. The choice of a programming language seems as sacred and personal as the choice of religion, and that choice often favors languages whose performance characteristics match computer architecture capabilities rather than the capabilities of the people who use programming languages.

"What We Do" sketches the activities we as computer scientists and software developers do and how folks outside our community view us. Here I talk a little bit about writing—which is dear to me—and how our assumptions about the obviousness of the importance of what we do might not and is not shared by the rest of the world.

"Life of the Critic" is an intellectual autobiography in which I hope to show how I arrived at my views and why I drifted toward the role of critic. I also hope to show that you don't have to start out with a silver spoon in your mouth to be able to make a contribution to humanity—that even someone with as checkered and failure-ridden past as I have can contribute. Many times in my life I despaired when I compared my progress with that of my fellows who never seemed to have had a slip in their careers, and part of my goal, therefore, is to show that someone of average intelligence and talents can do well, even in our modern world.

"Into the Ground" is the story of the company I founded—from its birth in 1984 until its death in 1994. The lessons to be learned from this experience center on the fact that the company carried out its technical agenda perfectly yet it failed miserably, and accompanied by circumstances almost unprecedented in Silicon Valley startup history.

My overall bias is that technology, science, engineering, and company organization are all secondary to the people and human concerns in the endeavor. Companies, ideas, processes, and approaches ultimately fail when humanity is forgotten, ignored, or placed second. Alexander knew this, but his followers in the software pattern language community do not. Computer scientists and developers don't seem to know it, either.

These essays . . . these essays aim to correct that.

જ   જ   જ

I would like to thank Christopher Alexander for his deep, prophetic work on architecture, patterns, and beauty; for writing the Foreword; and for providing original art. Katalin Bende, in Alexander's office, was most gracious in providing assistance with the artwork.

Some essays are reprinted with permission from the Journal of Object-Oriented Programming (copyright © 1991–1993 SIGS Publications, 71 West Twenty-third Street, Third floor, New York, New York 10010). Quotes from *Christopher Alexander: The Search for a New Paradigm in Architecture* by Stephen Grabow were provided by permission from International Thomson Publishing Services Ltd.

Bill Zobrist, Krysia Bebick, and Irene Pavitt of Oxford University Press provided tremendous editorial assistance and support during the preparation of this book.

Mountain View, Calif.   R.P.G.

Contents

V. Into the Ground

PART I

PATTERNS OF SOFTWARE

Reuse Versus Compression

Maybe it's my failing memory, but I recall that the hook that grabbed the mainstream world and pulled it toward object-oriented programming was reuse. One of the larger problems that development managers face is how to get big software projects done fast. Most people agree that maintenance is a big part of the overall software problem, but to organizations whose survival depends on getting out new projects or products, the important issue is getting the new software done.

Within each organization writing a lot of software—and among many organizations writing a lot of software—it seems that a lot of that software should be reusable. If this were true, then it would be possible to take some of the code that already exists and put it toward the new project, thereby reducing the time to produce the desired software, Furthermore, if code is reused, it is more likely to be well tested and possibly bug free, and even if it isn't, the maintenance of the various programs that use the reused code should be easier.

Reuse is not a new idea. For decades languages have supported the notion of libraries. A library is a set of subroutines, usually in a particular application area. Old examples are the scientific subroutine libraries for FORTRAN. A similar idea is the Collected Algorithms published by ACM years ago in an ALGOL-like publication language. I remember when I was a kid in 1968 looking up algorithms for sorting and searching in my first programming job.

However, what every manager learns is that reuse under these circumstances requires a process of reuse or at least a policy. First, you need to have a central repository of code. It doesn't help if developers have to go around to other developers to locate code you might be able to use. Some organizations are small enough that the developers can have group meetings to discuss needs and supplies of code.

Second, there has to be a means of locating the right piece of code, which usually requires a good classification scheme. It does no good to have the right piece of code if no one can find it. Classification in the world of books, reports, magazines, and the like is a profession, called *cataloging*. Librarians help people find the book . But few software organizations can afford a software cataloger, let alone a librarian to help find the software for its developers. This is because when a development manager has the choice of hiring another developer or a software librarian, the manager will always hire the developer. It's worth looking at why this is, and I'll return to it later.

Third, there must be good documentation of what each piece of code in the repository does. This includes not only the interface and its purpose but also enough about the innards of the code—its performance and resource use—to enable a developer to use it wisely. A developer must know these other things, for example, in order to meet performance goals. In many cases such documentation is just the code itself, but this information could be better provided by ordinary documentation; but again, a development manager would prefer to hire a developer rather than a documentation person.

For a lot of pieces of code it is just plain simpler to write it yourself than to go through the process of finding and understanding reusable code. Therefore, what development managers have discovered is that the process-oriented world of reuse has too many barriers for effective use.

Looking at the nature of this approach to reuse we can see that it is focused on reusing code from one project to another rather than within a project; the mechanism for reuse is an organization-wide process.

Enter object-oriented programming. The primary point of object-oriented programming is to move the focus of program design from algorithms to data structures. In particular, a data structure is elevated to the point that it can contain its own operations.

But such data structures—called *objects*—often are related to one another in a particular way: One is just like another except for some additions or slight modifications. In this situation, there will be too much duplication if such objects are completely separate, so a means of inheriting code—*methods*—was developed.

Hence we see the claim of reuse in object-oriented languages: When writing a single program, a programmer reuses code already developed by inheriting that code from more general objects or classes. There is a beauty to this sort of reuse: It requires no particular process because it is part of the nature of the language.

In short, *subclassing* is the means of reuse.

Despite this simplified view of reuse, the idea that object-oriented languages have reuse as part of their very essence proved to be a large attraction to the mainstream community. To be sure, there were other attractions as well; here are some:

- Objects and classes of objects are a natural way for programmers to organize programs.

- Systems written with objects and classes are simpler to extend and customize than traditionally constructed ones.

ൠ   ൠ   ൠ

However, the form of reuse in object-oriented languages hardly satisfies the broad goals of software development. What I want to suggest is a better word than *reuse* and maybe a better concept for the reuse-like property of object-oriented languages.

The word (and concept) is *compression*. Compression is the characteristic of a piece of text that the meaning of any part of it is "larger" than that piece has by itself. This is accomplished by the context being rich and each part of the text drawing on that context—each word draws part of its meaning from its surroundings. A familiar example outside programming is poetry whose heavily layered meanings can seem dense because of the multiple images it generates and the way each new image or phrase draws from several of the others. Poetry uses compressed language.

Here is a simple single-sentence example: *My horse was hungry, so I filled a morat with oats and put it on him to eat.*

This sentence is compressed enough that the meaning of the strange word *morat* is clear—it's a feed bag. Pronouns work because of compression.

Compression in object-oriented languages is created when the definition of a subclass bases a great deal of its meaning on the definitions of its superclasses. If you make a subclass of a class which adds one instance variable and two methods for it, the expression of that new class will be simply the new variable, two methods, and a reference to the existing class. To some, the programmer writing this subclass is reusing the code in the superclass, but a better way to look at it is that the programmer is writing a compressed definition, the bulk of whose details are taken from the context in which the superclass already exists.

To see this, note that the subclass definition is frequently some distance from the superclass definition, and so the programmer is relying on knowledge of the superclass to write the shorthand definition.

Compressed code has an interesting property: The more of it you write—the further down the class hierarchy you go—the more compressed the new code becomes. This is good in at least one way: Adding new code is very compactly done. For a development manager this *can* mean that the new code can be written more quickly.

Here is where the change of perspective can help us: Compression has clear disadvantages, and these disadvantages can help explain why object-oriented languages have not solved the software problem (of course, there are many reasons, but this is just the first essay, after all).

Compression is a little dangerous because it requires the programmer to understand a fair amount about the context from which compressed code will take its meaning. Not only does this require available source code or excellent documentation, but the nature of inherited language also forces the programmer to understand the source or documentation. If a programmer needs a lot of context to understand a program he needs to extend, he may make mistake because of misunderstandings.

Furthermore, even if the new code—the compressed code—is compact, it will take at least as much time and effort to write as it would to write the uncompressed code, unless the overall complexity and size of the total code is small or unless the person writing the code has the existing code firmly in mind.

Maintaining compressed code requires understanding its context, which can be difficult. The primary feature for easy maintenance is *locality*: Locality is that characteristic of source code that enables a programmer to understand that source by looking at only a small portion of it. Compressed code doesn't have this property, unless you are using a very fancy programming environment.

Compression has another obvious problem. If you build derived code that tightly depends on some base code, then changing the base code can be expensive and dangerous. If the developer of the base code is not the same person as the developer of derived code, the derived code can be in jeopardy. This is just the problem of all by-reference relationships. Compression in poetry is fine because the ultimate definitions of the words and phrases are outside the poet's mind. Not so for compression in programs: The meanings of the words—the classes—are determined by the programmer. This problem is not unique to class-based compression but applies to any abstraction-based compression.

I don't want to imply that compression is bad—in fact, it is an important resource for incremental definition—but abstractional problems like the risk of changing base code can get in the way.

Compression doesn't help interproject reuse, because to do so requires exporting classes that can be reused. This simply lands us in the classic reuse situation we had earlier, in which the primary barrier to reuse is one of process rather than of technology.

ॐ   ॐ   ॐ

Remember I stated that a development manager will always hire a developer over someone whose job is to effect reuse. Why is this?

Some of the reasons should now be apparent. First, reuse is easiest within a project instead of between them. A manager's success depends on performance on a given project and not on performance over several projects. And preparing code for reuse requires additional work, not only by the reuse expert but also by developers. Therefore, preparing for reuse has a cost for any given project.

Finally, a project's success often depends at least partly on the performance of the code that is developed. The development manager knows that plenty of code to be developed really is different from existing code if for no other reason than the new code has to be specialized to the particular situation to be fast enough. Therefore, in this situation reuse doesn't help very much.

What we've seen is that reuse is properly a process issue, and individual organizations need to decide whether they believe in its long-term benefits. Object-oriented languages provide compression, which can substitute for reuse within a program, but at a cost in maintenance.

Compression is not reuse, and both reuse and compression have their costs and savings.

~

Habitability and Piecemeal Growth

*The sun paints the scattered clouds red, paints the hills across the Bay
a deeper red. Moment by moment the sun's light flares windows in
the hills, moving upward as twilight approaches. The programmer
looks up from his screen to watch. He sees headlights moving one way
and taillights the other along either side of the highway spine. Home-
lights click on, and the Bay is a silhouette. His daughter: Will she be
too petrified to dance? Will she miss the cue? If only he could help her
pass by her fear. Reaching to the right of the mouse, he lifts his Coke
and drains it, saves his buffers, drifts his eyes to the sensual movement of the highway, pausing his mind as it passes over a detail in the
code he's just typed. The thought passes before crystallizing, so he puts
the CDs in his blue Kelty pack—and heads for the recital.*

Code is written by people. And people have a lot on their minds, they have lives to
lead, and those lives intrude on their thinking. You might pay a developer for a
full eight-hour day, but how much of that day is truly yours? Of course, not all of
us are software development managers, but the concerns of these managers
should rightfully be concerns of ours—concerns of language designers. The
astute software manager knows that just about every programmer except the
pathological workaholic trades his hours of overtime for hours of undertime. The
manager goes all out to ensure that the needs of the developer are met—home
terminals, sunny offices, minimal meetings, meals during the big push, and a
healthy ego boost from time to time.

If the software manager knows that people and their habits are the determining factor in software development, why don't language and system designers?
Here is what Stroustrup says about the design of C++:

> *C++ is a general purpose programming language designed to make
> programming more enjoyable for the serious programmer.* (Strous-
> trup 1987)

9

This is an interesting idea—no doubt it would be a surprise to most C++ programmers. But, Stroustrup goes on a little more honestly to say:

> C++ retains C's ability to deal efficiently with the fundamental objects of the hardware (bits, bytes, words, addresses, etc.). This allows the user-defined types to be implemented with a pleasing degree of efficiency.... Features that would incur run-time or memory overheads even when not used were avoided.... C++ types and data-hiding features rely on compile-time analysis of programs to prevent accidental corruption of data.... They can, however, be used freely without incurring run-time or space overheads.
> (Stroustrup 1987)

I suppose that the enjoyable part of programming that Stroustrup refers to is the pleasing degree of efficiency that a program acquires when it has no run-time or space overhead.

Like Stroustrup, R. D. Tennent starts out with an admirable goal for programming languages:

> A programming language is a system of notation for describing computations. A useful programming language must therefore be suited for both describing (i.e., for human writers and readers of programs) and for computation (i.e., for efficient implementation on computers). But human beings and computers are so different that it is difficult to find notational devices that are well suited to the capabilities of both. Languages that favor humans are termed high-level, and those oriented to machines low-level. (Tennent 1981)

He goes on to describe machine language as the most "powerful" low-level language, but he tellingly remarks:

> It might be thought that "natural" languages (such as English and French) would be at the other extreme. But, in most fields of science and technology, the formalized notations of mathematics and logic have proved to be indispensable for precise formulation of concepts and principles and for effective reasoning. (Tennent 1981)

Precise formulation and effective reasoning—again, not exactly what I had in mind. Finally, let's look at Modula-3, a modern, enlightened language:

> Modula-3 is a modern, general-purpose programming language. It provides excellent support for large, reliable, and maintainable applications.... The nature of programming has changed. For many years we were puzzle-solvers, focused on turning algorithms into sets of instructions to be followed by a computer. We enjoyed solving these

puzzles, and we often viewed both the complexity of the puzzle and the obscurity of the solution as evidence of our skill. . . . Aware of our human limitations, we have come to view complexity and obscurity as faults, not challenges. Now we write programs to be read by people, not computers. (Harbison 1992)

This is the best start, and its finish is not bad either:

> *There is a pleasure in creating well-written, understandable pro-grams. There is a satisfaction in finding a program structure that tames the complexity of an application. We enjoy seeing our algo-rithms expressed clearly and persuasively. We also profit from our clearly written programs, for they are much more likely to be correct and maintainable than obscure ones.* (Harbison 1992)

Although I think the goal of Modula-3 is not ideal, it is better than the precise formulation goal that Tennent advocates, and it is in a different league from Stroustrup's pleasure of efficiency.

There is, I think, a better goal, to which I want to draw your attention. It's a characteristic of software that you've perhaps not thought of and which perhaps should have some influence over the design of programming languages and cer-tainly of software methodology. It is *habitability*.

Habitability is the characteristic of source code that enables programmers, coders, bug-fixers, and people coming to the code later in its life to understand its construction and intentions and to change it comfortably and confidently. Either there is more to habitability than clarity or the two characteristics are different. Let me talk a little bit more about habitability before I tackle what the difference may be.

Habitability makes a place livable, like home. And this is what we want in soft-ware—that developers feel at home, can place their hands on any item without having to think deeply about where it is. It's something like clarity, but clarity is too hard to come by.

Habitability is related to a concept called *organic order* that Christopher Alex-ander, the architect, uses in his work:

> *Organic Order: . . . the kind of order that is achieved when there is a perfect balance between the needs of the parts and the needs of the whole.* (Alexander 1975)

How are architecture and software related?

I've heard Gregor Kiczales—one of the CLOS designers—say that he wishes that computer science practice could reach the level of engineering excellence that creates buildings like the Superdome in New Orleans. He points out that the design of the Superdome puts together pieces made from a variety of materials and from a range of engineering and building disciplines. The result is a monument to that engineering skill. This is a tempting picture, but I think it's off base.

Buildings like the Superdome lack habitability. In this instance people inhabit the building, but only for very short periods of time, and for very special occasions—and such buildings are not easily grown or altered. The Superdome is a static building, and therefore it can stand as a monument, being little else.

A modern skyscraper, to take another example, has a fixed inflexible interior, which is secondary to the designed beauty of the exterior. Little attention is paid to the natural light, and often the interiors are constructed as "flexible office space," which means cubicles. The flexibility is for management to set up offices for the company, not for the inhabitants—the employees—to tailor their own space. When you run out of space in the skyscraper, you build another; you don't modify the existing one or add to it.

Contrast this with the New England farmhouse. It starts as a small home with a barn out back. As the family grows and the needs of the farm grow, a back room is added to the house, then a canning room, then a room for grandma; stables are added to the barn, then a wing for milking more cows. Finally the house and barn are connected because it is too difficult to get from the house to the barn in a blizzard. The result is rambling, but each part is well-suited to its needs, each part fits well with the others, and the result is beautiful because it is a living structure with living people inside. The inhabitants are able to modify their environment because each part is built according to familiar patterns of design, use, and construction and because those patterns contain the seeds for piecemeal growth.

I think this should be the goal for computer science practice. Most programming languages are excellent for building the program that is a monument to design ingenuity—pleasingly efficient, precise, and clear—but people don't build programs like that. Programs live and grow, and their inhabitants—the programmers—need to work with that program the way the farmer works with the homestead.

This, I think, is the challenge of programming language design in the next generation: to recognize, finally, what programming really is and to address those issues, not issues of elegance and monumental programs.

What are some of the things that contribute to uninhabitable programs? Overuse of abstraction and inappropriate compression come to mind. But that's a topic for another day; today is just to explore the concepts of habitability and piecemeal growth.

In Alexander's definition of organic order applied to software, the concept of "needs of the whole" refers to the grand design or architecture of the piece of software under development, and "needs of the parts" refers to the inevitable changes the various parts of the software undergo. It's difficult to change the grand design of software: You cannot expect to evolve a window system into a spreadsheet.

Although the primary need of the whole is to remain true to its essence, the parts often must change. For instance, one sort of window system could evolve into another.

Software needs to be habitable because it always has to change. Software is subject to unpredictable events: Requirements change because the marketplace changes, competitors change, parts of the design are shown wrong by experience, people learn to use the software in ways not anticipated. Notice that frequently the unpredictable event is about people and society rather than about technical issues. Such unpredictable events lead to the needs of the parts which must be comfortably understood so they can be comfortably changed.

Consider bugs. Many a bug is the result of not anticipating a particular event or use and is not the result of a mistake—bugs are not always errors. Bugs tell us that we are not capable of producing a *master plan*. A master plan is a detailed design, and many projects consider critical their detailed designs. But a master plan is usually not possible, especially for extensive, long-lived software. Alexander writes:

> It is simply not possible to fix today what the environment should be like [in the future], and then to steer the piecemeal process of development toward that fixed, imaginary world. (Alexander 1975)

This simply acknowledges that it is impossible to predict the circumstances of a long-lived program. But there is a more important point:

> Master plans have two additional unhealthy characteristics. To begin with, the existence of a master plan alienates the users. . . . After all, the very existence of a master plan means, by definition, that the members of the community can have little impact on the future shape of their community, because most of the important decisions have already been made. In a sense, under a master plan people are living with a frozen future, able to affect only relatively trivial details. When people lose the sense of responsibility for the environment they live in, and realize that there are merely cogs in someone else's machine, how can they feel any sense of identification with the community, or any sense of purpose there?
>
> Second, neither the users nor the key decision makers can visualize the actual implications of the master plan. (Alexander 1975)

It should be clear that, in our context, a "user" is a programmer who is called upon to maintain or modify software; a user is not (necessarily) the person who uses the software. In Alexander's terminology, a user is an inhabitant. A client or software user certainly does not inhabit the code but instead uses its external interface; such a software user would be more like the city sewer, which hooks up to a building but doesn't live in it.

Several points come to mind. First, when you design software, let the implementers complete those parts of the design for which they are responsible.

Second, have you ever heard a good manager ask the group he or she manages "who owns this?" It's because the manager knows that the excellent employee needs to feel he or she has some authority over what they are responsible for. Further, a well-knit group has this same sense of ownership over what they work on plus a bond of "elitism" that holds them together and makes each member of the team feel responsible for the others' success.

Third, how do you enable a programmer to feel responsible for software developed earlier? Here is where habitability comes in. Just as with a house, you don't have to have built or designed something to feel at home in it. Most people buy houses that have been built and designed by someone else. These homes are habitable because they are designed for habitation by people, and peoples' needs are relatively similar. As I said earlier, a New England farmhouse is habitable, and the new owner feels just as comfortable changing or adapting that farmhouse as the first farmer was. But a home designed by Frank Lloyd Wright—though more habitable than most "overdesigned" homes—cannot be altered because all its parts are too rigidly designed and built. The needs of the whole have overshadowed the needs of the parts and the needs of the inhabitants.

Finally, if Alexander's lesson applies to software, it implies that a development project ought to have less of a plan in place than current thinking allows. This provides a mechanism for motivation and a sense of responsibility to those developers who later must work with the code.

Alexander goes on:

> The principle of organic order: Planning and construction [implementation, in our context] will be guided by a process which allows the whole to emerge gradually from local acts. (Alexander 1975)

This just piecemeal growth. Here is how Alexander puts it:

> [E]ach new building is not a "finished" thing. . . . They are never torn down, never erased; instead they are always embellished, modified, reduced, enlarged, improved. This attitude to the repair of the environment has been commonplace for thousands of years in traditional cultures. We may summarize the point of view behind this attitude in one phrase: piecemeal growth. (Alexander 1975)

Piecemeal growth is a reality. What gets in its way and prevents software habitability is overdesign, overabstraction, and the beautiful, taut monument of software. Alexander calls this *large lump development*:

> *Large lump development hinges on a view of the environment which is static and discontinuous; piecemeal growth hinges on a view of the environment which is dynamic and continuous. . . . According to the large lump point of view, each act of design or construction is an isolated event which creates an isolated building—"perfect" at the time of its construction, and then abandoned by its builders and designers forever. According to the piecemeal point of view, every environment is changing and growing all the time, in order to keep its use in balance; and the quality of the environment is a kind of semi-stable equilibrium in the flux of time. . . . Large lump development is based on the idea of* replacement. *Piecemeal growth is based on the idea of* repair. (Alexander 1975)

Recall that one of the tenets of encapsulation is that the interface be separate from the implementation because this permits the implementation to be replaced when needed.

The problem with traditional approaches to abstraction and encapsulation is that they aim at complete information hiding. This characteristic anticipates being able to *eliminate* programming from parts of the software development process, those parts contained within module boundaries. As we've seen, though, the need to program is never eliminated because customization, modification, and maintenance are always required—that is, piecemeal growth.

A better goal is to *minimize* or *reduce* the extent of programming, which implies providing mechanisms that allow small changes to largely already correct code.

One of the primary reasons that abstraction is overloved is that a completed program full of the right abstractions is perfectly beautiful. But there are very few completed programs, because programs are written, maintained, bugs are fixed, features are added, performance is tuned, and a whole variety of changes are made both by the original and new programming team members. Thus, the way a program looks in the end is not important because there is rarely an end, and if there is one it isn't planned.

What is important is that it be easy for programmers to come up to speed with the code, to be able to navigate through it effectively, to be able to understand what changes to make, and to be able to make them safely and correctly. If the beauty of the code gets in the way, the program is not well written, just as an office building designed to win design awards is not well designed when the building later must undergo changes but those changes are too hard to make. A language (and an accompanying environment) is poorly designed that doesn't recognize this fact, and worse-still are those languages that aim for the beauty and elegance of the (never) finished program.

Habitability is not clarity, I think. If it were, then Modula-3 would hit the nail on the head. Clarity is just too rare, and it's dangerous, too, in a funny way.

Books on writing tell you to be clear and simple, to use plain language. What can this mean? It is no advice at all because no one would ever try to be muddy and complex, to use obscure language as part of an *honest* attempt to be understood. But clarity is a quality that is rarely achieved—rare because it is difficult to achieve. However, even though only the rare writer or poet throws off an occasional clear sentence or paragraph, many of us are able to be understood with little problem, because our writing is habitable—not great, but easy enough to read, easy enough to change.

The danger of clarity is that it is uncompromised beauty; and it's real tough to to improve uncompromised beauty. Many second- and third-rate sculptors can fix a decent sculpture—I saw a group of them one summer making replacement gargoyles for Notre Dame Cathedral in Paris—but which of them would dare repair Michelangelo's *David*? Who would add a skyscraper to the background of *Mona Lisa*? Who would edit Eliot's poems? Clarity is dangerous.

If a programming language is optimized for the wrong thing—like pleasing efficiency, mathematical precision, or clarity—people might not be able to live with in or in it: It isn't habitable, piecemeal growth isn't possible, and the programmers who must live in the software feel no responsibility or ownership.

Abstraction Descant

The room fills with cold, conditioned air; outside the heat hazes, fil-
tered through greened glass windows: a new building hardly first-
populated. The speaker is wild-eyed, explaining new ideas like a
Bible thumper. His hair is a flat-top; his mouth frowns in near gri-
mace. He strides to my seat, looks down and says in a Texas drawl,
"and the key is simply this: Abstractions. New and better abstrac-
tions. With them we can solve all our programming problems."
(Gabriel and Steele 1990)

This scene, which occurred in the late 1980s, began my off-and-on inquiry into
the good and bad points of abstraction. All through my computer science education, abstraction was held up as the bright, shining monument of computer science. Yet when discussed in essays on the philosophy of science, abstraction is
routinely questioned. Here is what Paul Feyerabend says about Ernst Mach, scientist and philosopher:

> *We have seen that abstraction, according to Mach, "plays an impor-*
> *tant role in the discovery of knowledge." Abstraction seems to be a*
> *negative procedure: real physical properties . . . are omitted. Abstrac-*
> *tion, as interpreted by Mach, is therefore "a bold intellectual move."*
> *It can misfire, it "is justified by success."* (Feyerabend 1987)

Throughout the book abstraction is discussed in terms of its relation to reality
and to the "interests" of those who develop them. Here is what Bas Van Fraassen
says:

> *But in certain cases, no abstraction is possible without losing the very*
> *thing we wish to study. . . . Thus [study at a certain level] can only go*

*so far—then it must give way to less thorough abstraction (that is, a
less shallow level of analysis).* (Van Fraassen 1980)

Both Van Fraassen and Feyerabend seem to subscribe to the notion that abstraction in the realm of science—I doubt they would include computer science—is about ignorance. Abstraction ignores or omits certain things and operates at a shallow level of analysis.

The following is the definition of abstraction in computer science that I've used for years:

> Abstraction *in programming is the process of identifying* common patterns *that have* systematic variations; *an abstraction represents the common pattern and provides a means for specifying which variation to use.*
>
> *An abstraction facilitates separation of concerns: The implementor of an abstraction can ignore the exact uses or instances of the abstraction, and the user of the abstraction can forget the details of the implementation of the abstraction, so long as the implementation fulfills its intention or specification.* (Balzer et al. 1989)

This definition does not directly mention ignorance or omission, though it does imply them. The common pattern is omitted—in most types of abstraction the common pattern is replaced by a name, such as function name, a macro name, or a class name. The structure and behavior of the common pattern is lost except that the name of the abstraction denotes it and the definition of the abstraction (its implementation) contains it. And the foregoing definition does mention the interests of particular people—abstraction implementers and abstraction users.

Although I will return to the themes brought out by Feyerabend and Van Fraassen later, first I will set the scene. In the first two essays in this book I looked at three new concepts for programming: *compression, habitability,* and *piecemeal growth*, defined as follows:

> Compression *is the characteristic of a piece of text that the meaning of any part of it is "larger" than that particular piece has by itself. This characteristic is created by a rich context, with each part of the text drawing on that context—each word draws part of its meaning from its surroundings.*
>
> Habitability *is the characteristic of source code that enables programmers, coders, bug-fixers, and people coming to the code later in its life to understand its construction and intentions, and to change it comfortably and confidently.*

> Piecemeal growth *is the process of design and implementation in which software is embellished, modified, reduced, enlarged, and improved through a process of repair rather than of replacement.*

Habitability can be limited by various things; abstraction being one of them. Many of my comments about abstraction also apply to encapsulation, which is a strong variety of abstraction. But don't panic: Abstraction and encapsulation are good things; my point is that they should be used only in moderation.

One bad effect of abstraction on programs occurs when it is taken too far. This results in code that is structured like a big pyramid, in which one level of abstractions is built tightly on another with minimal interfacial glue. Wait, that's not right—abstractionists would have you believe that abstraction guarantees you'll build geometrically precise programs, but that's garbage. Even in single inheritance object systems (in which hierarchies look like pyramids), there are other use relationships besides inheritance. Let's try this paragraph again.

One bad effect of abstraction on programs occurs when abstraction is taken too far. This results in code that is structured like a big web, in which groups of abstractions are tightly interwoven with others by means of interfacial glue.

In such large tangles lies one of the problems. If one abstraction is used in many places and that abstraction's interface is wrong, then repairing it forces repair of all its uses. The more the abstraction is shared, the more repair will be needed. But such repair is dangerous because it is usually made with less deliberation than the original design and in the context of unexpected requirements. If the repairs are being made by people other than the original designers and much later than the design and original implementation, the likelihood of mistake or ugliness will be increased.

Such webs are examples of compression: The meaning of an expression written in the context of the web is determined by the contents of the entire web. If you need to change another part of the web, your compressed expression might change its meaning, what it does, or even whether it works at all. So when we build our tight inheritance hierarchy in object-oriented fashion—weblike or pyramid style—we might be falling into this trap.

The reason for this failure is the insistence on using abstractions throughout, at all levels. If, instead, there were a level at which the code became direct rather than indirect, this might be less likely to happen. The problem is that people are taught to value abstraction above all else, and object-oriented languages and their philosophy of use emphasizes reuse (compression), which is generally good. However, sometimes the passion for abstraction is so strong that it is used inappropriately—it is forced in the same way as it is with larger, more complex, and typically ad hoc abstractions.

Abstractions must be carefully and expertly designed, especially when reuse or compression is intended. However, because abstractions are designed in a partic-

ular context and for a particular purpose, it is hard to design them while anticipating all purposes and forgetting all purposes, which is the hallmark of the well-
designed abstractions.

This implies that abstractions are best designed by experts. Worse, average
programmers are not well-equipped to design abstractions that have universal
usage, even though the programming languages used by average programmers
and the programming language texts and courses average programmers read and
attend to learn their trade emphasize the importance of doing exactly that.
Although the designers of the programming language and the authors of texts
and course instructors can probably design abstractions well, the intended audience of the language—average programmers—cannot and are therefore left out.
That is, languages that encourage abstraction lead to less habitable software,
because its expected inhabitants—average programmers working on code years
after the original designers have disappeared—are not easily able to grasp, modify, and grow the abstraction-laden code they must work on.

Not everyone is a poet, but most anybody can write usable documentation for
small programs—we don't expect poets to do this work. Yet we seem to expect
that the equivalent of poets will use high-level programming languages, because
only program-poets are able to use them. In light of this observation, is it any
wonder that abstraction-poor languages like C are by far the most popular and
that abstraction-rich ones like Lisp and Smalltalk are niche languages?

Recall that one of the virtues of abstraction is that "the user of the abstraction
can forget the details of the implementation of the abstraction." Nonetheless, the
interface of a complex abstraction is likely to expose the implementation because
portions of the abstraction's interface are likely to be dedicated to accessing particular behavior. Inexpertly designed and ad hoc abstractions frequently suffer
from this shortcoming. Once the implementation is even partially revealed, it
becomes more difficult to change the abstraction's implementation without causing problems. If abstraction were limited to simple cases, especially those with a
fairly universal meaning—like the well-loved and ubiquitous stack, a favorite of
almost every paper on abstract types—this problem would be reduced.

Another problem with complex abstraction arises from the observation that
abstractions are about ignorance. The prime idea of encapsulation is that the
implementation is hidden, thereby preventing assumptions about the implementation. Some complex abstractions, however, contain information about the
implementation that is legitimately required, such as its performance, the algorithm, coding tricks, and resource usage—keep in mind that almost all interaction issues are about resource conflicts. When the implementation is truly
hidden, its user is forced to use real scientific methods to infer or discover the
needed information. Rather than preventing assumptions, hard encapsulation
tends to guarantee incorrect assumptions.

Furthermore, when the implementation is truly hidden and there is a need to make a change or add behavior, the user is reduced to reinventing; if the implementation is not only hidden but also protected, the user will need to copy and maintain a parallel version. This implies that later changes to the code will be less efficiently made because similar code must be implemented in several places. In fact, the programmer—especially a programmer new to the project—may be unable to find all the occurrences of the similar code.

Notice the dilemma: Complex abstractions sometimes reveal implementation, which limits the opportunity to change their implementations, and they also are intended to hide implementation, which forces programmers (inhabitants) into ignorance and its resulting frustration, ineffectiveness, and feelings of denied responsibility. Strict abstractionists would argue that it is far better to hide the implementation, but consider what Christopher Alexander said:

> When people lose the sense of responsibility for the environment they live in, and realize that they are merely cogs in someone else's machine, how can they feel any sense of identification with the community, or any sense of purpose there? (Alexander 1975)

Why put your programmers through this?

Most of these problems can be eliminated or reduced if the user is encouraged to build small abstractions only. This is easier if the language provides other mechanisms that help the programmer build the larger structures needed in a program, structures that would normally be constructed from abstractions.

When we couple this advice with that of building hierarchies slowly, keeping them shallow as long as possible, we might find that we have paved the way for habitability, piecemeal growth, and healthy, usable compression. In fact, if we put in place an explicit process of piecemeal growth, hierarchies will naturally grow slowly, and they are more likely to be correct, because their use evolves over time. The resulting compression also is natural, not forced, and it is less likely that the compression will backfire.

This same advice is more cynically arrived at by Martin D. Carroll and John F. Isner when discussing the design of the C++ Standard Components developed by UNIX Systems Laboratories:

> [W]e take the minimalist approach to inheritance. We use it only when it makes our components more efficient, or when it solves certain problems in the type system.
> We do not intend for our components to serve as a collection of base classes that users extend via derivation. It is exceedingly difficult to make a class extensible in abstracto (it is tenfold harder when one is trying to provide classes that are as efficient as possible). Contrary to a common misconception, it is rarely possible for a programmer to

take an arbitrary class and derive a new, useful, and correct subtype from it, unless that subtype is of a very specific kind anticipated by the designer of the base class. Classes can only be made extensible in certain directions, where each of these directions is consciously chosen (and programmed in) by the designer of the class. *Class libraries which claim to be "fully extensible" are making an extravagant claim which frequently does not hold up in practice. . . . There is absolutely no reason to sacrifice efficiency for an elusive kind of "extensibility."* (Carroll and Isner 1992, emphasis added)

Their argument comes more from efficiency than from the needs of habitability and piecemeal growth; in fact, their whole essay is about how to achieve what they consider the most important characteristic of a library—its efficiency. But notice that they make a very strong claim that being able to extend a class hierarchy is nearly impossible, though they don't say why precisely. One can try to puzzle out the reason; the best I can come up with is that many possible extensions require access to the internal implementation of a class, and the author of the class either does not know what parts are needed or wishes to retain the opportunity to change the implementation and therefore hides the implementation. In C++ there are other reasons, like the need for speed encourages class authors to make virtual as little as possible.

Regardless of the reasons behind it, if we accept Carroll and Isner's statement that unanticipated extension is difficult, their statement supports my claim that during the growth of an abstraction web, one must frequently go back to existing abstractions to repair them, such repair being a sort of delayed anticipation of the extensions.

Because abstracting a common pattern and using the abstraction is a process of replacing something directly expressed by a shorthand, adding an abstraction is like adding a new word to a real language: It requires learning a new vocabulary. Real languages rarely permit us to add new words, and such words are reserved for concepts, objects, actions, and qualifications that are basic or newly basic. We don't invent new words for dogs that can jump through hoops or automobiles modified to carry 300 gallons of fuel. First, there is no need for these words except within a small familylike circle, and even there the need soon dissipates when the name of the dog or a phrase like "Joe's big fueler" prove worthy and effective.

Second, these words would be meaningless outside the small circle that might need them, and encountering an enclave of odd-language users would negate the advantages of natural language. Similarly, we want to limit the use of abstraction to either common items—common to every programmer—or items inextricably linked to the application domain. Otherwise, unnecessarily abstracted code would be unintelligible to programmers fresh to a project, and hence it would not be habitable.

Van Fraassen hints at this idea: "But in certain cases, no abstraction is possible without losing the very thing we wish to study." He means that the object of interest is captured only by the name of the abstraction rather than by the thing itself. For example, when we speak of redness and *go no deeper*, redness disappears and all we have left is the name *red*.

Recall that one of the primary reasons that abstraction is overloved is that a completed program full of the right abstractions is perfectly beautiful—it is "justified by success" as Mach said. Of course, Christopher Alexander would probably not think such a program was beautiful—assuming he would even know how to read a program. Note what he said about completed, planned urban development:

> [P]lanned development is also generally not coherent . . . not in a deep-felt sense. It is supposed to be. But if we ask ourselves whether the final product of current urban design projects actually is coherent in the real, deep sense that we know from traditional towns, then we must say no. The order is superficial, skin deep, only in the plan or in some contrived orderliness of the arrangements. There is no deep inner coherence, which can be felt in every doorway, every step, and every street.
>
> And . . . this modern planned development which we think of as normal, certainly has NO power to evoke deep feeling. It can, at best, ask for some kind of admiration for "design." But of deep feeling there is no word, not a tremor, not a possibility. (Alexander 1987)

Alexander's area of study—architecture and urban development—has the advantage of having had a long history and, hence, examples of the sort of habitable, deeply felt homes and towns and cities with which he can contrast the products of the modern design approach. In software there are no large examples that I can point to with which we are all familiar. And so we can ask whether Alexander's words—which sound so nice when apply them to the field of software— pertain in any real sense to computer science. But that is a question for another essay.

Remember, piecemeal growth is the norm, and programs grow, change, and are repaired. Therefore, the perfectly beautiful program is possible only for very small programs, like the ones in books on programming or in programming courses.

Now let's return to my definition of abstraction. One thing that strikes me about this definition, now that I have used it for years and years, is the degree to which the fact is ignored or forgotten that there are two conditions for abstraction. There is not only a common pattern but also systematic variations. Sub– routines and functions are perfect examples: The common pattern is the code that ends up in the subroutine, and the systematic variations are the arguments that are passed—the mechanism for specifying the variation is the parameter.

What about common patterns without systematic variations? I will turn to this topic in the second part of this essay.

To some extent, object-oriented programming is about piecemeal growth. But in some languages, it is achieved by catching the excess-abstraction disease. This essay is not intended to convince you that abstraction is bad (or that I'm nuts), but to show that maybe some of the other concerns of software development—creating habitable software that can be effectively maintained, recognizing that the reality of software development is piecemeal growth and to plan accordingly, and to understand that the power of object-oriented programming is compression, which carries a terrific requirement for careful use of inheritance—relate to how we use abstraction and how much we use it.

ప ప ప

> In order for the building to be alive, its construction details must be unique and fitted to their individual circumstances as carefully as the larger parts. . . . The details of a building cannot be made alive when they are made from modular parts. (Alexander 1979)

Let's look again at the definition of abstraction I've been using:

> Abstraction *in programming is the process of identifying* common patterns *that have* systematic variations; *an abstraction represents the common pattern and provides a means for specifying which variation to use.*
>
> *An abstraction facilitates separation of concerns: The implementor of an abstraction can ignore the exact uses or instances of the abstraction, and the user of the abstraction can forget the details of the implementation of the abstraction, so long as the implementation fulfills its intention or specification.* (Balzer et al. 1989)

Unfortunately, such patterns are usually turned into abstractions, with the unsystematic variations being lumped in with the systematic ones, the result being an ad hoc interface. Using such ad hoc abstractions, client code—code using an abstraction—can end up being composed of glue code surrounding "invocations" of the ad hoc abstractions. The glue code, however, may only to contort the natural structure of the client code. Notice how this effect compounds another problem with abstractions: If an abstraction is composed of what amounts to a conglomeration of somewhat related operations, programmers are more likely to want to modify or add to the abstraction—it's ugly enough to begin with, so what's the harm?

Examples of this sort of abuse of abstraction abound in Common Lisp—though I like the language and don't intend to criticize it. A typical example is `mismatch`, which searches two sequences (a sequence is a Common Lisp data type) for the first index where the two sequences differ according to a test predicate. Common Lisp supports *keyword arguments*, which provide a means to supply a variable number of optional arguments by naming them. This mechanism helps clarify the meaning of (the possibly many) arguments to a complex function. The function `mismatch` takes a variety of optional arguments that specify the direction to search, a function to test whether two items are the same, and whether the predicate should be negated (even though there are mechanisms to negate predicates in the language and the negated predicate can be easily passed to `mismatch`). Clearly, Common Lisp, though a well-designed language, contains a number of common patterns without systematic variations.

Christopher Alexander's comment on modular parts, which began this essay, bears on this point. Contrast it with what Greg Nelson said about Modula-3:

> *The better we understand our programs, the bigger the building blocks we use to structure them. After the instruction came the statement, after the statement came the procedure, after the procedure came the interface. The next step seems to be the* abstract type.
> (Nelson 1991)

What Alexander seems to be saying is that if we try to use modular parts (solid building blocks not easily molded to the current circumstances), then the overall structure of the thing built with them may become overly constrained by their shape. In programming, if a set of large abstractions does nearly the right thing, it is tempting is to use them and to bend the structure of the surrounding program to fit them. This can lead to uninhabitable programs.

Worse: You can fight this temptation and choose *not* to use them. This choice also can lead to uninhabitable programs because you will be using parts similar but subtly different from possibly familiar ones. The only way to avoid this is to use small blocks rather than large ones, or to use blocks well-designed and tested by experts.

Large abstractions are large common patterns, and what is missing in programming languages is a treatment of common patterns. Such a treatment would need to support separating their use from their definition. Now, what would such a separation mean in ordinary abstractions? The key benefit is that there would be just one place the programmer has to look in order to repair or study it. There is no reason a language or—far better—a programming environment couldn't show the underlying common parts of a pattern. Later I'll cite an example of what this could be like.

What is an example of such a pattern? The idea of accumulating a result is one:

```
(let ((result ...)
       ...)
  ...
  (<loop> ... (setq result ...) ...)
  ...result...)
```

This isn't such an interesting example because the pattern is so familiar, but it is easy to see it as a pattern people learn and which cannot be easily captured by a traditional abstraction. There isn't too much one can do to systematically modify this pattern—it has so few common parts and so many potential variations—but there is a lot that programmers gain from knowing this pattern and later coming upon a piece of code that contained it: It would help them know why the obscure-looking variable is popping up from place to place; it would help them see in their mind's eye the whole pattern with the intervening portions elided.

One way to lay a foundation of common patterns is the same way we do with natural language: Teach people the most common patterns. We never think to teach people how to create words—poets do this frequently, and sometimes ordinary people become word-inventors—yet we teach budding programmers to create their own vocabulary but we don't provide a catalog of common patterns of usage.

I think this means that we need to spend more time teaching programming, and the increased time should be devoted to teaching patterns and reading "great" programs. How much time do we spend reading in our ordinary education? And from our reading we gain a foundation for writing. In turn, this foundation is sometimes expanded by careful instruction and tutoring in writing. Certainly many people who write for a living go through this process. But in programming we just learn the language and solve a bunch of short puzzles. Sort of like writing 50 limericks and then off to write books.

Let's look at a simple example of how abstractions and patterns interact. Consider the following code fragment:

```
(let ((result (mapcar f list))) ...)
```

This takes a function f, applies it to each element of the list list, and binds the list of the results of those applications to the variable result. Now, an ordinary programmer knows that mapcar traverses the list, so there should be some tricky way to make the mapcar do double duty, computing the length of the list as well. But try as you might, you won't find an easy way to modify f so that the length can be transparently obtained and abstraction boundaries heartily enforced—remember I said an easy way.

There will always be some object somewhere that is accumulating the length; we can bury the side-effecting code in a modified f, but there still is the access of that accumulator, whether it be a variable or some object. If you really wanted to have abstraction reign, you'd try to write something like this:

```
(let  ((result (mapcar f list))
       (len    (length list))) ... )
```

Here the shaded area indicates a place where a "sufficiently smart" compiler could try to fold the two computations into one. Actually, there are lots of ways to imagine an environment helping promote such transparent patterns. One is that this could be the environment's surface manifestation of an optimized section of code. In this case, the programmer might have made the optimization by hand, and the environment would be simply showing the unoptimized code; this environmental feature might also aid with piecemeal growth by maintaining a history of the software evolution.

This formulation also correctly respects the abstraction of both operations—the mapcar and the length computation—but it incorrectly overemphasizes abstraction because the unabstracted but common-pattern code is just fine:

```
(let ((length 0))
  (let ((result
          (mapcar
            #'(lambda (x)
                (incf length)
                (f x))
            list)))
    ...))
```

This code is obvious to even a novice (modern) Lisp programmer, and it requires a lot less mechanics than does the environmental approach just before it. Further, note that the length computation winds like a vine from the outside of the mapcar abstraction to its inside.

Let's look at another problem with abstractions: Data and control abstractions are generally best when they are codesigned and this is rarely done anymore. Consider, for example, the FORTRAN abstractions of arrays and iteration. Arrays are abstractions designed to represent vectors and matrices. Iteration is a control abstraction useful for traversing vectors and arrays. Think, for example, of how easy it is to implement summation over the elements of a vector. This is because arrays and DO loops were codesigned.

The codesign of mathematical data and control abstractions is not an accident. One could hardly ignore the need to refer to individual elements in a matrix or a sequence while performing nested sums and products in a numeric computation.

Partly the codesign was made by mathematicians before FORTRAN was created, and partly because when FORTRAN was developed there were no alternatives other than conditional and GO statements. The success of FORTRAN is due at least somewhat to the close match between the data abstractions (scalars, vectors, and arrays) and control abstractions that manipulate them (DO loops).

Even though there was a recognized need to be able to define data abstractions after FORTRAN was developed, there was never a recognized need to be able to define control abstractions. Some languages, like Lisp, adopted a powerful macro facility which enables programmers to define their own control abstractions. Of course, macros also enable programmers to define their own data structures by providing a means to define a protocol that is syntactically the same as ordinary function invocation.

But an interesting thing happened to Lisp in the early 1980s: the use of macros to define control structures became forbidden style. Not only did some organizations outlaw such use of macros, but the cognoscenti began sneering at programmers who used them that way. Procedural abstractions are acceptable, but not control abstractions. The only acceptable control abstractions in Lisp today are function invocation, do loops, while loops, go statements (sort of), non-local exits, and a few mapping operations (such as mapcar in Lisp).

The mismatch example shows how one sort of abstraction (a function) can be used to implement control abstractions. Some of the arguments specify the function's control behavior (which direction to search, how to extract the data of interest, how to test whether the item was found, and whether to negate the value of that test function). The common pattern—generalized search, generalized extraction, generalized test, and gratuitous negation—has been completely eliminated, and all hope of understanding a code fragment invoking this abstraction rests with being able to understand the name of the function and the meanings of its arguments. Common Lisp, at least, provides keyword arguments to name the role of the arguments. Does the following code fragment:

```
(mismatch sequence list :from-end t
          :start1 20 :start2 40
          :end1 120 :end2 140 :test #'baz)
```

seem easier to understand than this pattern of use:

```
(let ((subseq1 (reverse (subseq sequence 20 120))
      (subseq2 (reverse (subseq list 40 140)))))
  (flet ((the-same (x y) (baz x y)))
    (loop for index upfrom 0
          as item1 in subseq1
          as item2 in subseq2
          finally (return t) do
      (unless (the-same item1 item2)
        (return index)))))
```

This latter code fragment is an example of a common pattern. If you have been taught to see such patterns, they are as easily understood as the shorthand `mismatch` call. Furthermore, if you have not been trained to understand either the `mismatch` or the common pattern, you can still understand the common pattern just by reading it. The `mismatch` expression has two advantages over the common pattern one:

- System implementers can more easily guarantee that the implementation of `mismatch` is maximally efficient, coding it in assembler if need be (I'm sure you'll rest better tonight knowing that).

- It is harder to type the longhand common pattern than the `mismatch` expression, and it is just plain longer.

The first problem goes away when computers are fast enough (more on this later). The second goes away with a well-designed programming environment or doesn't matter at all when you consider the habitability gains from using an easily understood program. In fact, there is no reason that the shorthand `mismatch` expression could not be simply an abbreviation for the longhand common pattern. The programmer could decide which to see and could change either one. Then if the common pattern version strays too far, it will no longer be abbreviated (because it can't be).

Let's consider the scenario in which the interface to a data abstraction is being extended—we've added to the interface and we need to modify our program to invoke the new parts. For example, additional state must be initialized and maintained. The problem of adding invocations of the new part of the protocol is exacerbated by the fact that only mathematical, FORTRAN-like control structures are available. Over the years programmers have gotten into the habit of optimizing the use of these control structures for either efficiency or style. Typically the most compact control structure for the specific job at hand is often preferred to a more general formulation. Modifying such optimized control structures sometimes requires large a structural modification of a program when only small modifications seem necessary. For instance, the initialization information might not be available at the point we need it and must be reconstructed or saved somewhere, or only part of the initialization information might have been computed because, earlier, not all of it was needed.

This problem with abstractions stems from mixing a fixed set of (inappropriate) control abstractions with custom-designed data abstractions. If natural control abstractions were matched, they must be implemented nonabstractly using existing low-level primitives—that is, through other control structures. Even though there is a pattern of control, there is no way to abbreviate it except through procedural or functional abstractions.

Such lopsided use of data abstraction forces programs to be written at varying levels of abstraction. The result is that the programmer is reduced to switching mentally between these levels. Right next to a protocol invocation that represents the opening of a floodgate will be the assignment of 1 to a flag that tells a later part of the program that a certain initialization already took place. Furthermore and worse, the flag might be part of an otherwise completely application domain-level data abstraction.

The use of procedural or functional abstractions (combined with the fact that argument evaluation rules might thwart a need to pass expressions and not values) only pushes the problem down one level: Within the procedure or function the implementation of the control abstraction is fully exposed, even though objects being manipulated are high-level data abstractions.

Regardless of what you make of this view of data versus control abstraction, it is certainly true that because almost every programming language does not allow any sort of meaningful user-defined control abstractions, there is always a mismatch in abstraction levels between control and data. If there is a good reason for allowing data abstractions, why isn't that a good reason for allowing control abstractions; and if there is a good reason to disallow control abstractions, why isn't that a good reason to disallow data abstractions? Nevertheless, it is accepted practice to use existing control abstractions to implement others using common patterns. My argument is that perhaps we should be more willing to use common patterns for other things as well.

The real reason that common patterns are not used rather than tight abstractions is efficiency. It is more efficient to write abstracted, compressed code than uncompressed common patterns, and it is more efficient to execute abstracted code in some cases. For example, if we were to write the two lines that do mapcar and length, they would run about twice as slow as some complex compressed version. This wouldn't matter if computers were big enough and fast enough for the programs we need, but right now they aren't. So we continue to pay with the sweat of people so that computers can take it easy and users don't have to be inconvenienced. Perhaps someday the economics of this situation will change. Maybe not.

Common patterns are similar in nature though not detail to the patterns that Christopher Alexander uses in his so-called pattern languages. A pattern language is a language for generating buildings and towns with organic order. Patterns generally specify the components of a portion of a building or a place and how those components are related to other patterns. Here is an example of a pattern that every planner of developers' offices should know:

> *Locate each room so that it has outdoor space on at least two sides,*
> *and then place windows in these outdoor walls so that natural light*
> *falls into every room from more than one direction.* (Alexander 1977a)

The bulk of Alexander's written work over the last 15 years—and from which I have been freely quoting—describes the theory behind pattern languages and the patterns for building and urban development that he and his students and colleagues have devised. These patterns and the social process for applying them are designed to produce organic order through piecemeal growth. Clearly there is a connection between patterns as Alexander defines them and the common patterns that form half the definition of abstraction. But there is no room in this essay to explore it; perhaps in another.

Here are the lessons that I think the last two essays plus this one teach:

- Object-oriented languages gain their power from compression, which can lead to compact, efficiently expressed programs. Compression, though, can present problems if it is prematurely used.

- Software development is always through piecemeal growth and rarely through thorough design. Such planned development can lead both to technical problems because the future of a piece of software cannot be known and also to social problems because completely planned development alienates those developers who are not also the planners.

- Habitability is one of the most important characteristics of software. It enables developers to live comfortably in and repair or modify code and design.

- When taken to extremes, abstraction can diminish habitability and can result in premature compression. Beware of overabstracting or of abstracting when a common pattern will do.

- There is much to learn about software development, and we are just starting to do that.

The Quality Without a Name

In 1992 I started reading the more recent work of Christopher Alexander, the Berkeley architect who studies design. The work I'm referring to is captured in the books, *The Timeless Way of Building* (1979), *A Pattern Language* (1977b), *The Oregon Experiment* (1975), and *A New Theory of Urban Design* (1987). Computer scientists over the years have picked up on his writing, and now a small group of them are into "writing patterns." Patterns certainly have an appeal to people who wish to design and construct systems because they are a means to capture common sense and are a way to capture abstractions that are not easily captured otherwise.

My own trek into the space of Alexander's thought began slowly—I read the work, but I tried not to jump to conclusions about its relation to software design. I wanted to figure out what the corresponding points were between architecture and software. The first place where I think I differed with others' interpretation of Alexander's work was in defining the users or inhabitants of a piece of software as its coders and maintainers. At least one computer scientist identified the "user" of a piece of software as the end user. This appears to make sense at first, but when you read Alexander, it is clear that a "user" is an inhabitant—someone who lives in the thing constructed. The thing constructed is under constant repair by its inhabitants, and end users of software do not constantly repair the software, though some might want to.

In earlier essays I've hinted that my trek might also head in the direction of patterns, which are not quite abstractions, modules, or classes. Alexander himself proposes pattern languages as a way to approach design at all levels, from cities and towns to houses and rooms and even to construction techniques.

Now I am at the point of trying to figure out what corresponds to Alexander's patterns. To do this, though, requires figuring out as precisely as I can what the *quality without a name* is in the realm of software. This quality is at the heart of everything Alexander has done since the mid-1960s, and it figures heavily in his conception of pattern languages. Pattern languages are designed to generate towns, communities, neighborhoods, buildings, homes, and gardens with this quality. Alexander's search, culminating in pattern languages, was to find an objective (rather than a subjective) meaning for beauty, for the aliveness that certain buildings, places, and human activities have. The objective meaning is the quality without a name, and I believe we cannot come to grips with Alexander in the software community unless we come to grips with this concept.

In an interview with Stephen Grabow, Alexander stated:

> I was no longer willing to start looking at any pattern unless it presented itself to me as having the capacity to connect up with some part of this quality [the quality without a name]. Unless a particular pattern actually was capable of generating the kind of life and spirit that we are now discussing, and that [sic] it had this quality itself, my tendency was to dismiss it, even though we explored many, many patterns. (Grabow 1983)

Computer scientists who try to write patterns without understanding this quality are quite likely not following Alexander's program, and perhaps they are not helping themselves and others as much as they believe. Or perhaps they are doing harm. So what is this quality without a name?

The quality is an objective quality that things like buildings and places can possess that makes them good places or beautiful places. Buildings and towns with this quality are habitable and alive. The key point to this—and the point that really sets Alexander apart from his contemporaries and stirs philosophical debate—is that the quality is objective. First I'll try to explain the quality, then I'll explain what is so radical about the concept of such a quality. Here is what Alexander says:

> The first place I think of when I try to tell someone about this quality is a corner of an English country garden where a peach tree grows against a wall.
>
> The wall runs east to west; the peach tree grows flat against the southern side. The sun shines on the tree and, as it warms the bricks behind the tree, the warm bricks themselves warm the peaches on the tree. It has a slightly dozy quality. The tree, carefully tied to grow flat against the wall; warming the bricks; the peaches growing in the sun; the wild grass growing around the roots of the tree, in the angle where the earth and roots and wall all meet.
>
> This quality is the most fundamental quality there is in anything. (Alexander 1979)

At first the quality sounds like one reserved for art or architecture. But Alexander asserts that the patterns themselves in his pattern languages must have the quality, and it's fairly clear from what he says about the quality that almost anything can have it or not.

Let's try to figure it out. Alexander says:

> It is a subtle kind of freedom from inner contradictions.
> (Alexander 1979)

This statement reflects the origins of his inquiry into the quality. It started in 1964 when he was doing a study for the Bay Area Rapid Transit (BART) system based on the work reported in *Notes on the Synthesis of Form* (Alexander 1964), which in turn was based on his Ph.D. dissertation. One of the key ideas in this book was that in a good design there must be an underlying correspondence between the structure of the problem and the structure of the solution— good design proceeds by writing down the requirements, analyzing their interactions on the basis of potential misfits, producing a hierarchical decomposition of the parts, and piecing together a structure whose

> *structural hierarchy is the exact counterpart of the functional hierarchy established during the analysis of the program.* (Alexander 1964)

Alexander was studying the system of forces surrounding a ticket booth, and he and his group had written down 390 requirements for what ought to be happening near it. Some of them pertained to such things as being there to get tickets, being able to get change, being able to move past people waiting in line to get tickets, and not having to wait too long for tickets. What he noticed, though, was that certain parts of the system were not subject to these requirements and that the system itself could become bogged down because these other forces—forces not subject to control by requirements—acted to come to their own balance within the system. For example, if one person stopped and another also stopped to talk with the first, congestion could build up that would defeat the mechanisms designed to keep traffic flow smooth. Of course there was a requirement that there not be congestion, but there was nothing the designers could do to prevent this by means of a designed mechanism.

Alexander said this:

> *So it became clear that the free functioning of the system did not purely depend on meeting a set of requirements. It had to do, rather, with the system coming to terms with itself and being in balance with the forces that were generated internal to the system, not in accordance with some arbitrary set of requirements we stated. I was very puzzled by this because the general prevailing idea at the time [in*

> *1964] was that essentially everything was based on goals. My whole*
> *analysis of requirements was certainly quite congruent with the oper-*
> *ations research point of view that goals had to be stated and so on.*
> *What bothered me was that the correct analysis of the ticket booth*
> *could not be based purely on one's goals, that there were realities*
> *emerging from the center of the system itself and that whether you*
> *succeeded or not had to do with whether you created a configuration*
> *that was stable with respect to these realities.* (Grabow 1983)

A system has this quality when it is at peace with itself, when it has no internal contradictions, when it is not divided against itself, when it is true to its own
inner forces. And these forces are separate from the requirements of the system
as a whole. In software we hear about gathering requirements, through talking
to users or customers or by examining the problem space. In the world of computer-aided software engineering (CASE) we hear about traceability, which
means that every procedure or object can be traced back to the requirement that
spawned it. But if Alexander is right, then many of the key characteristics of a
system come from internal forces and not external requirements. So to what will
such parts of system trace? Perhaps to the requirement that a system have the
quality without a name.

Alexander proposes some words to describe the quality without a name, but
even though he feels they point the reader in a direction that helps comprehen-
sion, these words ultimately confuse. The words are *alive, whole, comfortable,*
free, exact, egoless, and *eternal.* I'll go through all of them to try to explain the
quality without a name.

The word *alive* captures some of the meaning when you think about a fire that
is alive. Such a fire is not just a pile of burning logs, but a structure of logs in
which there are sufficient and well-placed air chimneys within that structure.
When someone has built such a fire, you don't see them push the logs about with
a poker but you do see them lift a particular log and move it an inch or maybe a
half inch, so that the air flows more smoothly or the flame curls around the log in
a specific way to catch a higher-up log. Such a fire burns down to a small quantity
of ash. This fire has the quality without a name.

The problem with the word *alive* is that it is a metaphor—it is hard to know
whether something literally not alive, like a fire, is, in fact, *alive,* and when we try
to think of what makes a fire alive, we're not really sure.

Whole captures part of the meaning, because for Alexander a thing that is
whole is free from internal contradictions or inner forces that can tear it apart.
The analogy he uses is a ring of trees around the edge of a windblown lake: The
trees bend in a strong wind, and the roots of the trees keep the bank from eroding, and the water in the lake helps nourish the trees. Every part of the system is in
harmony with every other part. On the other hand, a steep bank with no trees is

easily eroded—the system is not whole, and the system can destroy itself: the grasses and trees are destroyed by the erosion, the bank is torn down, and the lake is filled with mud and disappears. The first system of trees, bank, and lake has the quality without a name.

The problem with this word is that *whole* implies, to some, being enclosed or separate. A lung is whole but it is not whole while still completely contained within a person—a lung requires air to breathe, which requires plants to absorb carbon dioxide and to produce oxygen. The system is much larger than the one that contains the lungs.

The word *comfortable* involves more that meets the eye. Alexander explains it this way:

> *Imagine yourself on a winter afternoon with a pot of tea, a book, a reading light, and two or three huge pillows to lean back against. Now, make yourself comfortable. Not in some way you can show to other people and say how much you like it. I mean so that you really like it for yourself.*
>
> *You put the tea where you can reach it; but in a place where you can't possibly knock it over. You pull the light down to shine on the book, but not too brightly, and so that you can't see the naked bulb. You put the cushions behind you and place them, carefully, one by one, just where you want them, to support your back, your neck, your arm: so that you are supported just comfortably, just as you want to sip your tea, and read, and dream.*
>
> *When you take the trouble to do all that, and you do it carefully, with much attention, then it may begin to have the quality with no name.* (Alexander 1979)

The problem with *comfortable* is that it has too many other meanings. For example, a family with too much money and a house that is too warm also is comfortable.

The word *free* helps define the quality by implying that things that are not completely perfect or overplanned or precise can have the quality too. It also frees us from the confines and limitations of *whole* and *comfortable*.

Free, of course, is not correct because it can imply reckless abandon or not having roots in its own nature.

The word *exact* counterbalances *comfortable* and *free*, which can give the impression of fuzziness or overlooseness. The quality *is* loose and fluid, but it involves precise, exact forces acting in balance. For example, if you try to build a small table on which to put birdseed in the winter for blackbirds, you must know the exact forces that determine the blackbirds' behavior so that they will be able to use the table as you planned. The table cannot be too low because blackbirds don't like to swoop down near the ground, and it cannot be too high because the wind might blow them off course, it cannot be too near to things that could frighten the birds like clotheslines, and it cannot be too exposed to predators. Almost every size for the table and every place to put it you can think of won't work. When it does work, the birdseed table has the quality with no name.

Exact fails because it means the wrong sort of thing to many people. Alexander says:

> *Usually when we say something is exact, we mean that it fits some abstract image exactly. If I cut a square of cardboard and make it perfectly exact, it means that I have made the cardboard perfectly square: its sides are exactly equal: and its angles are exactly ninety degrees. I have matched the image perfectly.*
>
> *The meaning of the work "exact" which I use here is almost the opposite. A thing which has the quality without a name never fits any image exactly. What is exact is its adaptation to the forces which are in it.* (Alexander 1979)

Egoless conveys an important and surprising aspect of the quality. I'll let Alexander say it:

> *When a place is lifeless or unreal, there is almost always a mastermind behind it. It is so filled with the will of the maker that there is no room for its own nature.*
>
> *Think, by contrast, of the decoration on an old bench—small hearts carved in it; simple holes cut out while it was being put together—these can be egoless.*
>
> *They are not carved according to some plan. They are carefree, carved into it wherever there seems to be a gap.* (Alexander 1979)

The word *egoless* is wrong because it is possible to build something with the quality without a name while retaining some of the personality of its builder.

Finally is the word *eternal*. By this word Alexander means that something with the quality is so strong, so balanced, so clearly self-maintaining that it reaches into the realm of eternal truth, even if it lasts for only an instant.

But *eternal* hints at the mysterious, and there is nothing mysterious about the quality. Alexander concludes his discussion of this quality with the following:

> *The quality which has no name includes these simpler sweeter qualities. But it is so ordinary as well that it somehow reminds us of the passing of our life.*
>
> *It is a slightly bitter quality.* (Alexander 1979)

This slightly bitter quality is at the center of Alexander's pattern languages. I believe that if we are to embrace pattern languages, we must also embrace this quality. But what is this quality in software? Certainly I am bitter when I think about some software I know of, but this isn't what Alexander is after. I'll return to this after explaining why this quality is regarded as revolutionary.

What is revolutionary about Alexander is that he is resuming the quest for an understanding of objective quality that science and philosophy abandoned in the modern era. In the seventeenth and eighteenth centuries, a tension developed in which mind and matter were separated by science and philosophy. From this came the separation of *fact* and *value*. After the separation, a fact had no value associated with it, a fact could not be good or bad, it just was. Science, then, tried to find theories that explained things as they were and no longer sought what was good or beautiful about things. That is, we no longer sought the objective characteristics of beauty, which is where Alexander started his quest.

Today it is hard for us to understand that fact and value once were tied together, and it is hard for us as software designers to think of what there could be about a software system that would exhibit Alexander's quality without a name. And, even if we could, it would be difficult to not dismiss it as something only in the eye of the beholder.

The study of beauty stopped because beauty became a mere contingency—whether something was beautiful didn't depend much or at all on the thing, only on the thing as perceived by an unnecessary observer. A thing was beautiful *to* someone: It was not simply beautiful.

Alexander stepped forward and tried to reverse the separation of fact from value. His program was not only to find patterns that explain the existence of the quality without a name but also to find patterns that generate objects with that quality. Furthermore, the patterns themselves must demonstrate the same quality.

Here is how Alexander puts it:

> *Myself, as some of you know, originally a mathematician, I spent several years, in the early sixties, trying to define a view of design, allied with science, in which values were also let in by the back door. I too played with operations research, linear programming, all the fascinating toys, which mathematics and science have to offer us, and tried to see how these things can give us a new view of design, what to design, and how to design.*
>
> *Finally, however, I recognized that this view is essentially not productive, and that for mathematical and scientific reasons, if you like, it was essential to find a theory in which value and fact are one, in which we recognize that here is a central value, approachable through feeling, and approachable by loss of self, which is deeply connected to facts, and forms a single indivisible world picture,* within which productive results can be obtained. (Alexander 1977a, emphasis in original)

For many, Alexander is merely pining for the days when quaint villages and eccentric buildings were the norm. But face it, the buildings he hates, you hate too; and buildings he loves, you love. If this is true, then maybe there is an objective value that we all can recognize.

Alexander is lucky that architecture has a very long history and that the artifacts of architecture from a lot of that history are visible today. This means that he can examine things built before science and philosophy relegated beauty to contingency. We in software are not so lucky—all of our artifacts were conceived and constructed firmly in the system of fact separated from value. But there are programs we can look at and about which we say, "no way I'm maintaining that kluge." And there are other programs about which we can say, "Wow, who wrote this!" So the quality without a name for software must exist.

One of the aspects of the quality with no name that Alexander seems clear on is that buildings with the quality are not made of large modular units. Some of his examples of buildings or things with the quality are built with bricks and other such small modular units, but not large ones. If you were thinking that Alexander is just talking about plain old highly abstract and modular code, perhaps you should think again. His pattern languages provide a well-thought-out abstract language for talking about buildings, and he encourages new pattern languages, but only when they embody the quality with no name—he does not endorse willy nilly pattern languages. Here is what he says:

> Suppose, for example, that an architect makes the statement that buildings have to be made of modular units. This statement is already useless to me because I know that quite a few things are not made of modular units, namely people, trees, and stars, and so therefore the statement is completely uninteresting—aside from the tremendous inadequacies revealed by a critical analysis on its own terms. But even before you get to those inadequacies, my hackles are already up because this statement cannot possibly apply to everything there is in the universe and therefore we are in the wrong ballgame. . . . In other words, I actually do not accept buildings as a special class of things unto themselves, although of course I take them very seriously as a special species of forms. But beyond that is my desire to see them belong with people, trees, and stars as part of the universe. (Grabow 1983)

If we look carefully at the buildings, towns, and cities that Alexander admires, we will see that they are European or perhaps even Third World. This suggests a couple of lines of inquiry into what the quality might be.

European building has an interesting constraint: There isn't much space. People and their buildings need to take up as little space as possible, and buildings, town layout, and common areas are cleverly put together to conserve what is precious. The same is true in many older cultures. Working under space constraints has a few interesting effects.

One effect is that things are on a smaller scale, where perfection is not as easily achieved and where regularity from irregular small parts is possible. Errors are seen as errors only in a context in which those errors are relatively large. When they are small, they form part of the attractiveness of approximate placement. One way to think about this is that nature has a regularity that is not captured well by precise prefractal geometry—such geometry is too precise, too exact to capture nature well. With fractals, though, we can simulate natural surroundings, and the approximate nature of small irregularities is mimicked by irregular placement and small errors.

Another effect is that of the creativity spawned by constraint, which is most easily explained by analogy to poetry. There are many reasons why poetry uses forms—specific meter, rhyme, and stanzaic structure. One reason is that such devices aid memory, and poetry was originally an oral art form. Another important reason is that by placing constraints on the form of a written statement, it becomes less easy to use a phrase or word that easily comes to mind, because it probably won't fit. And if it comes to mind easily, it is most likely a hackneyed phrase or at least one that the poet uses or hears frequently enough that it has lost its edge. By forcing the poet to write in a form, the easy, automatic phrase is eliminated, and the poet is forced to find other ways of saying what is meant. And when that isn't possible, the poet must look for other things to say. In both cases, the constraints force the poet to look for something new to say or new way to say it. Therefore, form in poetry is a device that helps create a climate or context for creativity and newness.

The same is true for construction: When there is no room to do the obvious or when a building must fit in a specific place, the architect must look for new solutions. Because constraint by form limits options, ways must be found to use a single space for multiple purposes.

Europe has a long history, and there are two more effects of that. One is that when people are put into a small space, building with flammable materials is dangerous. Therefore one must build with more durable and difficult materials. This implies that the standard of perfection must drop, and the results are buildings that look more like nature—more fractal-like.

The last effect is that today we see those buildings and towns that have survived because they are pleasant—there is a natural selection. It would be odd to see towns and buildings in Europe that are old and just plain ugly; they would not have survived.

Some of these things might be reasons to question whether the quality without a name really exists separate from the quality of looking like nature or the quality of being highly compressed.

Software has a situation corresponding to compression: bummed code. Bummed code is code that must perform a particular task in a highly constrained footprint because there just isn't any space to do the task in a straightforward manner. This often requires very clever encoding and multiple uses of single resources. Bummed code possesses a certain aesthetic quality, not unlike the compressed quality without a name. The indirectness of such code is pleasing to admire, though not, perhaps, to modify.

ℬ   ℬ   ℬ

I still can't tell you what the quality is, but I can tell you some things about software that possesses it:

- It was not written to an unrealistic deadline.

- Its modules and abstractions are not too big—if they were too big, their size and inflexibility would have created forces that would overgovern the overall structure of the software; every module, function, class, and abstraction is small and named so that I know what it is without looking at its implementation.

- Any bad parts were repaired during maintenance or are being repaired now.

- If it is small, it was written by an extraordinary person, someone I would like as a friend; if it is large, it was not designed by one person, but over time in a slow, careful, incremental way.

- If I look at any small part of it, I can see what is going on—I don't need to refer to other parts to understand what something is doing. This tells me that the abstractions make sense for themselves—they are whole.

- If I look at any large part in overview, I can see what is going on—I don't need to know all the details to get it.

- It is like a fractal, in which every level of detail is as locally coherent and as well thought out as any other level.

- Every part of the code is transparently clear—there are no sections that are obscure in order to gain efficiency.

- Everything about it seems familiar.

- I can imagine changing it, adding some functionality.

- I am not afraid of it, I will remember it.

I wish we had a common body of programs with the quality, because then we could talk about them and understand. As it is, programs are secret and protected, so we rarely see any but those we write ourselves. Imagine a world in which houses were hidden from view. How would Alexander have found the quality with no name?

Think about the quality without a name when you look at your software. Do you think your software possesses it? What would you do to make your software have it?

Pattern Languages

Christopher Alexander's work is based on the premise that the quality without a name is an objective characteristic of things and places. As an architect, Alexander wants to know where this quality comes from and, more important, how to create it, how to generate it. In the previous essay, "The Quality Without a Name," we learned of the divorce centuries ago of beauty from reality. That science could survive the divorce is understandable because science seeks to *describe* reality. Science can live and succeed a long time before it needs to concern itself with describing what makes something beautiful— when something is contingent, as beauty seems to be in modern science, there is little need to describe it. Art, on the other hand, cannot ignore beauty or the quality without a name because artists *create* things—paintings, sculptures, buildings—that are beautiful, that have the quality without a name. There are few fields that blend art and science: Architecture is one, and computer science is another. Architects must design buildings that can be built and architects have a "theory" about what they do—at least architects like Alexander do. In computer science we can describe theories of software, and we create software.

In a field that combines art and science, its practitioners are often divided into camps—one that cares about the raw science and traditionally objective characteristics of the field and another that cares about the beauty and elegance of its creations. In software we care a lot about good code, and we rave about the good coders that we know. In doing this we fall into a trap that Alexander wants us to avoid: separating design from construction.

Before we plunge into patterns, I want to set the stage for the accepted view of how architecture is done, at least in the pre-Alexander world. Architects are hired to solve the problem of how to construct a building or buildings that meet certain constraints as specified by the future inhabitants or people in a position to specify what those inhabitants will need. The architect generally interviews those future inhabitants, studies the site, refers to the local building code, observes neighboring buildings, considers the building materials and construction protocols in the area, and then is inspired, in the manner of all artists, to create a set of drawings which a general contractor, in occasional conference with the architect, reduces to a physical object.

This view of architecture should be familiar to software theorists: It corresponds to the Waterfall Model with a Niagara-sized waterfall. The analyst or designer studies requirements, construction techniques (choice of language), and the context (related software) and, in the manner of all artists, creates the design which he or she happily tosses over a large wall for someone else to implement.

Enlightened folks nowadays tend to view askance this methodology, preferring one or another variant of the Spiral Model. (To be fair, the original Waterfall Model contains backward arrows linking later stages to earlier ones in a feedback type of arrangement, so there actually is not as sharp a contrast between the Waterfall and other models as some would have us believe.)

In fields separated into theory and practice we frequently find that aesthetics are fragmented. The theorist is often interested in beauty of a nature akin to mathematical beauty. In computer science such beauty is exactly mathematical beauty—Occam's razor slicing away fat, eliminating ornamentation, the hard chill beauty of a compact, precisely clever theorem. In architecture the architect works with drawings and models. The beauty of a drawing is not the beauty of a building. A beautiful drawing has spare lines, simple geometric shapes. A home or town is involved, ornamented, shows a care for human interests. Only an inhabitant could know what really counts.

The first of Alexander's contributions to architecture was to reject the separate architect and builder model and to posit user-centered design—in which users (inhabitants) design their own buildings—and the architect-builder who would blend the activities of design and construction. This was viewed by architects as high treason enough, let alone the curious quest for an elusive quality that Alexander cannot name.

The mechanism he proposed to accomplish his new model was the *pattern language*. A pattern language is a set of patterns used by a process to generate artifacts. These artifacts can be considered complexes of patterns. Each pattern is a kind of rule that states a *problem* to be solved and a *solution* to that problem. The means of designing a building, let's say, using a pattern language is to determine the most general problem to be solved and to select patterns that solve that problem. Each pattern defines subproblems that are similarly solved by other, smaller patterns. Thus we see that the solution to a large problem is a nested set of patterns.

Of course, because usually several patterns can solve a given problem, and any pattern requires a particular context to be effective, the process is generally not linear but is a sort of constraint-relaxation process. These days we know all about this sort of process, but back when Alexander came up with pattern languages, it was relatively new. His initial work was done when Noam Chomsky's transformational grammar was first in vogue, and the idea of a human activity—especially a creative one—being subject to rules and generated by a language was hard to swallow.

One interesting aspect of this approach is that it isn't grounded ultimately in *things* but stays at the level of patterns throughout. Some patterns talk about particular construction materials, but rarely is anything like a kitchen or a toilet mentioned. This is partly to maintain a level of elegance—there are only patterns and patterns of patterns, not things and patterns mixed—but also because the patterns talk, in addition, about social and human activities. For example, a stove is really a relationship between a surface, heating elements, thermostats, and switches, and a stove is part of a pattern of activity—cooking a meal, perhaps in a social context. Viewed this way, a stove is also a pattern within a larger pattern which is the whole kitchen whose other patterns involve refrigerators, preparation surfaces, cupboards, utensils, dining areas, walls, natural light sources, gardens, doors, and possibly much, much more. Some of the patterns must be implemented physically near one other, adding a layer of constraints on the solution to the kitchen design/construction process.

The way Alexander motivates pattern languages is with the example of barns. A farmer in a particular Swiss valley wishes to build a barn. Each barn has a double door to accommodate the haywagon, a place to store hay, a place to house the cows, and a place to put the cows so they can eat the hay; this last place must be convenient to the hay storage location so it is easy to feed the cows. There must be a good way to remove the cow excrement, and the whole building has to be structurally sound enough to withstand harsh winter snow and wind.

If each farmer were to design and build a barn based on these functional requirements, each barn would be different, probably radically different. Some would be round, the sizes would vary wildly, some would have double naves, doubly pitched roofs.

But barns in Swiss valleys do not vary wildly, so each farmer must be copying something. The farmer is not copying a specific other barn, because the barns do vary somewhat. Each is a little different because of where it is located and each farmer's particular needs. Therefore, farmers do not copy particular barns. Alexander says that each farmer is copying a set of patterns which have evolved to solve the Swiss-valley-barn problem. Barns in any given Swiss valley are similar, as are all alpine barns. They also are similar to barns in other areas of the world—a family resemblance among buildings—but they do have differences. For example, California barns are generally larger although they share the same general shape.

Here, again, is my working definition of abstraction:

> Abstraction *in programming is the process of identifying common patterns that have systematic variations; an abstraction represents the common pattern and provides a means for specifying which variation to use.* (Balzer et al. 1989)

Patterns in Alexander's sense are a lot like the common patterns but without the systematic variations. For Alexander, the variations of a pattern depend on the other patterns it contains and those containing it, thus eliminating the possibility of systematic variations. Patterns are not well structured enough to have systematic variations—their variations are too context dependent.

This is the format of patterns as presented in *A Pattern Language* (Alexander 1977b):

> *First, there is a picture, which shows an archetypal example of that pattern. Second, after the picture, each pattern has an introductory paragraph, which sets the context for the pattern by explaining how it helps to complete certain larger patterns. Then there are three diamonds to mark the beginning of the problem. After the diamonds there is a headline, in bold type. This headline gives the essence of the problem in one or two sentences. After the headline comes the body of the problem. This is the longest section. It describes the empirical background of the pattern, the evidence for its validity, the range of different ways the pattern can be manifested in a building, and so on. Then, again in bold type, like the headline, is the solution—the heart of the pattern—which describes the field of physical and social relationships which are required to solve the stated problem, in the stated context. This solution is always stated in the form of an instruction— so that you know exactly what you need to do, to build the pattern. Then, after the solution, there is a diagram, which shows the solution in the form of a diagram, with labels to indicate its main components.*
>
> *After the diagram, another three diamonds, to show that the main body of the pattern is finished. And finally, after the diamonds there is a paragraph which ties the pattern to all those smaller patterns in the language, which are needed to complete the pattern, to embellish it, to fill it out.*
>
> *There are two essential purposes behind this format. First, to present each pattern connected to other patterns, so that you grasp the collection of . . . patterns as a whole, as a language within which you can create an infinite variety of combinations. Second, to present the problem and solution of each pattern in such a way that you can judge it for yourself, and modify it, without losing the essence that is central to it.* (Alexander 1977b)

Alexander's book contains 253 patterns covering regions, cities, towns, neighborhoods, transportation, homes, offices, work communities, relaxation areas, rooms, lighting, windows, gardens, waiting rooms, terraces, walls, building materials, and construction. One thing that strikes many readers of the pattern language is the degree to which Alexander talks about people and their activities in the patterns—the patterns are a response to his arguments about how life is best lived. Because of this, many regard *A Pattern Language* as a manual of how to live and how physical surroundings can support and enhance living.

The book is full of evocative black-and-white photographs of towns, parts of homes, scenes of life in Europe, Greece, the Middle East, Asia—all over—each demonstrating a place with the quality without a name and which the patterns are intended to create.

Alexander says:

> *And yet, we do believe, of course, that this language which is printed here is something more than a manual, or a teacher, or a version of a possible pattern language. Many of the patterns here are archetypal—so deep, so deeply rooted in the nature of things, that it seems likely that they will be a part of human nature, and human action, as much in five hundred years, as they are to-day. . . .*
>
> *In this sense, we have also tried to penetrate, as deep as we are able, into the nature of things in the environment. . . .*
> (Alexander 1977b)

Let me present an example pattern—I'll condense it quite a bit to save space.

> *179. Alcoves**
> . . . many large rooms are not complete unless they have smaller rooms and alcoves opening off them. . . .*
>
> ❖ ❖ ❖
>
> *No homogeneous room, of homogeneous height, can serve a group of people well. To give a group a chance to be together, as a group, a room must also give them the chance to be alone, in one's and two's in the same space.*
>
> *This problem is felt most acutely in the common rooms of a house—the kitchen, the family room, the living room. In fact, it is so critical there, that the house can drive the family apart when it remains unsolved. . . .*
>
> *In modern life, the main function of a family is emotional; it is a source of security and love. But these qualities will only come into existence if the members of the house are* physically able to be together as a family.

This is often difficult. The various members of the family come and go at different times of day; even when they are in the house, each has his own private interests. . . . In many houses, these interests force people to go off to their own rooms, away from the family. This happens for two reasons. First, in a normal family room, one person can easily be disturbed by what the others are doing. . . .Second, the family room does not usually have any space where people can leave things and not have them disturbed. . . .

To solve the problem, there must be some way in which the members of the family can be together, even when they are doing different things.

Therefore:

Make small places at the edge of any common room, usually no more than 6 feet wide and 3 to 6 feet deep and possibly much smaller. These alcoves should be large enough for two people to sit, chat, or play and sometimes large enough to contain a desk or table.

alcoves

❖ ❖ ❖

Give the alcove a ceiling which is markedly lower than the ceiling height in the main room. . . . (Alexander 1977b)

What's interesting to me is the argument about how families are served by alcoves. This seems to go well with Alexander's desire to emphasize that the quality without a name is concerned with life and living. In fact, he says:

You see that the patterns are very much alive and evolving.
(Alexander 1977b)

Part of Alexander's research program is to creative *generative* patterns—patterns that generate the quality without a name. Generativeness is an interesting trait. Typically something is said to be generative when it produces the generated quality indirectly.

A good example of a generative process is a random-number generator. Such programs perform simple arithmetic operations on simple starting quantities and produce a stream of numbers with have no simple relation to one other. If we look inside the generator, we don't see any structure or parts that are clearly related to the purpose of generating random numbers.

Another example from a different domain is advice on how to hit a tennis ball. The advice I'm thinking of is that you should not concentrate on hitting the ball at the point of impact but, instead, on hitting a point beyond the ball in the direction the racket is moving. The purpose of this advice is to avoid the effects of the muscles trying to slow down or stop at the point of impact. That is, if I ask you to hit a particular thing with a racket, your muscles will propel the racket toward the target, and just before hitting the target, the muscles controlling opposing movement will contract slightly in order to decelerate to the point of impact—though you will not, obviously, be decelerating to zero velocity, you will decelerate a little. The result of this small deceleration is to cause the racket to jiggle or jitter and for the impact to be less precise. If, on the other hand, you are told to hit something just beyond the target, your muscles will not involuntarily contract until you have hit the target, and as a result, the hit and trajectory will be smoother.

This is the same advice given to martial arts students who are attempting to break boards and bricks.

Such advice is generative: The goal is to hit smoothly and with full power, but this goal is not part of the advice. Rather, the advice is to do something else which has the side effect of achieving the goal.

Patterns in a pattern language are intended to be generative—they are supposed to generate the quality without a name. Just as the advice to write clearly and simply is not possible to follow—because writing clearly and simply is achieved by choosing words and syntax carefully, by choosing presentation order, and by deciding how to emphasize topics in sentences and paragraphs—neither is the advice to produce the quality without a name.

ୡ   ୡ   ୡ

The question we face is how pattern languages apply to software development. People who have tried to apply pattern languages to software have done what you might describe as the obvious thing: They started to develop patterns that are a prescription of how to solve particular problems that come up in development. This isn't new. For example, Knuth's *The Art of Computer Programming* (1969) is a multivolume book that contains exactly such information. This book presents programming situations and problems and describes, in the manner of a textbook, various solutions. A large consideration for Knuth is the performance—time and space complexity—of solutions, and he treats performance very mathematically.

Patterns provide several benefits to programmers and system developers. One is a common language. I've heard many discussions about programs in which the common reference points are algorithms and data structures Knuth describes—and the discussions frequently refer to such algorithms or data structures by citing Knuth's name for them and the volumes in which the descriptions can be found.

Another benefit is a common base for understanding what is important in programming. That is, every pattern in a program is a signpost that helps developers new to a program rapidly understand it. Each common pattern is both important and points out its important subpatterns. For example, in low-level programming languages, people often write `while` loops with the test at the end. When you first come across this style of loop, you wonder what it's all about— your ability to understand a program is challenged by the puzzle of why this loop is coded this peculiar way. Well, most people figure it out sooner or later or at least come to understand the purpose of the code. However, they can understand it more rapidly if they have read Knuth's `while`-loop optimization discussion— with such knowledge they can instantly recognize the Knuth `while` loop, and it is a matter of recognizing a pattern. The loop pattern is important, and the pattern highlights the meat of the loop—the part that is repeated—along with the loop test.

A third benefit is that with a corpus of patterns a programmer is able to solve problems more rapidly by having available a storehouse of solutions—a cookbook, if you will.

Among the folks who write software patterns is the Hillside Group. This group is at least spiritually led by Kent Beck and has met once or twice to talk about patterns and to gather them up—it's a sort of a writers workshop group for writing patterns.

This group, like many others concerned with patterns, focuses on objects and object-oriented programming. The idea is that behavior in object-oriented programs comes largely from configurations of objects and classes sending messages to one another according to protocols. The analogy to architecture should be plain.

Let's look at a pattern discussed by this group. I will, again, abbreviate it.

> Pattern: *Concrete Behavior in a Stateless Object*
> Context: *You have developed an object. You discover that its behavior is just one example of a family of behaviors you need to implement.*
> Problem: *How can you cleanly make the concrete behavior of an object flexible without imposing an unreasonable space or time cost, and with minimal effect on the other objects in the system?*
> Constraints: *No more complexity in the object. . . . Flexibility— the solution should be able to deal with system-wide, class-wide, and instance-level behavior changes. The changes should be able to take place at any time. . . . Minimal time and space impact. . . .*

Solution: *Move the behavior to be specialized into a stateless object which is invoked when the behavior is invoked.*

Example: *The example is debug printing. . . .* (Kent Beck, personal communication 1993)

The example actually explains the solution a lot better than does the solution description—the example is given in Smalltalk. The idea is that you define a side object (and a class) that has the behavior you want by defining methods on it. All the methods take an extra argument which is the real object on which to operate. Then you implement the desired behavior on the original object by first sending a message to `self` to determine the appropriate side object and then sending the side object a message with the real object as an extra argument. By defining the method that returns the side object you can get either instance-level, class-level, or global changes in behavior.

This is a useful pattern, and you can imagine how a book full of stuff like this would turn a smart but inexperienced object programmer into something a little closer to an expert.

Patterns seem to be a partial solution to the overabstraction problem I talked about in "Abstraction Descant." They are a way to take advantage of common patterns without building costly, confusing, and unnecessary abstractions when the goal is merely to write something understandable. That is, when there are more idioms to use, using them is far better than inventing a new vocabulary. There are lots of reasons that abstractions are used, and I'm not saying we shouldn't use them, but let's not confuse their convenience in some situations as proof of their unqualified usefulness. For example, abstractions allow us to avoid typing (fingers pounding the keyboard). However, avoiding typing is something a programming environment is supposed to help accomplish, and one can imagine a programming environment that would let people use a pattern about as easily as an ordinary abstraction. Keep in mind that the most useful patterns are quite large, like the one regarding concrete behavior in stateless objects. Furthermore, as Alexander points out, patterns interact with larger and smaller patterns in such a way that the actual manifestation of any given pattern is influenced by and influences several or many other patterns.

Alexander talks about the poetry of patterns. Poetry is at least partly distinguished from prose by its stronger use of *compression*. Compression is that characteristic of a piece in some language in which each word assumes many meanings and derives its meaning from the context. In this way, a small expression can perform a lot of tasks because the context is rich. This is one reason that inheritance works and is also a way that inheritance can go wrong. When you write a subclass, you can reuse the methods above it—and the code you write is compressed because it takes its meaning from the context of its superclasses. This is good, but if you have a deep or dense hierarchy, you could easily spend a lot of time understanding it in order to write correct, highly compressed code.

For patterns, you can have compression if several patterns are present in one space. Alexander says:

> *It is quite possible that all the patterns for a house might, in some form, be present, and overlapping, in a simple one-room cabin. The patterns do not need to be strung out, and kept separate. Every build-ing, every room, every garden is better, when all the patterns which it needs are compressed as far as it is possible for them to be. The build-ing will be cheaper; and the meanings in it will be denser.*
> (Alexander 1977a)

Compression is what we saw when we looked at the constraints of European and some Third-World architecture: small scale. With limited space, all the features that people require to live must be present in the space available. This forces people to be clever to design in all the parts in minimal space, most likely by over-lapping and causing this poetry—the poetry of compression. It also forces things into small, irregular pieces.

The question is: Is software that is compressed better than software that is not? I think there is a great deal of admiration for compressed software, but is it more maintainable?

❧   ❧   ❧

Patterns in software are a good idea, but I have rarely seen the attention to the human side—to living within software—that I see in Alexander's patterns. One architect commented on Alexander that he regarded the patterns as providing information, sort of heuristics, about architecture, and I have to admit the patterns I've seen about software do that—they provide information that the software practitioner just plain ought to know.

But the picture is not quite complete, and I fear it may never be. The use of patterns is clearly helpful, if for no other reason to capture in a common format programming lore and tips—a sort of better-organized *Art of Computer Program-ming*. The "but" concerns the quality without a name. Alexander hoped that his pattern language would generate towns, buildings, communities, homes, offices, gardens, and places with that quality. And he had the benefit of knowing what he was trying to generate. He could go to Florence and walk the piazzas, the colon-nades, the small hidden gardens, he could visit the temples in Kyoto, the perfect alcoves in Norway, white hilltowns of Greece. We as computer scientists do not have examples of programs exhibiting the quality without a name that we all can agree on or even just name. That's step 1. Step 2 is to understand the quality. I took a stab at it in "The Quality Without a Name," but I admit I was simply guessing.

The worst thing is this: Alexander had the chance in the 1970s to try out his pattern language. He observed the results of others trying it out and he even tried it out himself several times. And guess what: It didn't work. In one project in Mexicali, Alexander, his colleagues, students, and a community of people constructed a community. Alexander says he found hints of the quality in only a few places. Otherwise, the houses were "funky". That is, when Alexander tried out his theory, it failed.

The story is not over.

The Failure of Pattern Languages

We have been exploring the Christopher Alexander saga and it might surprise some to learn that Alexander completed by the early 1970s all the work I've reported so far—in what some would call the infancy of computer science. People have read his work and taken off from it—The Hillside Group and others are writing software patterns, believing they are doing something worthwhile—and they are. But are they doing for software what Alexander set out to do for architecture—find a process to build artifacts possessing the quality without a name? Or is the quality unimportant to what the software pattern writers are doing? Is it important only that they are accomplishing something good for software, and Alexander's original goal is unimportant, merely a catalyst or inspiration—the way fine drizzle drawing his eyes low, narrowing streetlights to a sheltering fog, can inspire a poet to write a poem of intimacy and its loss? Or the way an inept carpenter building an overly sturdy birdcage can inspire another person to construct a tiger's cage?

I think the quality without a name is vital to software development, but I'm not yet sure how, because I am not clear on what the quality without a name is in the realm of software. It sits zen in the midst of a typhoon frenzy of activity in both architecture and software. Alexander's story does not end with the publication of *A Pattern Language* in 1977. It went on and still goes on. And Alexander did not sit still after he wrote the patterns. Like any scientist he tried them out.

And they did not work.

Read Alexander's own words:

> *All the architects and planners in christendom, together with* The Timeless Way of Building (Alexander 1979) *and the* Pattern Language (Alexander 1977a), *could still not make buildings that are alive because it is other processes that play a more fundamental role, other changes that are more fundamental.* (Grabow 1983)

Alexander reached this conclusion after completing some specific projects. One was the Modesto Clinic. In this project an architect from Sacramento used Alexander's pattern language to design and build a medical clinic in Modesto (in the Central Valley of California). The building was a success in the sense that a building was actually constructed and its plan looked good on paper. Alexander noted:

> Up until that time I assumed that if you did the patterns correctly, from a social point of view, and you put together the overall layout of the building in terms of those patterns, it would be quite alright to build it in whatever contemporary way that was considered normal. But then I began to realize that it was not going to work that way. (Grabow 1983)

Even though the Sacramento architect tried hard to follow the patterns, the result was dismal. Alexander says about the clinic:

> It's somewhat nice in plan, but it basically looks like any other building of this era. One might wonder why its plan is so nice, but in any really fundamental terms there is nothing to see there. There was hardly a trace of what I was looking for. (Grabow 1983)

This wasn't an isolated failure, but one repeated frequently by other people trying to use the pattern language from bootlegged copies of A Pattern Language:

> Bootleg copies of the pattern language were floating up and down the West Coast and people would show me projects they had done and I began to be more and more amazed to realize that, although it worked, all of these projects basically looked like any other buildings of our time. They had a few differences. They were more like the buildings of Charles Moore or Joseph Esherick, for example, than the buildings of S.O.M. or I. M. Pei; but basically, they still belonged perfectly within the canons of mid-twentieth century architecture. None of them whatsoever crossed the line. (Grabow 1983)

Alexander noticed a more bizarre phenomenon than the fact that the buildings were no different from their contemporaries—the architects believed they were different, vastly and remarkably different. Alexander said:

> They thought the buildings were physically different. In fact, the people who did these projects thought that the buildings were quite different from any they had designed before, perhaps even outrageously so. But their perception was incredibly wrong; and I began to see this happening over and over again—that even a person who is very enthusiastic about all of this work will still be perfectly capable of

> *making buildings that have this mechanical death-like morphology,*
> *even with the intention of producing buildings that are alive.*
>
> *So there is the slightly strange paradox that, after all those years of*
> *work, the first three books are essentially complete and, from a theo-*
> *retical point of view, do quite a good job of identifying the difference*
> *but actually do not accomplish anything. The conceptual structures*
> *that are presented are just not deep enough to actually break down*
> *the barrier. They actually do not do anything.* (Grabow 1983)

Alexander determined that they failed because the geometry of the buildings was not as different from the standard modern geometry as it needed to be to generate the quality. One of his reaction he was to consider the *process* of building: the mortgage process, the zoning process, the construction process, the process of money flowing through the system, the role of the architect, and the role of the builder. By controlling the process, you control the result, and if the control retains the old, broken process, the result will be the old, broken architecture.

This resonates with what we see in software development: The structure of the system follows the structure of the organization that put it together, and to some extent, its quality follows the nature of the process used to produce it. The true problems of software development derive from the way the organization can dis-cover and come to grips with the complexity of the system being built while maintaining budget and schedule constraints. It is not common for organizations to try to put together a novel large artifact, let alone doing it on schedule. When an engineering team designs and builds a bridge, for example, it is creating a vari-ant of a well-known design, and so many things about that design are already known that the accuracy of planning and scheduling depends on how hard the people want to work, not on whether they can figure out how to do it.

Even while considering process, Alexander never lost sight of geometry.

> *[T]he majority of people who read the work, or tried to use it, did not*
> *realize that the conception of geometry had to undergo a fundamen-*
> *tal change in order to come to terms with all of this. They thought*
> *they could essentially graft all the ideas about life, and patterns, and*
> *functions on to their present conception of geometry. In fact, some*
> *people who have read my work actually believe it to be somewhat*
> *independent of geometry, independent of style—even of architecture.*
> (Grabow 1983)

From the time when buildings routinely possessed the quality without a name to the present when almost no buildings possess that quality, the process of build-ing has changed from the so-called renaissance building paradigm to the current industrial building paradigm, from one in which building was a decentralized activity in which the architect, if one was used, was closely associated with the building or even participated in the building, and material was handcrafted on site, to one in which an architect might design hundreds of homes which were then built by a contractor buying and using modular parts, perhaps minimally customizing them—for example, cutting lumber to the proper length. At the same time, because building became a high-volume activity, the process of funding building changed so that, now, a large sum of money needs to be allocated to produce any homes at all.

As I mentioned in "Habitability and Piecemeal Growth," one problem with the building process is *lump-sum development*. In such development few resources are brought to bear on the problems of repair and piecemeal growth. Instead, a large sum of money is dedicated to building a large artifact, and that artifact is allowed to deteriorate somewhat, and anything that is found lacking in the design or construction is ignored or minimally addressed until it is feasible to abandon the building and construct a replacement. This phenomenon also occurs in the mortgage process. The bank lends someone, say a developer, a large sum of money to construct a home. A homebuyer purchases this home by assuming a large debt. The debt is paid off over time, with the early payments dedicated mostly to paying the interest, which accumulates, and only at the end of the mortgage period is the principal taken down. The result is that a homeowner might pay $1 million for a house that cost $400,000 to build. The problem with this—aside from all the problems you can easily identify yourself—is that the additional $600,000 paid for the house is not available for repair and piecemeal growth. It is a fee to the bank. And the house is not improved in any way or only minimally during the payment period—10 to 30 years—at which point the house is sold to someone else who pays another (or the same!) bank another enormous fee. The key ingredient to long-term development—piecemeal growth—is thwarted.

Alexander started a lengthy process himself of constructing arguments to show that process itself was the root cause for the practical failure of his theory of the quality without a name and of his particular pattern language—that the process of construction encompassed so many things controlling geometry that the outcome had to be as flawed and disappointing as what he saw in the early, uncontrolled experiments.

First he needed to convince himself that process could be the primary determiner of the outcome of a generative process. He got this from D'Arcy Thompson; Alexander said:

> What Thompson insisted on was that every form is basically the end
> result of a certain growth process. When I first read this I felt that of
> course the form in a purely static sense is equilibrating certain forces
> and that you could say that it was even the product of those forces—
> in a non-temporal, non-dynamic sense, as in the case of a raindrop,
> for example, which in the right here and now is in equilibrium with

the air flow around it, the force of gravity, its velocity, and so forth—
but that you did not really have to be interested in how it actually got
made. Thompson however was saying that everything is the way it is
today because it is the result of a certain history—which of course
includes how it got made. But at the time I read this I did not really
understand it very well; whereas I now realize that he is completely
right. (Grabow 1983)

It's somewhat amazing that Alexander would fail to understand this right off, because his theory—patterns generating the quality without a name—is an example of it. His error, if there was one, was not to go far enough with his theory. Once he latched onto this insight he went hog wild. First he examined the process closely, identifying places where its details did not serve the quality without a name and geometry. Second, he performed several important experiments in which he controlled or nearly controlled the entire process.

These experiments were based on an alternative process developed by Alexander, which he called the "grassroots housing process." The basic idea is that a sponsor—a group of people, a corporation—would provide land at a reasonable price. There would be a builder who was actually an architect, a builder, and a manager rolled into one. Families would get an allotment of money to begin construction. The builder would help, and with the pattern language each family would build its own home. Each family would pay a fee per year with the following characteristics. The fee would be based on square footage and would decline from a very high rate in the early years to a very low one in later years. It was assumed to take around 13 years to pay off the fee. Materials for building would be free to families (of course, paid for by the fees). This means that families would be encouraged initially to build small homes. Because materials would be free and the only fees would be for square footage, each family would be encouraged to improve or embellish its existing space and the cluster's common space. As time passed and the fees dropped in later years, homes could be enlarged. These clusters would nest in the sense that there would be a larger "political" unit responsible for enhancing structures larger than any particular cluster. For example, roads would be handled in this way and the political unit would be a sort of representative government.

The existence of free materials and nested clusters would, Alexander hoped, create a mechanism for planning within a community and with a nearby or enclosing community.

The builder would help the families do their own building by instruction or by doing those jobs requiring the most skill. Each builder would have several apprentices who would be trained on the job. A builder would work with a cluster of families, and over time the builder would gradually move on to service another cluster, at which point the first cluster would become self-sufficient.

The way this scheme would work, of course, is the same way the banks work, but with a lower fee and with the community—the cluster—acting as the bank. Profits from the process would be used to sponsor other clusters.

After presenting this proposed process, Christopher Alexander was shocked to be quizzed about his views on Marxism. Nevertheless, two important concepts came out of it: the nested cluster with shared common areas and the architect-builder.

This led to several projects. One was to see whether local politics could be changed to support this new building process. To this end Alexander managed to get passed a Berkeley referendum in the early 1970s that put a moratorium on new construction and established a commission to look into a new master plan based on participatory planning of the sort talked about in *The Oregon Experiment* (Alexander 1975). The result was not quite what he had in mind: There was a new master plan, but one that asked local neighborhoods which streets could be closed. As a result, some of them were—if you drive through Berkeley today, you can still experience the results.

The most ambitious experiment was to build a community in Mexicali. The Mexican government became convinced that Alexander would be able to build a community housing project for far less than the usual cost, so they gave him the power he felt he needed to organize the project. The land was provided in such a way that the families together owned the encompassed public land and each family owned the land on which their home was built. The point of the experiment was to see whether with a proper process and a pattern language, a community could be built that demonstrated the quality without a name. Because of the expected low cost of the project and the strong recommendation of the University of Mexico regarding Alexander's work, the Mexican government was willing to allow Alexander to put essentially into practice his grassroots system of production. The details of this system hinged on the answers to these questions (all seven questions are from Alexander 1985):

1. *What kind of person is in charge of the building operation itself?*

   An architect-builder is in charge. This corresponds to the master architect of a software system who also participates in coding and helps his codevelopers with their work.

2. *How local to the community is the construction firm responsible for building?*

   Each site has its own builder's yard, each responsible for local development. This corresponds to putting control of the computer and software resources for each small project within that project. Local control and physically local resources are important.

3. *Who lays out and controls the common land between the houses, and the array of lots and houses?*

This is handled by the community itself, in groups small enough to come to agreement in face-to-face meetings. This corresponds to small group meetings to discuss and negotiate interfaces in a project. There is no centralized decision maker, but a community of developers sits down and discusses in the group the best interfaces.

4. *Who lays out the plans of individual houses?*

Families design their own homes. This corresponds to each developer designing his or her own implementations for a component.

5. *Is the construction system based on the assembly of standard components, or is it based on acts of creation which use standard processes?*

Construction is based on a standard process rather than by standard components. This goes against one of the supposed tenets of the object philosophy in which standardized class libraries are *de rigueur*. Nevertheless, many experiences show that the true benefits of reuse come from reuse within a project and not as much from among projects. Such successful reuse is based on being able to model the domain of the project so that classes defined to represent aspects of the domain can be used for several purposes within that same model. Typically such a model is called a *framework*.

6. *How is cost controlled?*

Cost is controlled flexibly so that local decisions and trade-offs can be made. This corresponds to giving a project a total budget number rather than breaking it down too far, such as one budget for hardware and another for developers.

7. *What is the day-to-day life like, on-site, during the construction operation?*

It is not just a place where the job is done but a place where the importance of the houses themselves as homes infuses the everyday work. Developers need to have their own community in which both the work and the lives of the developers are shared: meals, rest time together in play. It's called team building in the management literature, but it's more than that, and every development manager worth paying knows that this is one of the most important parts of a project.

You might wonder why Alexander (or I, for that matter) considers a project's day-to-day life to be important. It's because the quality of the result depends on the quality of communication between the builders or developers, and this depends on whether it is fun to work on the project and whether the project is important to the builder or developer in a personal sense and not just in a monetary or job sense.

Alexander tells the story of this project—including the sorts of meals the families had and their celebrations after completing major projects—in *The Production of Houses* (1985). At the end of that book Alexander tells about the failures of the project as seen close up—that is, before he was able to sit back and look at the results objectively. He says there were a number of failures. First, the Mexican government lost faith in the project and pulled the plug after five houses were built, leaving 25 unbuilt. Partly they lost faith because the buildings looked "traditional" rather than modern. Alexander said:

> The almost naïve, childish, rudimentary outward character of the
> houses disturbed them extremely. (Remember that the families, by
> their own frequent testimony, love their houses.) (Alexander 1985)

Another reason was that the government was dismayed by Alexander's experimentation with construction systems. The government felt that because Alexander was a world authority on architecture and building, he would simply apply what he knew to produce beautiful homes cheaply and rapidly.

One failure that seemed to disturb Alexander was that the builder's yard was abandoned within three years of the end of the project. He felt that the process would have continued without his involvement once the families saw that they could control their own living spaces.

But did the buildings and the community have the quality without a name? Alexander said at the time:

> The buildings, for example, are very nice, and we are very happy that
> they so beautifully reflect the needs of different families. But they are
> still far from the limpid simplicity of traditional houses, which was
> our aim. The roofs are still a little awkward, for example. And the
> plans, too, have limits. The houses are very nice internally, but they
> do not form outdoor space which is as pleasant, or as simple, or as
> profound as we can imagine it. For instance, the common land has a
> rather complex shape, and several of the gardens are not quite in the
> right place. The freedom of the pattern language, especially in the

hands of our apprentices, who did not fully understand the deepest ways of making buildings simple, occasionally caused a kind of confusion compared with what we now understand, and what we now will do next time. (Alexander 1985)

This chilling reference to the deep understanding required to build buildings with the quality without a name is echoed in the discussion of the builder's yard:

When their [the government's] support faded, the physical buildings of the builder's yard had no clear function, and, because of peculiarities in the way the land was held, legally, were not transferred to any other use, either; so now, the most beautiful part of the buildings which we built stand idle. And yet these buildings, which we built first, with our own deeper understanding of the pattern language, were the most beautiful buildings in the project. That is very distressing, perhaps the most distressing of all. (Alexander 1985)

Later, after some reflection Alexander became more harsh:

There was one fact above everything else I was aware of, and that was that the buildings were still a bit more funky than I would have liked. That is, there are just a few little things that we built down there that truly have that sort of limpid beauty that have been around for ages and that, actually, are just dead right. That's rare; and it occurred in only a few places. Generally speaking, the project is very delightful— different of course from what is generally being built, not just in the way of low-cost housing—but it doesn't quite come to the place where I believe it must.

. . . But what I am saying now is that, given all that work (or at least insofar as it came together in the Mexican situation) and even with us doing it (so there is no excuse that someone who doesn't understand it is doing it), it only works partially. Although the pattern language worked beautifully—in the sense that the families designed very nice houses with lovely spaces and which are completely out of the rubric of modern architecture—this very magical quality is only faintly showing through here and there. (Grabow 1983)

Alexander noticed a problem with using the word *simplicity* to refer to the fundamental goal of the patterns:

We were running several little experiments in the builder's yard. There is an arcade around the courtyard with each room off of the arcade designed by a different person. Some of the rooms were designed by my colleagues at the Center and they also had this unusual funkiness—still very charming, very delightful, but not calm at all. In that sense, vastly different from what is going on in the four-hundred year old Norwegian farm where there is an incredible clarity and simplicity that has nothing to do with its age. But this was typical of things that were happening. Here is this very sort of limpid simplicity and yet the pattern language was actually encouraging people to be a little bit crazy and to conceive of much more intricate relationships than were necessary. They were actually disturbing. Yet in all of the most wonderful buildings, at the same time that they have all of these patterns in them, they are incredibly simple. They are not simple like an S.O.M. building;—sometimes they are incredibly ornate—so I'm not talking about that kind of simplicity. There is however a kind of limpidity which is very crucial; and I felt that we just cannot keep going through this problem. We must somehow identify what it is and how to do it—because I knew it was not just my perception of it.

The problem is complicated because the word simplicity completely fails to cover it; at another moment it might be exactly the opposite. Take the example of the columns. If you have the opportunity to put a capital or a foot on it, it is certainly better to do those two things than not—which is different from what the modern architectural tradition tells you to do. Now, in a peculiar sense, the reasons for it being better that way are the same as the reasons for being very simple and direct in the spacing of those same columns around the courtyard. I'm saying that, wherever the source of that judgment is coming from, it is the same in both cases. . . . The word simplicity is obviously not the relevant word. There is something which in one instance tells you to be simple and which in another tells you to be more complicated. It's the same thing which is telling you those two things. (Grabow 1983)

Another part of the problem Alexander saw with the Mexicali project had to do with the level of mastery needed in the construction process. At the start of the project he felt that merely having the same person do both the design and the construction was enough, so that the important small decisions dictated by the design would be made correctly. But during the project and later on Alexander learned that the builder needed more.

Only recently have I begun to realize that the problem is not merely one of technical mastery or the competent application of the rules— like trowelling a piece of concrete so that it's really nice—but that there is actually something else which is guiding these rules. It actually involves a different level of mastery. It's quite a different process to do it right; and every single act that you do can be done in that sense well or badly. But even assuming that you have got the technical part clear, the creation of this quality is a much more complicated

*process of the most utterly absorbing and fascinating dimensions. It is
in fact a major creative or artistic act—every single little thing you
do—and it is only in the years since the Mexican project that I have
begun to see the dimensions of that fact.* (Grabow 1983)

Not only must you decide to build the right thing, but you also must build it
with skill and artistry. This leads to an obvious question: Are buildings with the
quality without a name just too hard to put together deliberately, and were they
created in older societies only by chance and survive only because of the quality?
Or even more cynically, is there a form of nostalgia at work in which everything
old is revered, because it comes from a more innocent and noble age?

There is another, chilling possibility: Perhaps it takes a real artist to create
buildings and towns possessing the quality without a name. If you think about it,
however, there is nothing really surprising or shocking about this.

Not everyone can write a great poem or paint a picture that will last through
the ages. When we go to museums, we see art with the quality without a name
and we are not surprised. And when we go to an adult-education art class we are
not surprised to see good art, but art that is a little funky and perhaps it's different
but it's not great.

The question is whether it is possible to write down rules or patterns for architecture—and software and art—so that ordinary people can follow the rules or
patterns and, by the nature of the patterns and using only the abilities of ordinary
people, beauty is generated. If this happens, then the rules or patterns are generative, which is a rare quality.

Art teachers can provide generative rules. For example, my father watched and
"studied" the various art programs on public television for 15 years, and I'll be
darned but he stopped painting like a fifth grader waiting for recess and started
being a pretty decent still-life and landscape painter. You won't see his work in a
museum in 20 years, but if you saw it on the wall in my house, you wouldn't bat
an eye.

What he learned about painting surprised me. I expected that the lessons
would talk about drawing skills and how to reproduce what you saw in reality by
attending to each detail in order to create an accurate reproduction. What he
learned instead was that by using the nature of the medium, the paint, the brush,
and brush strokes, he could create the same effects as those of reality through
reflected light and by the oil on canvas. So, instead—as I expected—of spending
hours painting each branch on a conifer, my father would dab and push with a
thick brush to create the effect of needled branches, and from a proper viewing
distance his conifers looked as real as real.

Let's recall what Alexander said about the people who helped build the houses
in Mexicali and who live there: "Remember that the families, by their own frequent
testimony, love their houses." Perhaps these houses did not live up to Alexander's

high artistic standards, but they were nice homes and served their users well. Like my father's paintings, they are better than the untutored could accomplish. And there's nothing wrong with that.

Perhaps Alexander's pattern language is working as well as it can—it's just that the artistry required to make buildings having the quality without a name wasn't present in any of the families who worked with Alexander or even in Alexander's team. The failure of the pattern language in the bootleg-designed houses and in Mexicali are maybe simply the failures of artistry.

Perhaps, and perhaps these are true failures, but this should not dissuade us from considering how to create things with the quality without a name.

It is easy to see that the process of constructing buildings has an obvious correspondent in software: The process of software construction is the single most important determining factor in software quality. Alexander's building process adapted to software could be called a form of *incremental development* because it advises the use of small groups with autonomy, architect-builders at the helm.

But what of geometry? Alexander always goes back to this. And one of his key questions is: What dictates geometry possessing the quality without a name—what is that thing that is falsely called *simplicity*?

What corresponds to geometry for us?

I think it is the code itself. Many talk about the need for excellent interfaces and the benefits of separating interface from implementation so that the implementation may vary. But few people talk seriously about the quality of the code itself. In fact, most theorists are eager to lump it into the category of things best not discussed, something to be hidden from view so that it can be changed in private. But think of Alexander's remarks: The quality comes in nearly equal part from the artistry and creativity of the builder who is the one whose hands most directly form the geometry that gives the building its quality and character. Isn't the builder the coder? And isn't the old-style software methodology to put design in the hands of analysts and designers and to put coding in the hands of lowly coders, sometimes offshore coders who can be paid the lowest wages to do the least important work?

Methodologists who insist on separating analysis and design from coding are missing the essential feature of design: The design is in the code, not in a document or in a diagram. Half a programmer's time is spent exploring the code, not in typing it in or changing it. When you look at the code you see its design, and that's most of what you're looking at, and it's mostly while coding that you're designing.

> *Poincaré once said: "Sociologists discuss sociological methods; physicists discuss physics." I love this statement. Study of method by itself is always barren. . . .* (Alexander 1964)

This could be a lesson for some of our software development methodologists: Study software, not software methods.

Patterns can help designers and designer-coders to make sure they put the right stuff in their software, but it takes a coder with extraordinary mastery to construct software having the quality without a name.

And what of simplicity? Can it be that blind subservience to simplicity in software development can lead to the same "death-like morphology" that it causes in architecture?

❧ ❧ ❧

In 1995, software developers are writing and publishing patterns, and the "patterns movement" is gaining momentum. What are they actually doing? Most of the patterns I've seen present solutions to technical problems. For example, a pattern language I'm familiar with explains how to produce a design for a program that will validate a complex set of input values presented on forms that the end user fills in. It's a very nice pattern language, but I'm not sure where the quality without a name is in this language. If I needed to write a system with a component that had to validate input fields, I would use it, but I doubt that the quality would emerge from what I learned from the pattern language.

From the pattern language I would learn the issues that go into an input validation component, and I would be able to get all the parts right, and perhaps folks later on maintaining my component would have an easier job of it for my having used the pattern language, but I doubt there would be any artistic merit in it or the quality.

When I look at software patterns and pattern languages, I don't see the quality without a name in them, either. Recall that Alexander said that both the patterns themselves and the pattern language have the quality. In many cases today the pattern languages are written quickly, sort of like students doing homework problems. I heard one neophyte pattern writer say that when writing patterns he just writes what he knows and can write four or five patterns at a sitting.

That patterns that I wrote neither possess the quality nor generate it is not surprising. Patterns are an art form, and they are designed to generate art within the domain about which they speak. Art is not created at the clip of four or five pieces per sitting. It takes time and the right context and the right preparation to write them.

My patterns are doggerel, just as are poems written quickly this way—four or five at a sitting. Poetic doggerel serves a purpose: therapy. And maybe so does pattern writing of the sort we're talking about.

Patterns written in this way will almost never generate the quality without a name, and it is likely that people who write patterns like this and see them fail will attribute the failure to the concept of patterns and pattern languages. And people who use the patterns and fail may do so as well.

But Alexander's pattern language is not doggerel: It was written by many people over many years, and each was subject to extensive discussion and criticism before being published. It is clear that the patterns themselves have the quality without a name, and I think this is because Alexander and his colleagues are pattern artists.

It just seems that the experiments that Alexander's team did in Mexicali were not done by artists or that the muse didn't visit them during the process.

⁋   ⁋   ⁋

Alexander's story is nearly up to date, but to many it disappears at the point we've left him here. Our modern-day pattern writers are content to stop with *A Pattern Language* and *The Timeless Way of Building* and to go off writing patterns. They ignore the failures that Alexander himself saw in his own processes at that point. The next chapter of his story takes him back to geometry and art. It's probably a story that has only the most metaphorical application to software because it has to do with beads, beauty, art, geometry, and Turkish carpets.

The Bead Game, Rugs, and Beauty

People in software research continue to find inspiration in the work of Christopher Alexander—they find his concept of pattern language a means to codify design skills. Some of them, though, don't see the relevance of the quality without a name, and anyhow some doubt there is anything about older building styles than they have survived through time by a process of natural selection—the old buildings we see today in Europe, let's say, are nicer because the cruddy ones were torn down and the nice ones imitated.

To many software patterns folk the quality without a name doesn't apply to things like software anyhow. I agree that most software—at least the software I see—doesn't have such a quality, but does that mean it couldn't? I find it odd, though, to take so much inspiration from the simple, mechanical parts of a person's work—the form of the pattern language and terms like *forces*—but to ignore the heart of it. I'm not so sure the quality without a name is irrelevant.

When we last left Christopher Alexander, he had apparently despaired in his quest for the quality without a name based on his experiences with the Modesto and Mexicali projects. In those projects his pattern language was used to construct a clinic (Modesto) and a small community (Mexicali). In Modesto the architect in charge was not able to control the process of spending and building as Alexander advocated in his "grassroots housing process." In the Mexicali project, where Alexander was in charge and had a special arrangement with the Mexican government, he had all the control he needed. But the results were disappointing. Alexander felt the buildings were "funky" and only in places demonstrated a hint of the quality.

It is at this point that Alexander went off in search of a universal formative principle, a generative principle governing form that would be shared by both the laws of nature and great art. If the principle could be written down and was truly formative, then aesthetic judgment and beauty would be objective and not subjective, and it would be possible to produce art and buildings with the quality without a name.

If there were such a universal principle, any form that stirred us would do so at a deep cognitive level rather than at a representational level, where its correspondence to reality is most important. That is, the feeling great form in art gives us would be a result of the form operating directly on us and in us rather than indirectly through nature; and nature would share the same forms because the principle is universal. Many philosophers from Plato onward believed in this deeper level of form, including Alexander. According to Herbert Read,

> *The increasing significance given to* form *or* pattern *in various branches of science has suggested the possibility of a certain parallelism, if not identity, in the structures of natural phenomena and of authentic works of art. That the work of art has a formal structure of a rhythmical, even of a precisely geometrical kind, has for centuries been recognised by all but a few nihilists. That some at any rate of these structures or proportions—notably the Golden Section—have correspondence in nature has also been recognised for many years. The assumption, except on the part of a few mystics, was that nature in these rare instances, was paying an unconscious tribute to art; or that the artist was unconsciously imitating nature. But now the revelation that perception is itself a pattern-selecting and pattern-making function (a Gestalt formation); that pattern is inherent in the physical structure and functioning of the nervous system; that matter itself analyses into coherent patterns or arrangements of molecules; and that the gradual realisation that all these patterns are effective and ontologically significant by virtue of an organisation of their parts which can only be characterised as* aesthetic—*all this development has brought works of art and natural phenomena on to an identical plane of inquiry.* (Grabow 1983; Read 1951)

Alexander took this point of view seriously and proposed the "bead game conjecture," a mechanism that unifies all forms—science, art, music, society.

> *That it is possible to invent a unifying concept of structure within which all the various concepts of structure now current in different fields of art and science, can be seen from a single point of view. This conjecture is not new. In one form or another people have been wondering about it, as long as they have been wondering about structure itself; but in our world, confused and fragmented by specialisation, the conjecture takes on special significance. If our grasp of the world is to remain coherent, we need a bead game; and it is therefore vital for us to ask ourselves whether or not a bead game can be invented.* (Alexander 1968)

"Bead game" refers to Hermann Hesse's imaginary game in which all forms—art, science, nature—can be represented in a single way.

As I noted in "The Failure of Pattern Languages," Alexander attributed this failure of his pattern language to two things: The first was that the level of mastery of the pattern language and of the building and design skills needed to produce the quality without a name were in fact limited in the folks doing the work; and the second was that the participants—the architects and builders—did not sufficiently appreciate the geometrical aspects of beauty and the quality. Alexander said:

> I had been watching what happens when one uses pattern languages to design buildings and became uncomfortably aware of a number of shortcomings. The first is that the buildings are slightly funky—that is, although it is a great relief that they generate these spontaneous buildings that look like agglomerations of traditional architecture when compared with some of the concrete monoliths of modern architecture, I noticed an irritatingly disorderly funkiness. At the same time that it is lovely, and has many of these beautiful patterns in it, it's not calm and satisfying. In that sense it is quite different from traditional architecture which appears to have this looseness in the large but is usually calm and peaceful in the small.
>
> To caricature this I could say that one of the hallmarks of pattern language architecture, so far, is that there are alcoves all over the place or that the windows are all different. So I was disturbed by that—especially down in Mexico. I realized that there were some things about which the people putting up the buildings did not know—and that I knew, implicitly, as part of my understanding of pattern languages (including members of my own team). They were just a bit too casual about it and, as a result, the work was in danger of being too relaxed. As far as my own efforts were concerned, I realized that there was something I was tending to put in it in order to introduce a more formal order—to balance this otherwise labyrinthine looseness.
>
> The other point is that even although the theory of pattern languages in traditional society clearly applies equally to very great buildings—like cathedrals—as well as to cottages, there was the sense that, somehow, our own version of it was tending to apply more to cottages. In part, this was a matter of the scale of the projects we were working on; but it also had to do with something else. It was almost as if the grandeur of a very great church was inconceivable within the pattern language as it was being presented. It's not that the patterns don't apply; just that, somehow, there is a wellspring for that kind of activity which was not present in either A Pattern Language (1977a) or The Timeless Way of Building (1979). (Grabow 1983)

More important, I think, is the fact that people did not quite understand the geometrical nature of what Alexander was talking about. The geometrical nature of the quality is brought out in Chapter 26 of *The Timeless Way of Building*, called "Its Ageless Character." Let me quote some passages from that chapter to give you a flavor:

> *And as the whole emerges, we shall see it takes that ageless character which gives the timeless way its name. This character is a specific, morphological character, sharp and precise, which must come into being any time a building or a town becomes alive: it is the physical embodiment, in buildings, of the quality without a name. . . .*
>
> *In short, the use of languages does not just help to root our buildings in reality; does not just guarantee that they meet human needs; that they are congruent with forces lying in them—it makes a concrete difference to the way they look. . . .*
>
> *This character is marked, to start with, by the patterns underlying it. . . .*
>
> *It is marked by greater differentiation.*
>
> *If we compare these buildings [the ones with the quality without a name] with the buildings of our present era, there is much more variety, and more detail: there are more internal differences among the parts.*
>
> *There are rooms of different sizes, doors of different widths, columns of different thickness according to their place in the building, ornaments of different kinds in different places, gradients of window size from floor to floor. . . .*
>
> *The character is marked, in short, by greater differences, and greater differentiation.*
>
> *But it is marked, above all, by a special balance between "order" and "disorder".*
>
> *There is a perfect balance between straight lines and crooked ones, between angles that are square, and angles that are not quite square, between equal and unequal spacing. This does not happen because the buildings are inaccurate. It happens because they are more accurate.*
>
> *The similarity of parts occurs because the forces which create the parts are always more or less the same. But the slight roughness or unevenness among these similarities, come from the fact that forces are never exactly the same. . . .*
>
> *And it is marked, in feeling, by a sharpness and a freedom and a sleepiness which happens everywhere when men and women are free in their hearts. . . .*
>
> *It is not necessarily complicated. It is not necessarily simple. . . .*

It comes simply from the fact that every part is whole in its own right.

Imagine a prefabricated window which sits in a hole in a wall. It is a one, a unit; but it can be lifted directly out from the wall. This is both literally true, and true in feeling. Literally, you can lift the window out without doing damage to the fabric of the wall. And, in your imagination, the window can be removed without disturbing the fabric of what surrounds it.

Compare this with another window. Imagine a pair of columns outside the window, forming a part of the window space. They create an ambiguous space which is part of the outside, and yet also part of the window. Imagine splayed reveals, which help to form the window, and yet, also, with the light reflected off them, shining in the room, they are also part of the room. And imagine a window seat leaning against the window sill, but a seat whose back is indistinguishable from the window sill, because it is continuous.

This window cannot be lifted out. It is one with the patterns which surround it; it is both distinct itself, and also part of them. The boundaries between things are less marked; they overlap with other boundaries in such a way that the continuity of the world, at this particular place, is greater. . . .

The timeless character of buildings is as much a part of nature as the character of rivers, trees, hills, flames, and stars.

Each class of phenomena in nature has its own characteristic morphology. Stars have their character; rivers have their character; oceans have their character; mountains have their character; forests have theirs; trees, flowers, insects, all have theirs. And when buildings are made properly, and true to all the forces in them, then they too will always have their own specific character. This is the character created by the timeless way.

It is the physical embodiment, in towns and buildings, of the quality without a name. (Alexander 1979)

Notice the possibly disturbing implications for software if we are to take Alexander at face value: In an Alexandrian system there is never any sense of modularity at any level of detail. Our definition of abstraction ("Abstraction Descant") allows for variations in the abstractions, but systematic ones. Is this definition flexible enough to capture the sense of freedom we get from Alexander's descriptions? For example, in his description of a window, we sense that every part of the abstraction—the panes, the frame, the relation to parts not specifically part of the window—is a little different in each instance depending on the forces at work at the window site. Instances of classes can acquire some of this flavor by varying the state of each object, each one different according to its role in the system; but is it enough?

Windows are windows because of their behavior vis-à-vis people: You can look through them, open them for air and spring smells; they provide light, and sometimes they act like seats or meeting places. Certainly this seems like the sort of variation we can expect from an object system—to be able to define a class of object very abstractly according to its behavior—but are we, perhaps, expecting too much in the variations? For instance, some windows provide light and air, but others act as chairs if they have sills so constructed. And windows can be ambiguous in their surroundings—can we possibly accommodate this in a modern, structured software design? Perhaps; perhaps if we drop some of our expectations regarding reuse, for instance, and universal applicability of abstractions. I'll say more about this later.

Alexander felt that people did not understand the geometrical nature of the quality, but he is partly to blame. It is sometimes hard to extract the importance of geometry from *Timeless Way* and *Pattern Language* possibly because he does not want people to think that modern architecture, with its obvious simplified geometry—large rectangular buildings designed to be looked at and not lived in—is an example of good architecture. He laments:

> *I've known from various readings that the book has had, that most people do not fully understand that chapter [Chapter 26]. It's just too short and it does not fully explain itself—although I was aware that in that book I just could not do the topic justice. In other words, I became increasingly aware of the fact that my own understanding of this, among other things, existed at a very highly developed geometrical level and that all of what* The Timeless Way of Building *(1979) was about—all of its human psychological and social content, and all of its political and constructional content—could actually be seen in the geometry. That is, there was a particular morphological character that exists in buildings which have this quality and which does not exist in buildings which lack it—and furthermore, that this geometrical character is describable and quite clear. But although I knew that to be so, and thought that I had written about it, I actually had not. I thought that Chapter 8—which has to do with the morphological processes in nature—together with the patterns, and together with Chapter 26, must make this clear. But in fact they do not.*
> (Grabow 1983)

Alexander was surprised that people didn't understand that the geometrical nature of his pattern language was fundamental. He felt he always knew that the geometry had to be right, and he always knew that he could tell quickly that it was right or wrong. I don't think that even after Mexicali he fully appreciated the importance of geometry, certainly not to the extent he seems to in his study of Turkish carpets. The problem in Mexicali wasn't obviously that everything was fine except for a lack of appreciation for geometry—it was that and also that the general skill level was low and that families participating in the design were unfamiliar with the language and process. But from his experience Alexander began to believe that maybe there was more to the geometry than even he appreciated and that perhaps it was something the could be codified. Alexander said:

> The point is that I was aware of some sort of field of stuff—some geometrical stuff—which I had actually had a growing knowledge of for years and years, had thought that I had written about or explained, and realized that, although I knew a great deal about it, I had never really written it down. . . .
>
> In a diagnostic sense, I can say that if this geometrical field is not present in something then there is something wrong there and I can assess that fact within a few seconds. (Grabow 1983)

What is this geometrical field of stuff? We can understand some of it from two things he did: a series of experiments with black-and-white serial patterns and an analysis of his Turkish rug collection.

I'll start with the series of experiments because it predates the Turkish rug studies, although the results of the experiments make more sense in the context of understanding the rugs.

In the 1960s at Harvard, Alexander performed an experiment in which he asked subjects to rank-order a set of strips from most coherent and simple to least coherent and simple. There were 35 strips, each consisting of three black squares and four white ones. Here are two examples:

If there was good agreement among the subjects about which were simpler and more coherent, then there would probably be some truth to the conjecture that there is an objective quality of wholeness or coherence or simplicity. It turned out there was excellent agreement; as Alexander wrote:

> First, Huggins [Alexander's coinvestigator] and I established that the relative coherence of the different patterns—operationally defined as ease of perception—was an objective quality, that varied little from person to person. In other words, the perceived coherence is not an idiosyncratic subjective thing, seen differently by different people. It is seen roughly the same by everyone. (Alexander 1993)

At the top of the next page are the 35 strips ordered according to the test subjects from most coherent at the top left, moving down the first column and then down each column from left to right, with the least coherent at the bottom right.

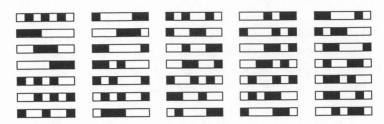

Next Alexander asked whether there was some way to explain this ranking. Oddly—I think—there is a way. It has to do with counting what Alexander calls *subsymmetries*. A subsymmetry is a symmetrical subsegment. Coherence is strongly correlated with the number of subsymmetries. Here's how you calculate this number: Consider all the subsegments of sizes 2, 3, 4, 5, 6, and 7. There is 1 subsegment of length 7, 2 of length 6, 3 of length 5, and so forth—21 in all. Here are the subsegments of length 3:

Now we simply count the number of subsegments that are symmetric. A subsegment is symmetric if it looks the same reversed. Let me repeat the previous figure with the number of subsymmetries to the right of each strip:

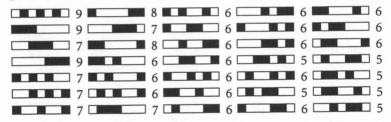

That there is such a correlation is remarkable. I can't say that I'm convinced that the ordering made by Alexander's subjects seems right to me; for example, I would have put the strip at the bottom of the first column ahead of the ones just above it. However, let's assume the data is accurate and try to understand the idea of subsymmetries.

It seems that people prefer symmetries that appear on all levels—so in Alexander's formula, small symmetries count as much as large ones. The first strip (upper left) has symmetries all over the place, and it is pleasant to look at, but is it really more coherent than the one at the bottom of the first column? It seems more regular in some ways, and it is certainly more interesting—it seems more complex, but it seems easier to remember, since there is a simple alternation rather than the 1-2-1-2-1 of the other. Maybe it's more coherent. The idea of subsymmetries seems to take this into account, perhaps a little too simplistically. Alexander wrote:

Thus, apparently. the perceived coherence of the different patterns
depends almost entirely on the number of symmetrical segments
which they contain. Since each of the segments which is symmetrical
is a local symmetry I summarize this whole result, by saying that the
most coherent patterns are the ones which contain the largest number
of local symmetries or "subsymmetries." (Alexander 1993)

When we look at his carpets, we'll see the same thing.

I spent a couple of hours playing with some variations on his computation and found one that correlated slightly better with experimental data and which fits his remarks on rugs as well. My computation adds additional bias in favor of doubled outer boundaries that diminishes exponentially as the boundary grows smaller.

For example, a strip like this has a bias added to its subsymmetry count (it is not a legal strip in his experiment):

This serves to boost the score of the strip that is third from the top in the first column and the one at the bottom of that same column. But the improvement is marginal. I suspect that perfect correlation requires a general algorithm like Alexander's, along with special cases for strips of overwhelming power. For example, it's hard to get the third strip from the top in the first column ( ) to come out third best when in general subsymmetries or something like them have to count in order to get the simple alternation strip to come out first—in Alexander's subsymmetry algorithm it comes out as low as ninth, and in my revised one it comes out fifth.

Notice that although there is an algorithmic way to determine whether a strip is coherent (to some degree of accuracy), there is not yet a formative rule for it, though I suspect there would be, perhaps a context-free grammar. But Alexander didn't find one.

When he moved into a study of Turkish carpets, he moved into a vastly more complex world. Next we'll look at his surprising look into the carpets, and, even more surprisingly, we'll see some glimmer of connection to software.

য়ৈ   য়ৈ   য়ৈ

Alexander's foray into rugs follows the strip-research vein, but on a far less scientific basis. There are no studies, there are no numbers (though he does talk about the number of "centers" in a carpet correlating with its "wholeness"). And in general the results there are a little less compelling as argument but much more compelling in beauty.

In the early 1970s Alexander began buying Turkish carpets, religious Turkish carpets. He said:

> *I was extremely innocent when I started out. I simply liked them. My*
> *main concern was actually in their color. I was completely absorbed*
> *by the question of color but never thought it would have any serious*
> *connection to my work. Also, I never thought of my interest in these*
> *rugs as having to do with geometry.* (Grabow 1983)

He spent a lot of money—even getting into financial trouble; he became a rug
dealer for a while—and he became known to Bay Area rug collectors. In fact, his
carpets were once shown in a special exhibition at the DeYoung Museum in San
Francisco.

Most people who collect rugs have a special interest, such the village where the
rugs were woven or the treatment of a particular theme, but Alexander's rugs
weren't in such neat categories—they were chosen because they had something
special about them. Because he had so little money compared with the cost of
each carpet, he spent a lot of time looking at them before he bought them. He
wasn't especially aware of the special quality that set some carpets apart—even
though his interest in carpets began in the midst of his quest for the quality without a name. His friends mentioned to him that his carpets had some special
something and he said:

> *When people started telling me this I began to look more carefully to*
> *discover that there was indeed something I was attracted to in a half-*
> *conscious way. It seemed to me that the rugs I tended to buy exuded*
> *or captured an incredible amount of power which I did not under-*
> *stand but which I obviously recognized.*
>
> *In the course of buying so many rugs I made a number of discov-*
> *eries. First, I discovered that you could not tell if a rug had this special*
> *property—a spiritual quality—until you had been with it for about a*
> *week. . . . So, as a short cut, I began to be aware that there were cer-*
> *tain geometrical properties that were predictors of this spiritual*
> *property. In other words, I made the shocking discovery that you*
> *could actually look at the rug in a sort of superficial way and just see*
> *if it had certain geometrical properties, and if it did, you could be*
> *almost certain that it had this spiritual property as well.*
> (Grabow 1983)

Alexander taught some courses on the geometry of his rugs and discovered that
the carpets shared this magical property with religious buildings and religious art
as well. Over the next 20 years he prepared a book about it, recently published,
called *A Foreshadowing of 21st Century Art: The Color and Geometry of Very Early
Turkish Carpets* (1993). This is a remarkable book. It's about 9 x 12 inches and
excellently bound. The paper is the sort you find in high-quality art-print books,
and the reason is that it is full of gorgeous reproductions of his carpet collection.

The sad thing—for you—of course is that I cannot possibly reproduce any of the art from this book in such as way as to do it justice, so some of my comments will necessarily be a little on the abstract side (those of you who believe whole-heartedly in the power of abstraction to solve all the world's problem will have no trouble with this at all). However, I will try my hand at reproducing some of his examples. But for the real impact—and the beauty of his stunning carpets—buy or borrow the book and enjoy.

In this book Alexander says some pretty darn unbelievable things. First is that the beauty of a structure—a building, for instance—comes from the fine detail at an almost microscopic level. He takes the grain size for noticeable structure from that used in the carpets: one eighth inch. He wrote:

> *In short, the small structure, the detailed organization of matter—controls the macroscopic level at a way that architects have hardly dreamed of.*
>
> *But twentieth century art has been very bad at handling this level. We have become used to a "conceptual" approach to building, in which like cardboard, large superficial slabs of concrete, or glass, or painted sheetrock or plywood create very abstract forms at the big level. But they have no soul, because they have no fine structure at all. . . .*
>
> *It means, directly, that if we hope to make buildings in which the rooms and building feel harmonious—we too, must make sure that the structure is correct down to $\frac{1}{8}^{th}$ of an inch. Any structure which is more gross, and which leaves this last eighth of an inch, rough, or uncalculated, or inharmonious—will inevitably be crude.* (Alexander 1993)

Second is that color and feeling also comes from this fine structure:

> *The geometric micro-organization which I have described leads directly to the glowing color which we find in carpets. It is this achievement of color which makes the carpet have the intense 'being' character that leads us to the soul.* (Alexander 1993)

Alexander feels that artists of the past—often of the distant past but as recently as Matisse, Bonnard, and Derain—had a better hold on beauty and that it is the task of late twentieth century artists to try to recapture the knowledge that seemed, perhaps, so obvious to these earlier artists as to be intuitive. Carpets provide a way to study this mastery because they are pure design, pure ornament, and their construction is so completely unconstrained by the materials of their construction as to allow the artist's true mastery to come forward. Alexander:

> *In a carpet, we have something which deals almost entirely with pattern, ornament. There is really nothing else: just the geometry and the color of the plane. As I began to enjoy carpets, I realized that the earliest carpets, especially, deal with this problem with enormous sophistication. The design of the carpet is essentially made of tiny knots—each knot usually about an 1/8 of an inch by an ⅛ of an inch. Each knot is a separate bit of wool, and may be any color, without any reference to the underlying warps and wefts. So it is a pure design, made of tiny elements, and which the structure (the design structure, the pure organization of the geometrical arrangement) is the main thing which is going on.* (Alexander 1993)

This is just a bitmap, but, as we'll see, with perhaps quite a number of color bits per pixel.

What is fascinating about this book is that Alexander is not afraid to come out and say that the power of these carpets comes at least in part from the need of these early artists to portray their religious feelings and needs. In fact, Alexander boldly tells us in the first paragraph of Chapter 1:

> *A carpet is a picture of God. That is the essential fact, fundamental to the people who produced the carpets, and fundamental to any proper understanding of these carpets. . . .*
> *The Sufis, who wove most of these carpets, tried to reach union with God. And, in doing it, in contemplating this God, the carpet actually tries, itself, to be a picture of the all seeing everlasting stuff. We may also call it the infinite domain or pearl-stuff.*
> (Alexander 1993)

The color of the carpets is paramount, and Alexander points out that usually the oldest carpets—even though they are the most faded—have the brightest and most brilliant colors. He says this is partly because the master dyer was an equal, in the twelfth century, to the master weaver. Such a master dyer served a 15-year apprenticeship, after which the apprentice was required to produce a color no one had seen before. Only after that could the apprentice become a master. Alexander notes that this training is the equivalent today of training as a theoretical physicist followed by training as a brain surgeon. Perhaps a dyer did not learn as much as someone would for either of these two professions, but it certainly says a lot about the importance of the dyer to Turkish society.

The depth of feeling in a carpet is related to a concept Alexander calls *wholeness*:

> *Both the animal-being which comes to life in a carpet, and the inner light of its color, depend directly on the extent to which the carpet achieves wholeness in its geometry. The greatest carpets—the ones*

which are most valuable, most profound—are, quite simply, the car-
pets which achieve the greatest degree of this wholeness within them-
selves. (Alexander 1993)

Alexander proposes that wholeness is an objective concept—it has nothing to
do with preferences or subjective feelings about the object that might display it.
Like the strips we saw in earlier, Alexander gives the reader a test to prove it, in
which he shows us two pairs of carpets and asks an unusual question:

If you had to choose one of these two carpets, as a picture of your own
self, then which one of the two carpets would you choose? . . .
     In case you find it hard to ask the question, let me clarify by asking
you to choose the one which seems better able to represent your
whole being, the essence of yourself, good and bad, all that is
human in you. (Alexander 1993, emphasis in original)

We are presented with two pairs of carpets. The first pair is the Berlin prayer
rug and the Kazak from the Tschebull collection; the second pair is the Flowered
Carpet with Giant Central Medallion and the Waving Border Carpet, both from
Alexander's collection.

Alexander claims that almost everyone will pick the same carpet from each
pair, because an objective something, a wholeness or oneness, comes through.

Up to this point in reading the book I thought maybe Alexander had gone a little off his nut and I was ready to quit, so I took the test to prove he was getting a
little too fanciful at this stage of his career. I stared at the two carpets in the first
pair and spent some time trying to second-guess him. Then I kept looking at the
first rug until I felt as calm as I could looking at it. After, I looked at the second
one, again until I became the most peaceful I could feel. Then I asked myself the
questions Alexander posed, and I chose the one that made me more at ease while
thinking about myself. I chose the Berlin prayer rug. This was the choice he predicted.

At this point I felt nervous.

He pointed out that the Berlin prayer rug is very well known, and sometimes
people have seen it and perhaps don't remember it but unconsciously choose it
because it is familiar. He then invites us to try it on the previously unpublished
pair from his own collection: the Flowered Carpet with Giant Central Medallion
on the left and the Waving Border Carpet on the right.

I looked at the Waving Border Carpet—the right-hand one—which has a large
central octagon with four surrounding smaller octagons. They are mostly blue
with intricate interlocking patterns inside. The large octagon has some red, white,
and beige subpatterns. All the octagons are in a field of red. At the ends of the central part of the carpet are triangular pyramidal indentations—sort of partial

shapes pressing into the center portion containing the octagons. These are darker, a deep blue-black—they are like an awakening into the center.

The primary feature of the carpet, though, is the waving border made of a degenerating vine. It is not very symmetric when you look closely at it, and it contains a recurring hook motif. Each bend of the vine contains a flower—maybe a tulip form—or a goddesslike figure—very abstract but distinct. The effect is that the motion of the border is so demanding that it enhances the calmness at the center of the carpet. I was immediately attracted to it.

But then I started to wonder how I was being gamed by Alexander—what was he trying to do? I looked at the other carpet—the left-hand one. It is partly destroyed—the upper right quarter and half of the very central portion are completely missing. The border is partly chewed away; the colors seem faded. The border is clearly less dramatic than the Waving Border Carpet. But the central part of the rug has spandrels of a color I had never seen before, a lace interlock of a deep green-black, but shimmering on a bed of slightly dark red. Sometimes the green comes to the fore, sometimes the red. The interlace is symmetric only at the grossest level, with almost every detail that should be the same, actually different. Each of the three existing spandrels are different from the others but seem of a kind. I found I was drawn to the upper-left spandrel, which is denser, more involved—a complexity that I followed and focused on for 10 minutes without noticing the time. I would be pulled in then pulled out, and as I moved my eyes from one spandrel to another, I crossed the central medallion, a simple blue, yellow, and red flower motif bordered in an Escher-field of abstract animal figures.

But it was clear that the first rug was the more profound and impressive to a trained eye, although I really wanted to look at the second one longer. Foo on you, Alexander, I said, you and your idiosyncratic punctuation and crazy theories—I'm choosing this lesser rug—the left-hand one—and this will prove that your damn ideas that I've puzzled over for years are worthless.

> I believe that almost everyone, after careful thought, will choose the left-hand example. Even though the two are of roughly equal importance, and of comparable age, I believe most people will conclude that the left-hand one is more profound: that one feels more calm looking at it; that one could look at it, day after day, for more years, that it fills one more successfully, with a calm and peaceful feeling. All this is what I mean by saying that, objectively, the left-hand carpet is the greater—and the more whole, of the two. (Alexander 1993)

My domestic partner made the same choices, feeling as I did that the left-hand carpet of the second pair showed significant flaws that mirrored something in her, though it was obviously the lesser carpet in some formal sense. (Later that week nine of 10 people I quizzed made the same choices.)

I kept reading.

The book is in four parts: a theoretical discussion of where the quality of wholeness comes from, a discussion of dating the carpets and how they fit into a progression, pictures and descriptions of the carpets themselves, and finally a comparison of two carpets, the first at the start of the progression and the second at the end—using them Alexander shows us how far the art has degenerated. I want to talk only about the origins of wholeness.

A carpet is whole to the degree that it has a thorough structure of *centers*. Alexander starts us out with this definition:

> *As a first approximation, a "center" may be defined as a psychological entity which is perceived as a whole, and which creates the feeling of a center, in the visual field.* (Alexander 1993)

This definition doesn't help much, so he gives us some examples.

The following is an example of a center from a round blossom from the Blossom fragment:

Notice that this figure has a strong center—in the very middle. But that's not the main point. Each of the lighter octagons and diamonds forms another center, the darker dots at the centers of the smaller blossoms form others. The asymmetrical black leaves are kinds of centers. The sharp indentations of the outer press toward the middle, reinforcing the center. The Blossom center gives the impression that centers are all like mandalas—somewhat circular and concentric. Not so.

Here is a sketch from the niche of the Coupled column prayer rug:

This form is a center because of the hexagonal archway, the steps, the arms with hexagons at the ends, and the lily at the top—not because of the overall shape.

The next point Alexander makes is that for wholeness, it isn't that a carpet has a single center but that it has a multiplicity of centers that reinforce one another by influence and by their structure, and that's what makes the difference.

Alexander says:

> *The degree of wholeness which a carpet achieves is directly correlated*
> *to the number of centers which it contains. The more centers it has in*
> *it, the more powerful and deep its degree of wholeness.*
> (Alexander 1993)

In fact, the more centers there are and the more intertwined and interlaced they are, the more whole the carpet becomes because the centers are denser. At the top of the next page is an example of this from the border of the Seljuk prayer carpet. Both the dark design elements and the lighter background form centers wherever there is a convex spot, wherever linear parts cross, and at bends. There are perhaps a dozen or more centers here.

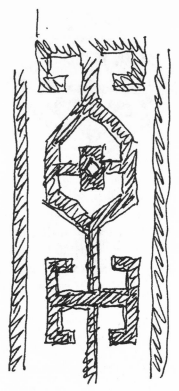

Centers are made up of local symmetries.

> *1. Most centers are symmetrical. This means they have at least one bilateral symmetry.*
>
> *2. Even when centers are* asymmetrical, *they are always composed of smaller elements or centers which* are *symmetrical.*
>
> *3. All centers are made of many internal local symmetries, which produce smaller centers within the larger center (most of them not on the main axis of the larger center), and* have a very high internal density of local symmetries. *It is this property which gives them their power.* (Alexander 1993)

One of the interesting things about the carpets is that the sense of symmetry remains even when the parts that are supposed to correspond are not exactly alike. At the top of the next page is an interesting example. Look at it quickly and decide whether you think it is symmetric. Looking closely at it, it's clear that it is crudely symmetric, but this is enough for most people to see it as very symmetric. There is actually something remarkable at work here: It is not just that the crudeness of this form—both in the original and in my even cruder reproduction—does not get in the way of its beauty; in fact, it enhances that beauty. On the wall above my writing place I have a photograph of a Greek "shack" taken by

Barbara Cordes. The shack is made of stone with a red-tile roof. Each stone is of a different size—some roughly cut, others seemingly randomly selected. The roof tiles are all different colors and roughly arranged. There is a deep blue frame window, and the shack sits behind a dead bush. The reason I have the picture there is that it is relaxing and helps me write. Its beauty, somehow, comes from the irregularity of the construction. Here is what Alexander wrote about a similar building, the famous House of Tiles in Mexico City:

> *We have become used to almost fanatical precision in the construction of buildings. Tile work, for instance, must be perfectly aligned, perfectly square, every tile perfectly cut, and the whole thing accurate on a grid to a tolerance of a sixteenth of an inch. But our tilework is dead and ugly, without soul.*
>
> *In this Mexican house the tiles are roughly cut, the wall is not perfectly plumb, and the tiles don't even line up properly. Sometimes one tile is as much as half an inch behind the next one in the vertical plane.*
>
> *And why? Is it because these Mexican craftsmen didn't know how to do precise work? I don't think so. I believe they simply knew what is important and what is not, and they took good care to pay attention only to what is important: to the color, the design, the feeling of one tile and its relationship to the next—the important things that create the harmony and feeling of the wall. The plumb and the alignment can be quite rough without making any difference, so they didn't bother to spend too much effort on these things.* They spent their effort in the way that made the most difference. *And so they produced this wonderful quality, this harmony . . . simply because* that is what they paid attention to, and what they tried to produce.
> (Alexander 1991, emphasis in original)

The reason that American craftsmen cannot achieve the same thing is that they are concerned with perfection and plumb, and it is not possible to concentrate on two things at the same time—perfection and the field of centers.

In our time, many of us have been taught to strive for an insane per-
fection that means nothing. To get wholeness, you must try instead to
strive for this *kind of perfection, where things that don't matter are*
left rough and unimportant, and the things that really matter are
given deep attention. This is a perfection that seems imperfect. But it
is a far deeper thing. (Alexander 1991, emphasis in original)

At this point it is clear that Alexander's earlier work on subsymmetries plays
right into the wholeness of rugs: The strips with more subsymmetries were seen
as more coherent than those with fewer. A subsymmetry is like a center, and the
more centers the more whole the carpet is. Furthermore, subsymmetries range
from the size of the entire strip down to the smallest place where symmetry is
possible—pairs of squares. The same is true of centers: They must exist at all levels of scale. In fact, carpets with all the other characteristics for wholeness but
lacking centers at all levels will not achieve wholeness and so can be boring. Alexander states the rule thus:

A center will become distinct, and strong, only when it contains,
within itself, another center, also strong, and no less than half its own
size. (Alexander 1993)

This is true not only for the same reasons it is true in the strips but also
because without large structure, the design cannot hold together—it becomes
merely a jumble of isolated design elements, each of which might hold attention
but without the large glue it will not be calm and whole—it would be like gluing
together several masterpiece paintings at the edges. With this definition it is
apparent that the goal of a carpet is to present a single center—the one at the largest scale—which necessarily must be constructed from other centers that support
it.

One of the things I noticed about the Flowered Carpet with Giant Central
Medallion was that the interlaced green and red spandrels held my attention. This
is an example of Alexander's notion of the strong use of *positive space*. In such use
both the positive and negative spaces have good shape and form centers. In this
way the density of centers can be higher, and the degree of wholeness stronger.
This concept should be familiar because it is like those Escher drawings of fish, for
example, in which both the figure and ground can be seen as fish. It is a little
more subtle in this niche, which appears at the top of the next page.

The shapes of the white convexities are strong as are the black convexities that
are white concavities. The figure is bilaterally symmetric and leads us to strong
centers at the half-hexagon at the top and in the spandrels.

Now that we have centers—lots of them—we need to make them distinct—the
centers need to be differentiated; recall that in Alexander's *A Timeless Way* (1979),

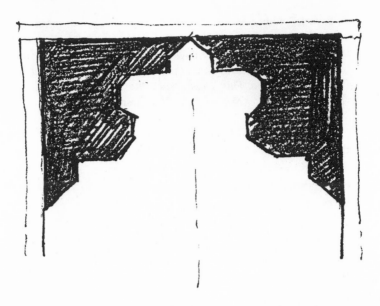

Alexander talked at length about differentiation. At the top of the next page is a very rough sketch of the central star of the star Ushak rug.

Alexander says the star achieves its distinctiveness from five sources:

> 1. *The centers next to the figure—those created by the space around it—are also very strong.*
> 2. *These strong centers are extremely* different *in character from the star itself—thus the distinctness is achieved, in part, by the differences between the centers of the figure, and the centers of the ground.*
> 3. *There are very strong color differences between field and ground.*
> 4. *The complex character of the boundary line seems, at least in this case, to contribute to the distinctiveness of the form. . . .*
> 5. *The hierarchy of levels of scale in the centers also help create the effect, by increasing the degree to which the form is perceived as a whole, entity, or being in its own right.* (Alexander 1993, emphasis in original)

The definition of a center now is:

> *Every successful center is made of a center surrounded by a boundary which is itself made of centers.* (Alexander 1993)

That this is a partially circular definition seems to startle Alexander, although we computer scientists and mathematicians find it simple. It reminds me of the definition of *system*, which I'll talk about once we're through with Alexander's wild ride.

Alexander goes back to the bead game and talks about the difficulty of finding two-dimensional patterns with high degrees of subsymmetries like the strips we saw earlier. He points out one that is seen in a couple of rare Konya carpets—it is a figure that is almost immediately familiar and unique (top of the next page).

There clearly are many centers here, and the figure ground distinction is amazing. There are embedded crosses, giving the entire figure the feeling of a being, and there are almost smaller beings within the larger one.

This figure lies in an 11 x 15 grid. It is one shape out of 10^{47} possibilities. Because of this, Alexander is enthralled by the creative process require to find it. He says something interesting about this process, which we can liken to the design process in software:

> [T]he greatest structures, the greatest centers, are created not within the framework of a standard pattern—no matter how dense the structures it contains—but in a more spontaneous frame of mind, in which the centers lead to other centers, and the structure evolves, almost of its own accord, under completely autonomous or spontaneous circumstances. Under these circumstances the design is not thought out, conceived—it springs into existence, almost more spontaneously, during the process by which it is made.
>
> And, of course, this process corresponds more closely to the conditions under which a carpet is actually woven—since working, row by row, knot by knot, and having to create the design as it goes along,

without ever seeing the whole, until the carpet itself is actually fin-
ished—this condition, which would seem to place such constraint
and difficulty on the act of creation—is in fact *just that circumstance*
in which the spontaneous, unconscious knowledge of the maker is
most easily released from the domination of thought—and thus
allows itself most easily to create the deepest centers of all.
(Alexander 1993, emphasis added)

The implication is clear: When we carefully design or work from a standard pattern, we do not achieve artifacts of the deepest meaning and wholeness. Perhaps the results are pleasant, but they are eventually boring and funky—perhaps they are commonplace or do not serve their purpose as well as they could. Alexander says he has evidence for his bold statement—he leaves it to the next book (not yet published) in the sequence, *The Nature of Order*—but there is not enough room in such a small book as *A Foreshadowing* to go into it.

This is also the way the best (creative) writing is done. When you sit down at your writing place, sometimes you are transformed into a mere scribe as the power of the story or poem takes over—it is an adventure to see where it will lead. Many writers have a ritual or set of superstitions that they hope will lead them to this magic place where the story becomes guide. When asked why they write, some writers say it is to find out what happens in the end.

I write poetry and fiction as well as essays. In all three, but especially in poetry, I am often shocked to read what I wrote, because it rarely corresponds to any plan I've made. Books on writing—at least the most recent ones—tend to discourage overplanning the story or poem. The question becomes—and you must answer this for yourself—does this clearly creative process have a place in a software process?

The last topic Alexander addresses is one I casually brought up just a bit ago—the emergence of beings.

I'll leave it to Alexander to introduce the topic:

I now present the culmination of the argument. This hinges on an extraordinary phenomenon—closely connected to the nature of wholeness—and fundamental to the character of great Turkish carpet art. It may be explained in a single sentence: As a carpet begins to be a center *(and thus to contain the densely packed structure of centers. . .),* then, gradually, the carpet as a whole also begins to take on the nature of "being." *We may also say that it begins to be a picture of a human soul.*

The subject is delicate, because it is not quite clear how to discuss it—not even how to evaluate it—nor even in what field or category to place it. It opens the door to something we can only call "spirit" and to the empirical fact—a fact of psychology if of nothing else— that after all, when a carpet does achieve some greatness, the great- ness it achieves seems to lie in the realm of the spirit, not merely in the realm of art. (Alexander 1993, emphasis in original)

What is a being? It's a powerful center that transcends the merely fascinating. It is a center that takes over and reflects the human and perhaps god-spirit. It is autonomous, a "creation unto itself." The figure at the top of the next page is the being that appears in the Seljuk prayer carpet.

I think it's rather impressive.

Alexander ends his book by telling us:

I see the beginnings of an attitude in which the structure may be understood, concretely, and with a tough mind—not only with an emotional heart. And I see the rebirth of an attitude about the world, perhaps based on new views of ethics, truth, ecology, which will give us a proper ground-stuff for the mental attitude from which these works can spring.

I do not believe that these works—the works of the 21st century— will resemble the Turkish carpets in any literal sense. But I believe some form of the same primitive force, the same knowledge of struc- ture, and the same desire to make a work in which the work carries and illuminates the spirit—will be present.

I am almost certain, that in the 21st century, this ground-stuff will appear. (Alexander 1993)

Perhaps.

Well, what can this possibly have to do with software? Maybe not too much, but Alexander's definition of center sounds familiar to me. Here is a definition of system I've been using:

A system *is a set of* communicating components *that work together to provide a comprehensive set of capabilities.*

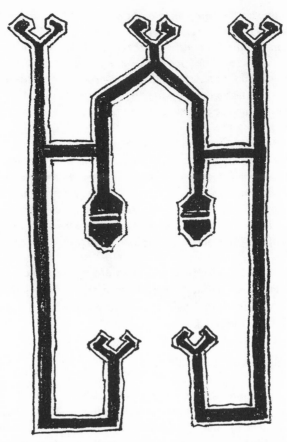

Of course, a component is another system. The nature of a system is such that at almost any granularity it looks the same—it is a system. This is easy: A system is composed of subsystems that achieve certain effects by exhibiting behavior in response to requests. The system and each subsystem are defined behaviorally according to the roles and responsibilities of that system or subsystem. Each subsystem can be viewed as a center, and the near circularity of Alexander's definition of center is reflected here: The goal is to build a system which is necessarily made up of other systems.

We can compare this with the definition of *autopoietic system*, which is a term from a field that studies systems from the point of view of biology—you could call it a field that has a mechanistic view of biological systems.

> *An* autopoietic system *is organized as a network of processes of production of components that produces the components that: (1) through their interactions and transformations continuously regenerate and realize the network of processes that produced them; and (2) constitute it as a concrete entity in the space in which they exist*

by specifying the topological domain of its realization as a network.
(Varela 1979)

If you read this definition carefully, you will find that it isn't so very different from my definition of "system" or Alexander's definition of "center". When we put together an object-oriented thing, it is a system, not a program. The difference between a program and a system is precisely the characteristic of a system having many centers or ways of approaching it—from the vantage point of any sub-system, the rest of the system is a server—whereas in a program, you generally have a single way of viewing it, usually from the top down.

The most wonderful thing can happen if you construct a system that can be customized or specialized—it becomes a *framework*.

> A framework *is a system that can be customized, specialized, or extended to provide more specific, more appropriate, or slightly different capabilities*

If you have a framework, you can use it for different purposes without having to recode it all. It is in this sense—and in this sense only—that objects and object technology provide reuse. There is no such thing as (easy) reuse in a general sense in which you can stockpile components except for the most trivial and inconsequential.

Building a system is like making a Turkish carpet: It requires an enormous amount of work, concentration, inspiration, creativity, and, in my opinion, it is best done piecemeal exactly the way the best Turkish master makers did it—by starting with an idea and partly designing it and then seeing where it goes.

Only in some systems does the being emerge, the framework that can be used and reused which gives systems and objects their spirit.

Like the best Turkish carpets the best systems are unique, but the work will not be wasted if you can continue to use it for new but related purposes. It is an asset and an inspiration to others who follow to try to do as well. A system can afford to be different—and perhaps over time we will develop mechanisms in our overly speed-conscious programming languages and system-building languages to make it easier to produce highly differentiated and center-full systems—I have hopes for the twenty-first century too.

What are patterns, then? Perhaps they are for Alexander what they are by analogy for computer scientists: just a way to remember what we've forgotten about buildings so that when we set out to build towns and buildings, cottages and homes, paths and places to congregate, we don't forget the stuff we need to help create the centers, to give them life, give them the quality without a name, the being that emerges at last.

PART II
~
LANGUAGES

~

Language Size

The Lisp world has had numerous and lengthy debates on the relative worth of large versus small programming languages. Large languages like Common Lisp have a relatively small core of true primitives with a large library of functionality, but—a big but—there is no distinction made between the primitives and the library in the language specification itself. Thus it appears to a casual observer as if the language were just plain big.

This is relevant to object-oriented programming because a point of the largeness of Common Lisp is to provide a useful corpus of reusable components in the form of functions. If there is a fundamental reason that large languages are believed inferior or less useful than a small one, the hope for the ubiquity of reusable components is in trouble.

It probably matters whether the library is included as part of the language or whether it is an acknowledged library. When a library is part of a language, as it is with Common Lisp, you cannot easily choose to ignore it, and later maintainers cannot easily know what parts of the language are used. When a library is packaged as a library, there is at least the possibility of documentation that states what libraries are actually used.

Let me take a minute to outline enough about the history of Common Lisp and its size woes to give you an idea of the context in which the debate exists. In 1980 there were two main dialects of Lisp—InterLisp and MacLisp—each vying to be the one true Lisp. But MacLisp had multiplied into a variety of similar subdialects, some on Lisp machines and some on stock hardware. InterLisp, on the other hand, was relatively stable and apparently about to win the Lisp sweepstakes. The MacLisp folks really didn't like InterLisp winning out—just as the Eiffel folks appear to dislike C++ winning out—and so they got together to define a description of a family of languages, called *Common Lisp*, but the effort changed over time so that Common Lisp became a true dialect. In the beginning it was relatively small: 772 defined symbols, including function names, macro names, global variables, and constants. When the rest of the world saw Common Lisp on the rise, an ISO Lisp effort began, and the United States responded with an ANSI effort. Well, this opened the floodgate for every would-be Lisp language designer to join and start flailing away at Common Lisp. The result is that ANSI Common Lisp has about 1,000 defined symbols and its specification is 1,300 pages long.

Part of the expanded Common Lisp is its object-oriented component (called CLOS for "Common Lisp Object System"), a generalized iteration construct called LOOP, and a full-blown condition system. Even though dozens of people contributed to the final design, it is relatively clean, given its starting point. For example, CLOS meshes very well with the rest of Common Lisp so that the only real places where the seam is visible are the (ordinary) functions that are not generic functions and the types that are not classes.

The standardization process lasted from around 1987 until 1995, and during that period, Lisp companies changed from enjoying a booming business to being just barely in business. There are probably lots of reasons for this—the bad business judgment of artificial intelligence (AI) companies being not the least—but one that has been proposed is that Common Lisp was just too big to run fast and produce small executables. Actually, the AI businesses tried to blame their business failures on Lisp and switched to C/C++ instead.[*] The Lisp community—always ready to aim for the simplistic answer—looked at the features that C/C++ have and contrasted them with Lisp features and tried to conclude that the differences were what made C/C++ successful. These different features boiled down to "small and fast."

The problem of size is what I want to address. While researching language size, I talked with a number of people on this issue. One person wrote this:

> There is a basic tension here between small, elegant languages and large, efficient languages. The reason for efficient languages being large is that typically the price for efficiency is specificity, so in order to have a general-purpose efficient language, the number of constructs must grow. (anonymous)

A common belief is that a language is large because the designers wish it to be efficient. For example, Scheme has no multidimensional arrays (only vectors) and there is an argument in the Scheme community about whether to add them, thus increasing the size of the language. The argument for arrays is that programming

---

[*] This seemingly nonsensical decision actually makes sense, because large companies that bought AI software usually required the source be put in escrow, planning to take over maintenance if the supplier went under. It was thought cheaper and easier to hire C/C++ programmers than Lisp programmers to maintain and enhance the source.

with them is common and so should be supported; the argument against is that you could roll your own arrays (using vectors of vectors) and the only difference would be speed—therefore, because multidimensional arrays can be expressed in terms of other more primitive constructs, Scheme would become less elegant by admitting redundant constructs. That is, to the Scheme community, adding multidimensional arrays would decrease Scheme's elegance while merely providing fast arrays.

There are more compelling reasons than efficiency, however, for adding constructs. If a data structure is commonly used, it should be supported as well as it can be. If a useful and frequently used function is difficult to implement correctly, it probably should be supported. A good example of this latter point focuses on one of Common Lisp's most ridiculed features, format, which is inspired by FORTRAN's FORMAT statement and is used to output strings. As you'd expect, format is used for printing floating-point numbers in a variety of ways and for printing tables and all sorts of things. As you might not expect, it can perform iteration, conditional execution, and non-local exits. With it you can construct pretty nice error messages and diagnostics. Here is an example: Suppose you have a compiler and you want to report the number of errors and warnings when it completes. You can define the following:

```
(defvar *compiler-format-string*
        "Done.~^ ~@(~R~) warning~:P.~^ ~@(~R~) error~:P.")
```

Then if there are no warnings or errors, you write

```
(format t *compiler-format-string*)
```

which prints

```
Done.
```

If there are three warnings you write

```
(format t *compiler-format-string* 3)
```

which prints

```
Done. Three warnings.
```

If there is 1 warning and 5 errors you write

```
(format t *compiler-format-string* 1 5)
```

which prints

```
Done. One warning. Five errors.
```

Notice a couple of things. First, there apparently is some control structure encoded in format strings—a format string can determine whether there are remaining arguments and can abort if there are none. Second, the syntax of such strings is obscure at best. Third, the encoding of format strings is compact, so that complicated instructions don't take up much space. Fourth, `format` allows you to express things normally difficult to express, such as the names of numbers spelled out, capitalization, and determining plurals. (Not shown are things like printing comma-delimited lists without breaking words across newlines and justifying text.) Fifth, `format` is powerful enough that there really isn't much excuse to forgo nice diagnostics in your programs.

What are the trade-offs? `Format` strings don't look like Lisp, and they constitute a non-Lispy language embedded in Lisp. This isn't elegant. But, the benefit of this is compact encoding in such a way that the structure of the fill-in-the-blank text is apparent and not the control structure. Consider the `format` string above—don't worry, I won't explain it to you or make you understand it. You can see that it prints basically three sentences:

"Done. _ warning_. _ error_."

The control structure that tells `format` to end early is encoded by ~^. It's thereby out of the way; were there no way to encode an early exit, the basic structure of the message would be lost, tangled up in conditionals and maybe exits expressed in ordinary Lisp code. It is unlikely that people will implement `format` on their own, and it is almost equally unlikely that people will bother writing the code to produce nice, readable diagnostics. Instead, we are likely to be stuck with messages like this:

```
Done. 1 warnings. 1 errors.
```

Of course, `format` could be part of a library, which isn't a problem as long as the library is universally accepted and available. With `format` part of the language, everyone uses the same function, and code is more readable.

However, consider proving that a compiler written using this `format` statement outputs correct messages. There is no access to the source, neither for proving nor for improving. And some would argue that libraries shouldn't supply source.

I won't even comment on the apparent linkage the first commenter made between "small" and "elegant."

Another person wrote:

> *It's easier to reason about an algorithm expressed in a small language, because the primitives of a small language have simpler, more intelligible, and (often) better-defined semantics. So it's easier to*

show that algorithms so expressed satisfy their specifications and to analyze their complexity. (John David Stone, personal communication 1993)

It is probably true that algorithms have specifications, but this isn't true very often of "regular" code, which has been constructed by a process of piecemeal growth. The difficulty of a proof of correctness, though, is at least partly dependent on the size of the text. In a small language, text is large, because either things are spelled out in situ or there are auxiliary functions (or programs). In either event, the proof of correctness will likely have lemmas corresponding to chunks of the program text—just to make the proof manageable—and these chunks will be equivalent to the constructs you'd find in a large language. So, I don't think proofs would be substantially easier based on size considerations alone. Any difference would be because one language might have a formal semantics, whereas another might not. A small language defined by a group of mathematicians or would-be mathematicians might have a usable formal semantics, and people who wish to prove correctness would be in luck with such a language. But—I hate to be the one to break the news—I've been in industry for over 10 years, and I don't see a whole lot of people proving correctness; I see them reasoning about their programs, but they don't need a formal semantics to do that.

Informal reasoning about a program using a complex language construct, however, can be difficult when only a small portion of the construct is used in a particular case. It's a matter of conjecture whether it is easier to prove the correctness of a reduced use of functionality than to code and prove correct your own reduced version of it. Certainly there is less reuse in the latter case.

The same writer made this remark:

> *The conclusions one reaches by reasoning about an algorithm expressed in a small language are more likely to apply to actual computer executions of the algorithm, because a small language is more likely to be correctly implemented on a computer.* (Stone 1993)

This is bad news for libraries. If you can't trust the implementers of a language to implement correctly something well specified in a standards document, how can you trust a library implementer? Indeed, since we know that language implementers discouragingly often get it wrong. But the key here is how to get to a correct program in the face of its size and its piecemeal origins. Better put, how can we retain a correct program as it evolves? Clearly, if correctness is important, you need to maintain that correctness incrementally just as the program grows.

He also said this:

> *It's easier and quicker to learn a small language.* (Stone 1993)

When I asked Stone to be more specific about how long it should take to learn a programming language he added,

> *One semester of thirteen or fourteen weeks, for one's first language.*
> - *Four to eight working days of eight to twelve hours each, for any subsequent language. After a couple of months of programming in a new language, maybe one or two more working days; after the promulgation of a new language standard or the acquisition of a new major revision of the translator, maybe one more working day.*
>
> *Let me turn it around: If a company hires a new B.S. in computer science of average ability and throws a new programming language at him and after a month he's still not using the resources of that language effectively, then probably the language is too big.* (Stone 1993)

If we think in terms of habitability, it seems amazing that learning a language would take time measured in days or weeks. Sure, you can learn the constructs of a language and its rules of composition in such a time, but do you really know the language? For instance, Lisp aficionados just laugh and laugh when they read code produced by someone who first learned FORTRAN and then spent four to eight working days learning Scheme (a small language according to the second commenter). This is because such code is just FORTRAN code transliterated, and FORTRAN is imperative whereas Scheme is quasi functional.

I think there is a useful distinction to be made between learning a language and being a master of it. You use a programming language to communicate to both a computer (or a compiler) and also to people, the people who will maintain and grow and alter your code after the original authors no longer maintain it. Because of this, the code you write must communicate well using familiar idioms and patterns of use. This is not learned by studying a book but by years of experience, including reading great programs.

If this is true—that mastery takes a long time—then the real question becomes whether the time for mastery differs for small and large languages. If the small language is augmented by libraries, there will be no difference between large and small languages, and if you need to reinvent or acquire idioms to make writing code faster and easier in a small language, there will probably be no difference either. Only if the language is illogical or so poorly designed or so syntactically obscure that it hinders common sense will the language itself be the high-order bit on mastering it.

When I made this argument to the first commenter, he replied:

> *Yes, but learning programming languages is only a very small part of mastering the profession of programming—and the smaller the better, unless it actually makes a visible difference in the quality of the programs produced. I can see taking years to learn the art of user-*

interface design; I can see spending three months every two years becoming acquainted with new hardware and its capabilities; I can see and approve endless learning about algorithms and data structures. But I can't see that a professional programmer who has instead spent the equivalent amount of time becoming a master of COBOL, PL/I, and Ada is really much of an ornament to her profession.
(anonymous)

It's hard for me to see how a language can be mastered outside many of the activities he mentioned, such as working with new algorithms and data structures and generally solving all the exercises one needs to solve in order to master computer programming—and sadly, I have no doubt that a lot of people become masters only of their language and not their professions. I mean, how can one possibly master a programming language without programming, and how can one program without learning about data structures, algorithms, and stuff like that?

Think about learning to be an architect. You have to become acquainted with mechanical drawing skills, which takes one or two semesters. Then you start designing buildings, studying them, studying their plans, making your own. During all this you are honing your mechanical drawing skills. Part of your effort is in mastering the "language" of your profession, but this is hidden beneath the fabric of learning the facts and techniques of that profession.

But drawing is not the only language of architecture. Remember Alexander's thoughts about architecture: Those who study only design and not pattern languages—languages that enable building habitable buildings and towns—are not, in general, capable of doing their jobs as well as they might. Another way to put this is that architects fail when they ignore the task of becoming masters of the languages they need to master.

Let's think about mastering English. I mastered English by using it to study history, philosophy, even mathematics, and by writing 20 to 50 e-mail letters every day for the past 20 years, by writing grant proposals and a dissertation (along with stories and poetry). I graduated the sixth grade having learned English; I mastered it 30 years later.

Consider the ways to approach writing software documentation. The best way is to have a developer who is an excellent writer. The next best way is to have an excellent writer interview a developer or start with notes written by a developer. The third best way is to let a developer write it. Finally, an excellent writer with no knowledge of the topic is worst. I think I wouldn't want to read the documentation written by the last two: One wouldn't make much sense, and the other would not tell me much—hard to guess, really, which would be worse. This supports partially the remark by the commenter that knowledge of the area is important, that knowing only how to write (English or a programming language) is not nearly enough. But the two best alternatives require good writers, so skill and mastery of writing and English do count for something.

When we think about how to apply this lesson to mastering programming languages, the best alternative is an excellent designer (for lack of a better term—I really need a word that denotes a great developer who doesn't necessarily know the programming language very well) who is also a master of the programming language; the next best is a great designer along with a language master; the third best is a great designer only; and the worst is a language master.

Applying Alexander's lessons, habitability and piecemeal growth require that software be developed with idioms, common patterns, small abstractions, and well-written, straightforward code. The real question we need to answer is whether such code can be more easily written with a small language, and we can not really know the answer to this without scientific studies.

English provides an example, even though it's hard to apply accurately to programming languages the lesson of the example—Basic English. In the 1920's and continuing through the 1930s, C. K. Ogden developed and promoted a sort of subset of English for the purposes of providing an international language, a gentle introduction to "full" English, and a plain English. The "Basic" in Basic English is an acronym for *British, American, Scientific, International,* and *Commercial.*

Originally there was a fixed analytic word order, six affixes (*-s, un-, -ed, -ing, -ly,* and *-er*), rules for compounding (*farmhouse, teapot*), and a reduced vocabulary: 400 general words, 200 picturable words, 150 adjectives, 82 grammatical words, and 18 operators (verbs like *put* and *get*). Operators were used to replace some verbs (*get* replaced *receive, obtain,* and *become*) and to form phrases to replace other verbs (*get money for* replaced *buy* and *put together* replaced *assemble*). In addition were numbers, names, and technical words for various disciplines.

Basic English is like a small programming language except that word compounding is the only way to define new words; that is, it has no abstraction capabilities. Even with support from Churchill and Roosevelt and with dictionaries published until the late 1980s, Basic English never made it. Part of the reason has to be that sentences in Basic English are longer and in some ways less pretty or at least more contorted than ones in regular English. Here is an example from "Time in Philosophy and Physics." In English:

> *The final word on this was said by St. Augustine. "What is time?" he asked, and replied "if no one asks me, I know; if I want to explain it to a questioner, I do not know."* (Dingle 1979)

The same passage in Basic English:

> *The statement which says the most it is possible to say about it was made by St. Augustine. His answer to the question "what is time" was "if no-one puts the question to me, I am certain about it; if I have a mind to give a questioner an account of it, I am uncertain."*

The second version is longer, more contorted, and, I daresay, uglier (except for the nice phrase "if I have a mind to give a questioner an account of it"). Code in small languages is like this: convoluted, longer, and a little harder to understand than it could be. With universally accepted libraries the expressiveness is better.

The same commenter I quoted earlier continued:

> *Someone who has learned a small language is generally familiar with almost all of its constructs and can therefore read most of the programs written in that language. Someone who has spent an equal amount of time learning a large language has only a passive and sketchy knowledge of many of its constructs and will have a harder time understanding many programs because they use unfamiliar parts of the language. Hence, programs written in a small language are often more easily maintained and ported.* (Stone 1993)

Offhand this sounds like a case of not having spend enough time mastering a language, but there is a truth here: If a language is too convoluted, illogical, or nonorthogonal, it won't be possible to master it, and programmers will tend to program in subsets, and the effect the commenter described will occur. This is all too likely, because

> *[s]mall languages tend to be better designed than large ones, showing fewer signs of ad hoc compromise between conflicting aesthetic principles and design goals.* (Stone 1993)

Aesthetic principles and design goals don't excite me, because often they have nothing to do with how people really program (habitability and piecemeal growth) but more often reflecting mathematical or abstract considerations and look-Ma-no-hands single-mechanism trickery. One cannot deny, however, that a small set of principles and goals applied to designing a small language usually results in a consistent concise language.

Large languages just cannot be as consistent as small ones—large languages necessarily address more problems, and it makes sense to do this only if those problems vary. With a small language with a large class library—for example, Smalltalk—you have exactly the same problem. The success of Smalltalk is due to the consistent and careful design of those class libraries coupled with a uniform access technique (message passing). It certainly didn't hurt that most of the libraries were designed by essentially the same people who designed the language.

I want to end with two quotations. The first is part of the introduction to the *Revised⁴ Report on Scheme*, and the second is from one of the CLOS designers.

> *Programming languages should be designed not by piling feature on top of feature, but by removing the weaknesses and restrictions that make additional features appear necessary. Scheme demonstrates that a very small number of rules for forming expressions, with no restrictions on how they are composed, suffice to form a practical and efficient programming language that is flexible enough to support most of the major programming paradigms in use today.*
> (Clinger and Rees 1993)

The problem with this approach, as Scheme itself demonstrates, is that one can fall into the trap of adding a feature that, because of its power, indeed reduces the number of features but is so powerful that it cannot be used safely and programs written using it are incomprehensible. I refer, of course, to `call-with-current-continuation`, which essentially eliminates the possibility of knowing how many times a statement is executed unless all the code in the program is available for inspection. In the presence of side-effects (which Scheme has) this can be a disaster.

> *Here are three widely-believed arguments about small versus large languages. In spite of the contradictions among these arguments and a certain amount of flawed reasoning inherent in them, many people believe one or more of these arguments and each of them contains some truth.*
>
> • *Small programs are better than large programs because small programs fit on fewer diskettes, which cost less postage to mail and take less time to feed into the diskette drive. Small languages are better than large languages because small languages produce small programs and large languages produce large programs.*
>
> • *The most important aspect of product development is time to market. Large languages are better than small languages because large languages allow products to be developed more quickly, since they contain more reusable components.*
>
> • *The most important aspect of product development is time to market. Small languages are better than large languages because small languages allow products to be developed more quickly, since they don't require as much time to learn all the reusable components.*
>
> *The above arguments assume the library is part of the language, as do most of the Scheme versus Common Lisp arguments. If we grant that the library is part of the language, and the library includes such*

things as the user interface toolbox, then there is no such thing as a serious small language today.

If we look only at core languages and not libraries, the size of the core language has more to do with elegance perceived by language connoisseurs than with size or time to market of delivered applications. A small core language probably does lead on the average to easier compilability and a higher quality of implementation, although size of core language is just one of many forces affecting those qualities.

If any of this sounds sarcastic, well what can I say, I meant it seriously. (David A. Moon, personal communication 1993)

There is something to these remarks. It isn't clear right away whether using a library will hurt or help the speed of development. It is not just learning the reusable components but also adapting the code that uses them. We saw this in an earlier essay: If a module is rigidly defined, the code that uses it must be written so that it can be used as is (if the door you bought is two feet wide and 10 feet high, that's how big you have to make the opening). Furthermore, good luck if there is a problem inside one of the components—a problem is not necessarily a bug, it can be something you (or one of your customers) will want to change.

If there is some difference in effectiveness or usefulness between a small and large programming language, we will need scientific studies to tell us what they are. No amount of reasoning from first principles can inform half as well as can a few carefully done studies.

The End of History and the Last Programming Language

In April 1993 Guy Steele and I gave our "Evolution of Lisp" paper at the ACM History of Programming Languages II Conference (Steele and Gabriel 1993). The histories of the following languages were presented there: ALGOL 68, Pascal, Ada, Lisp, PROLOG, FORMAC, CLU, Icon, Forth, C, and C++. According to the program committee's requirements, the only languages considered for the conference were those that had been in existence for a long time and have had a significant impact, measured in an indeterminate manner.

Two days before the conference started, Steele and I sat in his living room in Lexington, Massachusetts, trying to decide what to present—we had not yet prepared our talk, contrary to the strict rules of Jean Sammet, the conference chairwoman. We noted that with only two exceptions, every language being presented was dead or moribund. The exceptions were C and C++. We thought for a while about the history of Lisp and noticed that at that time, though there were new Lisp sprouts pushing up through the earth, Lisp could be characterized as having gone through two periods of expansive growth, the first followed by a minor consolidation and the second followed by a major consolidation which dwindled to its then-current stagnant state. This stagnation, it seemed, was typical of all programming languages, and we set out to figure why.

Even though we did come up with a theory that seemed to explain why the field of general-purpose programming languages is currently dead and predicted the death of a currently expanding language, we decided against presenting the material because it might be too controversial. Little did we know that during the concluding panel session of the conference—entitled "Programming Languages: Does Our Present Past Have a Future?"—the general remarks would hint that our feeling was shared by at least some in attendance. Our feeling was also bolstered by the average age of the papers' authors, somewhere in the 50- to 60-year-old range.

In this essay I will present our theory, but first a word about general-purpose versus application-specific languages.

Languages can be broken into two categories: application specific and general purpose. Some languages are fairly obviously application specific, such as simulation packages, spreadsheet programming languages, and even 4GLs. In some ways these languages are the most prevalent, particularly if you consider COBOL to be an application-specific language. A case can be made that COBOL is such a language by arguing that it is applicable only to business-related computations such as payroll, inventory, and accounts receivable. When you lump COBOL into this category, the size of the general-purpose programming language population (in lines of code) is somewhat small. Later in this essay I will present some figures that show this.

If you group COBOL with the general-purpose programming languages, you have to conclude that it renders all the others essentially irrelevant, except one or two. Again, we'll see the figures later.

ॐ ॐ ॐ

There are four parts to the theory:

- Languages are accepted and evolve by a social process, not a technical or technological one.

- Successful languages must have modest or minimal computer resource requirements.

- Successful languages must have a simple performance model.

- Successful languages must not require users have "mathematical sophistication."

ॐ ॐ ॐ

Let's look at how languages are accepted and evolve. My theory, which Steele seems to accept, is that a number of factors enable a language to flourish:

- The language must be available on a wide variety of hardware.

- It helps to have local wizards or gurus for the language.

- It must be a minimally acceptable language.

- It must be similar to existing popular languages.

The process is social because it relies on the actions of people in response to a language. Many of us, particularly academics, hope that the nature of the language would be the dominant factor. I want to put people ahead of the language so that we all realize it is not the abstract nature of the language that is critical but the way that human nature plays into the acceptance process.

The acceptance process is not unique to languages—it works well and sometimes better with other things such as application programs and operating systems.

ﻉ   ﻉ   ﻉ

The language must be on every platform the *acceptance group* needs—an acceptance group is a potential population of users that is large enough and cohesive enough to make a difference to the popularity of the language. This can be accomplished if developers port the language to every such computer, but often it is better to make a portable implementation or a particularly simple implementation and let local wizards or gurus do the porting for you.

ﻉ   ﻉ   ﻉ

It's sometimes hard to get started with a new language—basics to master, tricks to learn. It helps to have a local wizard to help with this, and what better way to develop a wizard than porting the language to the local computers? Having a wizard can make a huge difference. Because information is local you have some control over when you can get it and how much you get—the source is not an impersonal voice on the other end of a phone or some words with a return e-mail address, nor is there some hidden problem more important than yours that keeps your informant from answering you.

With a local wizard who is at least a porter, both you and the wizard have a personal attachment to the new language through the power to control it—the language is not completely someone else's master plan: you share in it. This is important for two reasons. First, people generally prefer to use something over which they are granted some degree of control; this is just human nature. It is especially difficult to have accepted a language whose designers and proponents hold it out as an untouchable panacea. Second, this tends to reduce the risk by putting the key technology in your hands. Would you risk your job on a new language whose implementation might be wrong and out of reach?

This implies something else: A proprietary language has little chance of success. Of course there are exceptions—the most notable being Visual BASIC— but I think it would be hard to buck this logic.

ﻉ   ﻉ   ﻉ

Despite the required simplicity of the language, it must be acceptable, and there must be a reason to move to it. In general the reason is that it solves a new problem well or makes certain tasks easier to do. Sometimes the only benefit needs to be that it makes existing tasks more reliably done.

The effect of the whole process as outlined so far is that a simple language with a minimal implementation takes hold through the vehicle of solving a new problem, for example, along with the local wizardry to make such a change sufficiently risk-free. Then, when the language is established, it can be improved. Improvements are always easier to accept than a new language is.

This last point is important. People who design and promote an exotic new language always try to defeat in the minds of users a simpler language by explaining why that simple language is no good, vastly inferior to the new one. But in time, the simpler one usually is improved, eroding the argument. Furthermore, if the simpler language is entrusted to local wizards, they will not only port it but improve it. In effect, the simpler language traveling by way of popular demand has an army of people trying to improve it; all the more reason proprietary languages are crippled in the language sweepstakes.

If we think about this model as developed so far, it resembles that of a virus. A simple organism that can live anywhere eventually attaches itself to widespread host organisms and spreads.

୨෧ ୨෧ ୨෧

The language must be similar to existing languages. I think some people find this point hard to understand because it sounds too conservative or pessimistic. But I compare it to two of the major processes for change we see in the world around us: the free market and evolution.

The free market works like this: It is in business's best interest to have frequent small releases that cost money. Innovation costs too much and is too risky. If the innovation is technological, it is least risky to apply the innovation conservatively and then improve or expand its application. This way you can spend either a lot of money or most of your money on quality, which builds brand loyalty. Much of the automotive and consumer electronics markets work like this. (More on the general workings of free markets will be explored in the essay, "Money Through Innovation Reconsidered.")

This works well with languages: With a simple language and implementation, you can spend time to make sure that it just plain works the first time every time. If you need to innovate over and over just to get the thing off the ground, its quality will be low and peoples' first taste will be a bad taste.

In the marketplace, adapting to innovation requires a long learning curve, and rarely is a compelling payoff in sight for the learning. People had trouble learning Lisp in the 1980s even when they believed they would achieve extraordinary productivity gains and when the price of admission to the artificial intelligence sideshow was a working knowledge of Lisp. Because of the difficulty learning Lisp, they were unable to learn it properly and gained almost none of the benefits. Also, it was never clearly shown that the higher productivity of Lisp programmers wasn't due to their greater natural ability—let's say better mathematical aptitude—of those who *could* learn Lisp.

The free market works like this because people don't like to take risks, especially by adopting a new language or any new way of doing things. People prefer incremental improvement over radical improvement. We are conditioned for this in all sorts of ways. Very little in public education prepares us for it. Our mothers didn't teach us to risk. And who wants to risk a job needlessly by using an exotic new language—there is always a safe alternative in the language domain.

People don't like to be different; being an early adopter of a radical thing is to really be different. When you're different, people notice you and sometimes laugh, especially when you are different for no particular reason. Different is risky. Why bother?

We can take an analogy from evolution. (Remember, this is an analogy only and has no compelling argumentative force except to comfort us that this radically conservative view of how things progress is common.) People normally consider that the primary purpose of natural selection is to promote small improvements— and this does happen. But there is no inexorable push from single-celled organisms through rats through monkeys and apes to humans. Rather, progress is made in fits and starts, and the main purpose of natural selection is to reject harmful changes, not to promote large leaps.

Only those things that are relatively worthless change rapidly and dramatically. These worthless things provide variety: Someday an environmental change can make one of those changes or a related group of them important to survival, and this one or this group will then join the ranks of the natural-selection protected, and perhaps some formerly static parts will no longer be essential and thus can begin changing.

In other words, natural selection provides very little incremental improvement: Almost all dramatic change occurs because the environment changes and makes the worthless invaluable. This is part of a larger argument regarding a theory of technological improvement and adoption called *Worse Is Better*, and in the essay called "Money Through Innovation Reconsidered" I will expand the evolution argument.

When applying the lesson from evolution to programming language design, there are two important features of languages that I think cannot be changed at the moment: a simple performance model and a need for only minimal mathematical sophistication. This leads us to the last two points of our quadripartite theory.

❧   ❧   ❧

The requirement to be on popular platforms has important technical fallout. Invariably the most prevalent commercial platforms are those that have been in the field for a year or two or more, which implies that they are one to three technology generations behind current hot boxes. The language must run well on such computers, which means it must not be a resource hog in any sense of the word, and in fact, it must be comparatively tiny.

This also implies that the language cannot attempt to break new ground in language design if doing so would require resources. Furthermore, breaking new ground sometimes requires time and testing, which delays the release of the new language while competitors—new or old—become established. This also applies to systems such as operating systems, and the example I use to show this point comes from UNIX.

An operating system provides services to a user program, and such services are provided by system calls. However, in most operating systems the end user can interrupt the execution of a program. Typically this is handled in the operating system by saving the user-level program counter and minimal context information in a save area such as the stack. Notice, though, that the user-level program counter does not adequately capture the execution point when the program is executing a system call. For instance, if the program is opening a file for reading, the operating system may be allocating a buffer. The operating system designer has three choices: Try to back out of the call, try to save the true state, or return a flag from the system call that states whether the call succeeded. The first two are very hard to do technically. One operating system I know from the past required approximately 60 pages of assembly language code to back out of the call in all cases. UNIX does the third. This requires almost no coding by operating system implementers, but it does require each application writer to write code to check the flag and decide what to do. This behavior—considered quite ugly and, well, stupid in modern operating system circles—has not harmed UNIX's success.

One can only imagine how much worse DOS must be.

The lesson is that you should choose carefully the problems you spend time solving by means of innovation. In this case, using innovation to solve the interrupt problem correctly served the purpose of merely bloating the operating system—the end users just did not care. The designers of the correctly functioning operating system probably thought that because computers do so many things correctly by design, they ought to be perfect. UNIX designers probably thought that it was OK for computers to be like anything else—lousy, and they were right: I've seen people grumble when they try to resume a UNIX program they've control-c'ed out of, but they just run the program again.

To a large extent the sophistication of a programming language is limited by the sophistication of the hardware, which may be high in terms of cleverness needed to achieve speed but is low in other ways to maintain speed, such as inexpensive large memory systems and secondary storage.

ᛤᚪ   ᛤᚪ   ᛤᚪ

One of the things I learned by watching people try to learn Lisp is that they could write programs that worked pretty well but they could not write fast programs. The reason was that they did not know how things were implemented and assumed that anything in the language manual took a small constant time. In reality, for example, there are many Lisp operations whose running times are linear in the length of one or several of their arguments. When you assume the constant-time model, the programs these novices wrote make perfect sense.

Another thing I learned from watching software businesses is that speed is king. In some cases a company would switch compilers for as little as 2% speed improvement and 1% of space, even though the cost of the change could be work years of effort. People will sacrifice all sorts of excellent features and significant personal productivity for a fast tool: Notice that vi is the editor of choice for UNIX, not Emacs, which is vastly "better" in some sense.

People can program effectively and happily when they feel they have mastered their craft, which means when they can write fast programs. People are quite capable of understanding the von Neuman architecture, and so a language whose performance model matches that architecture is a shoo-in.

A final point is that the marketplace does not care how much it cost a company to produce a software product; what customers really care about is price and speed. If your program costs too much, forget it; if it's too slow, forget it. The CEO who saves money on development by using a language with high productivity and (necessarily) poor performance is a fool.

ᛤᚪ   ᛤᚪ   ᛤᚪ

The second mandatory feature is that the language cannot require mathematical sophistication from its users. Programmers are not mathematicians, no matter how much we wish and wish for it. And I don't mean sophisticated mathematicians, but just people who can think precisely and rigorously in the way that mathematicians can.

For example, to most language theorists the purpose of types is to enable the compiler to reason about the correctness of a program in at least skeletal terms. Such reasoning can produce programs with no run-time type errors. Strict type systems along with other exemplary behavior, moreover, enable certain proofs about programs.

Well, the average programmer might be grateful somewhere in his heart for the lack of run-time type errors, but all he or she really cares about is that the compiler can produce good code, and types help compiler writers write compilers that do that.

Furthermore, types that try to do more than that are a hindrance to understanding. For example, abstract data types allow one to write programs in which the interface is completely separate from the implementation. Perhaps some large programming teams care a lot about that, but a lot of programming goes on in ones and twos, maybe threes. Types of this variety, with complicated syntax and baffling semantics, is a hindrance to programming for many of these folks. Sure, someday this will be important as the size of programming teams increases and as the level of mathematics education increases (no laughing, please), but today it is not.

Inheritance and polymorphism are examples of programming language concepts requiring mathematical sophistication to understand.

ℬ   ℬ   ℬ

The three parts of the theory work together like this: The first part—an acceptance process—provide a means for a language with the right ingredients to be spread and accepted. This shows why certain modest languages succeed over others. Furthermore, the first part describes the best acceptance process. The second, third, and fourth parts are hard requirements for a language to be accepted, but without them, a language cannot succeed merely by following the process described in the first part.

Let's look at some examples of this theory in action. The first programming languages were machine language and assembly language. Assembly language is just a symbolic machine language. There are no types. No mathematical sophistication is required at all. The performance model is the machine model. Every computer comes with an assembler, and often local wizards are needed to bum the tightest loop.

After that came FORTRAN, which has a simple machine performance model. Until 1990, the majority of non-application-specific programming took place in assembly language and FORTRAN.

FORTRAN allows one to program small integers and floating-point numbers stored in variables or arrays. Many computers support these operations directly. Types enable the compiler to produce good code. The level of mathematical sophistication required is minimal, but remember mathematicians or people very like them are programming in FORTRAN. Over the years FORTRAN came to run on every machine. FORTRAN can be considered an application-specific language because it is used so heavily in scientific computation.

In the early 1980s we saw the next step in the evolution of assembly language make its major move in acceptance—C. C also is the first language to use the acceptance process described in the first part of the theory.

The performance model of C is essentially the same as assembly language. The primary purpose of types in the original C (K & R C) is for performance. C allows one to manipulate bits, bytes, words, and very simple recordlike structures. C is easy to implement on almost any computer, and there are many local wizards. No mathematical sophistication is required to program in it. Because it follows either the virus model (through such things as gcc from the Free Software Foundation) or the assembly language model (through the hardware manufacturer), it runs on every machine.

COBOL has a simple performance model and requires absolutely no mathematical sophistication. Like FORTRAN, it doesn't follow the acceptance model, but it can also be considered an application language.

Lisp has a complex performance model and requires a great degree of mathematical sophistication to program in it. It has a functional flavor and many programs require recursive functions or higher order functionals. Some Lisp dialects and implementations follow the acceptance model, but only the smallest Lisps can run on all computers.

PROLOG has a very complex performance model based on backtracking and unification and requires very high degree of mathematical sophistication to master. In many ways PROLOG is like a proprietary language because it is rarely moved forward by the preferred acceptance model.

Pascal has a simple machine model for performance but requires a small degree of sophistication to understand its type system. However, because its type system is rudimentary, this level is still quite modest. I would say its performance model is less directly that of the machine than C, and its required mathematical sophistication is significantly higher. Pascal runs on every computer but does not follow the acceptance model.

Let's see how we're doing with usage numbers. First we'll look at lines of code. The following numbers indicate the percentage of lines of code worldwide in the languages I've mentioned in 1992 (Dataquest 1992):

Language	Percentage (lines of code)
COBOL	44%
FORTRAN	12%
Assembly	11%
C	3%
Pascal	3%
Lisp	<6%
PROLOG	<6%

Not fair, you might think, to look at total number of lines of code. OK, let's look at the usage by programmers in 1992 in North America in the technical programming segment.

Language	Usage
Assembly	88%
C	80%
Pascal	33%
Lisp	<6%
PROLOG	<6%

In this study the technical world is defined in such a way to as exclude COBOL and FORTRAN.

So far we can see that the theory can "explain" the relative proportions of existing languages. The real test comes with predictions.

The next interesting candidates are the object-oriented languages, Smalltalk and C++. Smalltalk, though designed for children to use, requires mathematical sophistication to understand its inheritance and message-passing model. Its performance model is much more complex than C's, not matching the computer all that well from a naïve point of view. Smalltalk does not run on every computer, and in many ways it is a proprietary language, which means that it cannot follow the acceptance model.

C++ is an interesting case because it is an attempt to develop C in a particular direction. This direction is not, by the way, an object-oriented direction but one that allows two things: more sophisticated user-defined types than is possible in C (something resembling abstract data types with encapsulation) and a little more safety from type errors and some other errors. However, C++ is intended to retain the C performance model when specifically C++ features are used. Best yet, C++ uses the virus model, just as C does.

Unfortunately, I believe the theory predicts that C++ will fail, even though it is clearly in the C camp and uses the acceptance model. It will fail because the performance model is too much like Smalltalk's—it is not simple— and the degree of mathematical sophistication required to use it is much greater than Smalltalk's.

Our theory predicts that C++ will do better than Smalltalk because C++ follows the acceptance model whereas Smalltalk is more like a proprietary language.

When we add Smalltalk and C++ to the second table we get the table at the top of the next page.

ঞ   ঞ   ঞ

Language	Usage
Assembly	88%
C	80%
Pascal	33%
C++	6%
Smalltalk	<6%
Lisp	<6%
PROLOG	<6%

As we look at the history of programming languages, we sit in an era where, basically, only assembly language and C are in use in the technical arena, and only COBOL, FORTRAN, and assembly language are in use worldwide. The 1980s saw some grand experiments with higher-level and more sophisticated languages like Lisp and PROLOG, but both those failed.

Languages like Modula-3 and Oberon are interesting to the language designer, but according to our theory, sadly they fall far short of Pascal in terms of acceptability. The great object-oriented experiment is under way, but the theory predicts failure there, too. Of course, like natural selection the theory is not static—it depends on when you apply it. In the early days of computers, the theory would predict that FORTRAN would not succeed, and it didn't for many years, but like the natural world, the environment changed with the need for scientific computing, and FORTRAN grabbed a big chunk of the computing world. Likewise, the need for larger programming teams might provide the environmental discontinuity that languages like Smalltalk and C++ need. The business world at large, though, resists such discontinuities.

One questioner at the HOPL II conference noted that only one language of those represented at the conference is alive: C. Looking at the last table, I would add assembly language to the list.

Right now the history of programming languages is at an end, and the last programming language is C.

~

Productivity: Is There a Silver Bullet?

For decades we computer scientists have been out trying to slay the dragon—poor programming productivity. How long does it take to develop 100 lines of production code, code that ends up in a commercial product or a delivered system? A month? Two months? Over the decades the "productivity" index has increased, by my estimate, from maybe 10 lines a month to a few hundred. Part of this productivity increase is due to better programming languages, some to better tools like better diagnostics in compilers, some to faster computers, some to symbolic debuggers, and probably most to better education. Some people claim 1,000 lines per month. However, in most cases this level of productivity seems difficult to sustain—if you had a programmer who could produce 1,000 lines a month of production code, you probably couldn't count on that programmer to produce 1,000 lines a month for two years running on one large project.

As object technologists—don't you love names like this?—we believe that we can increase productivity through object-oriented languages and design techniques. We are ever the technologists and always look toward technology for the answer. But maybe that is not the best place to look for productivity.

The word *productivity* itself is somewhat loaded. Do programmers working at some company wish they were more "productive"? Probably not. Such programmers wish they were more effective, that their tools were better, that there were fewer barriers to getting work done, that management was more competent, that working conditions were better, that there was some direct link between the success of the company and the efforts of the programmers, and that it wasn't a struggle for the company to survive from quarter to quarter. *Productive* is a term that management uses to describe what an employee is or isn't. When an employee is productive, the corporation can enjoy a better return on investment and profits. An employee who is not productive is a candidate for layoff. (The law says that you cannot lay off people for poor performance—you can eliminate only those positions not required for the success of the company. However, most development managers and vice presidents I know secretly and not so secretly consider a layoff an opportunity to let natural selection take its toll by eliminating weak, nonproductive people; when hiring starts up again—often about three months later—they hire new people and do not even consider laid-off employees for re-hire.)

Productivity is often associated with "effort"—a developer is less productive because he or she is exerting less effort than is required. (One CEO I know of once gave the order to his engineering manager to prepare a layoff list in which the sole selection criterion was effort. The CEO was willing—and eager—for the manager to eliminate people who got good results but whose effort and enthusiasm was lacking. That manager used the "gold watch" strategy: He measured each developer by the difference between what that developer could accomplish and what he or she actually did accomplish, as judged by the engineering manager and by the developer's direct manager. When the engineering manager's layoff list included the chief architect—who worked exactly eight hours a day for family reasons— and the principal user-interface guy, the CEO let the engineering manager determine his list in his own way.)

The point is that productivity is not simply something between a developer and a software problem—it has to do with management skills and realistic goals. Investment at proper levels is very rare in American software companies. Frequently I hear of companies going to market with products that the developers themselves say are not ready—this is especially devastating when the products are targeted at developers. That developers are so out of the business loop sometimes amazes me when they could be such an asset to business planning. Alas, they don't have that crucial ingredient: a business education. (This point is interesting with regard to abstraction: American companies are almost universally run by people educated in business schools rather than in schools that teach the content of the business area. Executives learn about locating and developing marketplaces, managing money, and handling managers, marketing people, sales people, people who produce the goods sold, people who service the goods, people who ship the goods, and so forth. In other words, executives treat their own companies as a set of abstractions whose insides they never know. In the United States, 80% of all CEOs of engineering-based companies are trained in business, whereas in Japan 80% of all such CEOs are engineers trained in the business domain area.)

Developers are salaried employees, and during parts of a project, in order to make the deadline, they are called upon to work 60 to 90 hours per week. However, they are not granted overtime for this extra work. In my experience, developers average 60 hours a week year-round. When the projects are fresh and exciting, working these hours can be not only acceptable but not noticeable to the developer. Inevitably, though, this leads to burnout, and the developer moves on to the next exciting project at another company. It seems to me inhuman to expect 60-hour weeks unless there is a routine bonus program or overtime.

ờ ờ ờ

Now let me tell you a story about a development group I heard about. It is the Borland Quattro Pro for Windows (QPW) development group, and I am taking the story from a paper by Jim Coplien entitled "Borland Software Craftsmanship: A New Look at Process, Quality, and Productivity" (1994).

This group developed a new, modern spreadsheet specifically designed for the Windows environment. The team included two people who had experience with the product area—one was an acknowledged expert on internal spreadsheet engines, and another had experience with implementing user interfaces of a sort similar to what they needed. The other programmers were of very high caliber— as the group itself put it, they had professionals not hired guns. The core development team consisted of four people who developed the architecture and early prototypes—two major prototypes were developed. Core development took about a year, and then four more team members, more or less, were added, and QA and documentation began.

The QPW group, consisting of about eight people, took 31 months to produce a commercial product containing 1 million lines of code. This elapsed time includes the prototypes, but the line count does not. That is, each member of this group produced 1,000 lines of final code per week. Product reviews for the first release were very good.

One of the most intriguing things about this example is that the team did not use a standard software process or methodology. Rather their process was iterative and partly prototype driven, and when they were asked what roles each developer played, they were able to easily describe that as well as what they were trying to do and where they were along the way and what was next. So in some real sense, they were really following a process.

The final coding was in C++, so although the language was probably not a positive productivity factor, it provided a mechanism to separate implementation from interface, and this turned out to be important to the group's productivity. As I noted in "Abstraction Descant," when implementation is separate from interface in a complex object-oriented design, the ripple effect that results from changing an interface can be devastating, causing many other interfaces and then their implementations to change in response. This team recognized the problem and adopted a process of almost-daily meetings to discuss architectural issues, interfaces, algorithms, and data structures. These meetings lasted several hours a day. People who have a lot of experience with meetings tend to view them as counterproductive, and indeed they are when the primary—often hidden—topic is turf and protecting credit for good results. At these meetings, however, the team was able to minimize the interface-ripple problem by giving everyone a view of all the changes—in this way the team members could immediately go off and change or extend their implementations to accommodate the interface changes, thereby quickly validating (or rejecting) them. Moreover, by keeping the architecture public, it did not get swept under the rug. Instead, it was gradually improved and extended. That the language supported the separation of implementation from interface was important because it meant that there was a clear line between what was discussed in the meetings and what was not.

An additional benefit of the frequent meetings was that all members of the team knew exactly what everyone else was doing and how their own pieces fit into the picture. This also contributed to a rich communication pattern among the group members.

The QPW group rarely used code reviews, and code reading and walkthroughs were rare or nonexistent. Each member of the team had tremendous faith in and respect for the abilities of the other team members. After a year, the team was filled out with technically savvy individuals, even in management and marketing positions.

During the first year of development, system-related technical issues—rather than marketing and sales issues—determined the architecture and design: Early decisions never appeared in marketing collateral and early customer visibility discussions.

The schedule was realistic and largely determined by development needs, though there was pressure to get things done quickly. This is unlike most companies I know about in which the marketing, sales, and upper management accept as the real date the earliest date they hear a manager utter, usually in the context of a bonus discussion. I have even heard of a marketing head and a CEO cutting 18 months off the development manager's schedule—the result was the predictable disaster.

Of course, you should recognize that QPW's process was inherently iterative with a series of increasingly stable prototypes until the product was completed.

Of particular interest is the relationship between how the QPW group saw what it was doing and the concepts of habitability and piecemeal growth we've been exploring. Habitability was encouraged by the frequent interface meetings in which the effects of changes in the necessarily global interface space were made public. Team members were naturally aware of what was public and private in the system, and patterns could emerge gracefully. About this, one of the team members said, "software is like a plant that grows," and Coplien interpreted this team member's comments like this: "You can't predict its exact shape, or how big it will grow; you can control its growth only to a limited degree" (1994).

When I asked Coplien what he thought was a good average for US software productivity, he said that many organizations can "muster 1,000 to 2,000 non-commentary source lines per programmer per year," and that this number was constant for a large in-house program over its 15-year lifetime—so that original development and maintenance moved at the same pace: slowly. Note that this estimate is lower than mine. Since Coplien has been studying process and productivity somewhat rigorously, let's use his numbers.

A thousand lines a year is about four lines a day. There is a software crisis. But is there a silver bullet?

The experience of the QPW group indicates that it is possible to achieve several orders of magnitude improvement over the industry average using common tools—C++ and a simple environment. Granted that the team in question was talented beyond that available to most organizations—but still of the several orders of magnitude perhaps a few factors, say three to five, should be available for ordinary programmers—this is asking only that programmers be able to produce 12 to 20 lines a day. The programmers in the QPW group did about 200 a day.

The way to approach this is, I think, as science. High-productivity development organizations are a natural phenomenon. The QPW group sits at the far end of a productivity spectrum; I have personal experience with several groups that demonstrated similar productivity levels. For example, during protracted development, I watched Lisp programmers produce 1,000 lines of Lisp/CLOS code per month per person, which is roughly equivalent to 350 to 1,000 lines of C++ code per week. Therefore, such productivity is not isolated, and we should figure out how to improve.

Unfortunately, to do this science requires doing some simple but expensive and time-consuming things. Here is a partial list:

- We need to determine goals, which can include higher productivity, higher quality, lower maintenance costs, better documentation, and easier extension and improvement (habitability and piecemeal growth).

- We need a reliably measured productivity baseline so we know whether we are making progress—we need well-documented numbers.

- We need to study rigorously the effects of programming language choice on productivity; that is, we need numbers from controlled experiments. Earlier I claimed that Lisp/CLOS provides a factor of 1.5 to 4 in productivity over C/C++. I based this on my personal experience with several large projects—in both Lisp and C++—but I did not perform rigorous measurements.

- We need to study the effects of various kinds of tools on productivity—environments and faster computers, for example. It seems offhand that good tools make for better productivity, but is this really true? And if so, how much does this contribute?

- We need to study all existing development methodologies and determine the factors that contribute to productivity. We must do experiments to find the best ones. I suspect that management in many companies will not like studies that assume it is possible that the best development processes do not mix with tight management control. Furthermore, tradition, law, government policy, and conventional wisdom probably do not sit well with this assumption. So we must allow neither engineers nor managers nor tradition nor law to influence the outcome or the experimental setup.

- It's possible that we cannot achieve all the goals for "productivity" at once—perhaps high productivity means a little lower quality. This may not be a fatal flaw if we know precisely what the trade-offs are, so we need to study the relationship between productivity and our other goals.

- Perhaps the best processes have not yet been discovered. So we should study new, perhaps wild alternatives such as those implied by the work of architect Christopher Alexander.

- If a proposed ideal methodology is developed, it should be tested with controlled experiments and numbers gathered. We should determine the relative contributions of the different factors in the process.

- If there is a proposed ideal methodology, we should develop the technology to support the infrastructure for it and figure out how to introduce it to industry in such a way that it will take hold. This could require a large investment cleverly designed and implemented.

I expect there to be surprises, surprises that the establishment will not like. For example:

- Only some aspects of programming languages will matter for productivity but not by more than 30% better or worse. My experience with C++ development started with a group just learning C++ and ended with quite an expert group. At the start I estimated the productivity advantage of Lisp/CLOS over C/C++ at a factor of three to four; at the end I set it at 30%. But I think this 30% is inherent in some languages, an advantage due to unpopular characteristics of those languages, such as dynamic types. I expect a lot of language designers' egos to get thumped when we learn that what they consider important for languages is trivial or counterproductive. I think ill-placed concern is the inevitable result of letting mathematicians design programming language principles, although I dearly love mathematicians and I'm sort of one myself.

- We'll find that traditional software development methodologies are among the least productive and possibly produce the lowest quality. Such methodologies are governed by the need for management control and repeatability—that is, management wants costs to be predictable. On the other hand, developers want revenues to be predictable, too, but for some reason, this is not possible to achieve.

- We'll find that traditional management has a crazy view of what motivates developers and that motivation is one of the larger productivity enhancers. The first thing that I think will fall is the view that management is there to tell developers what to do, to set schedules, and to act as a conduit for upper-management-supplied "team-player" dictums. A manager should be like the sweeper in curling: The sweeper runs ahead of the stone and sweeps away debris from the path of the stone so that the progress of the stone will be smooth and undisturbed—does this sound like your manager? The traditional view of management seems to be based on military-style thinking. The best managers, in my view, are those that combine a strong desire to help his or her developers with strong leadership abilities. In fact, I believe that leadership will prove more important than management. Very few managers are good leaders, and I feel that American MBA programs and large corporations do not produce leaders. Here is a quote from Ken Haas, who started as corporate lawyer at IntelliCorp, became its CFO, and then became its president and CEO:

> *Shortly after I joined IntelliCorp, I became perplexed by the fact that a couple of managers in the product development group got terrific results from their people (in terms of adherence to schedule as well as innovation) without apparently doing much managing—planning, organizing, controlling. Although I did not realize it at the time, these managers were practicing the art of leadership, creating a vision for their group, aligning their group behind that vision, and motivating them towards it. . . . While management and leadership skills are both important for the well-rounded executive, American companies are over managed and under led, so there's a premium on the latter. For years, I learned from my peers in product development and their ornery crew ("strong leaders choose poor followers"), and I even tried to implement some of their techniques within the administrative groups reporting to me. Although I believed in my heart that visioning, aligning, and motivating could not have much success in the highly structured realms of accounting, human resources, and facilities management, I was absolutely wrong, Leadership is for everyone, even CFOs.* (Haas 1993)

The second thing that will fall will be the attitude that motivation is purely based on reward. There is a CEO I know whose motto is "Tell me how I'm measured and I'll tell you how I'll act." His view is that if a developer is told that following the schedule set by some manager will result in a bonus or a raise, the developer will follow the schedule. A lot of times a manager-set schedule assumes that there will be no architectural changes. Even though a detour to repair the architecture will often result in no lost time or even saved time, management that rewards developers based on following schedules might very well get what they want—a product developed on schedule. But also they will likely get one that cannot be extended, improved, and grown, and which does not fit the market's actual needs. If you want someone to be more of a developer, try being more of a manager.

- The physical environment will prove a larger factor than previously believed. Alexander believes this, but management seems to think that a one-time savings in setting up offices, computers, and so on is more important than recurring productivity losses. If your organization is pooping along at four lines a day per person but you saved $100,000 by using those cheap cubes, and mine is humming at 200 per day, who is laughing all the way to the bank?

- We'll find that very frequent, large meetings to settle interfaces will prove to be helpful. Some developers will find this distasteful.

- The goal of total design before implementation will prove to be very unhelpful. Piecemeal growth will prove the right way to go—that "software is like a plant."

- Reuse will prove to be a factor in only limited ways and limited situations. Some of the reuse guys won't like this too much. Reuse is important, but it is important to piecemeal growth. Many people hope there will be a way of storing up pieces of code in a library that can supply a basis for arbitrary reuse. Sadly, although I once believed this myself, I have abandoned that hope. Even with fairly common operations like sorting, it is difficult to come up with a piece of code suitable for all sorting applications. Some of the problems have to do with language choice, data structure choice, performance characteristics, names, and calling conventions. On the other hand, patterns of sorting routines are handy and popular, giving credence to the hope of the patternists such as the Hillside Group.

The real basis for reuse is frameworks. A framework is a model for the basic operation of some aspect of your problem space or business. When this model is properly implemented in an object-oriented manner to do certain tasks, it is easy to add additional tasks by reusing the framework and its code. For example, if you write software to track purchase orders from receipt through shipment and maintenance, you can easily add code to grab addresses for marketing mailings. Another way to put this is that object-oriented programming encourages you to model the *entity* not the *function*, and entities, not functions, are reused.

- The result of this research will be a silver bullet: We will find that productivity and quality can be increased by two or three orders of magnitude averaged over a long term. This will be fabulous, but I fear industry will not easily accept the means to achieve it.

This last point is sad. What I expect to find is that the mechanisms that do work will work best over a longer period of time than is traditional in American business circles. Therefore, they will not be adopted because the traditional way results in short-term savings at the expense of long-term growth. Furthermore, although the QPW group had management accepting whatever it took for good development, very few companies are as open-minded. My experience is that management distrusts developers and feels held hostage by them. I have heard many discussions in which software-company CEOs look forward to the day when software development does not require hiring those pesky programmers. They would rather not spend all that money buying better computers, putting in home equipment, supplying private window offices, and providing caffeine-laced drinks.

Yet the saddest thing of all is that there are no sources of funding for such work. I recently attended a meeting at which a government agency was seeking ideas for projects aimed at economic improvement in the software area—and there was $20 million to $200 million available per year for it. However, the requirement was that there be a *technological barrier* to the improvement, in addition to an unwillingness or inability for any given company to fund the work. That is, the ultimate goal was enviable but ultimately aimed at funding the same old tinker-toy sorts of technology-busting boondoggles.

You know, sometimes it's a people problem, not a technology problem.

PART III

WHAT WE DO

What We Do

Every now and then, I think, it makes sense to sit back and think about what we do. By "we" I mean computer scientists and especially those working in object-oriented technologies. It seems to most of us that we are doing good things for the world and propelling it forward, easing the drudgery of day-to-day life, providing technology that enriches people's lives and makes them happy.

But this isn't always the case. Think of the scientists who worked on nuclear fission just before the start of the Manhattan Project—especially think of the theoretical physicists working long before. It's likely only few of them thought deeply about the destructive uses of the application of their work; and if they had thought about those uses, perhaps they would have thought twice about it.

We don't think much about the uses of our work partly because we are never in a position to hear valid criticism of that work. Sure, we hear things like computer databases are misused by corporations and individuals, and sometimes we hear people say that by increasing productivity in the workplace we are indirectly denying people their jobs. These problems, though, are indirect: If people did not have greedy or other ignoble motives, databases would not be misused; if the economy were in better shape, increased productivity would result in more products and jobs, not layoffs or fewer jobs.

Networks and hypertext are examples of a technology we developed that is regarded by a number of people as dangerous and detrimental to entire industries and culture as well, even when those technologies are used exactly the way we intend by people with lofty motives.

In August 1993 I was at the Bread Loaf Writers' Conference in Vermont. While there I was just another poet sitting in the Burgess Meredith Little Theater listening to poets, fiction writers, editors, and publishers read their work and talk about it. Up on the mountain in central Vermont during cool, dry, early autumn reflecting at an unhurried pace about one's work and passion—we as computer scientists should do things like this. While there I heard a speech by Paul Zimmer, director of the University of Iowa Press on two topics. One was his battle with the NEA (National Endowment for the Arts) over prior restraint and censorship during the recent Frohnmeyer regime there. Zimmer led the way in protest, refusing to follow the restrictive new rules (since lifted) and we all saw him as a hero. Then he turned his attention to networks and hypertext.

There is a storm on the horizon he told us. With computers now able to display text reasonably well on the screen, with screens becoming better and smaller and more portable, with networks being better and more available, with authors being able to write and produce their own texts and to send them out over networks, the role of the editor and publisher could vanish. Soon there could be no intermediaries between the author and his or her audience. Worse, distribution could become a matter of software distribution companies providing floppy disks containing unedited and unselected stories, books, and poems.

Zimmer added that part of the repulsion for him is the thought of people not being able to sit quietly in a warmly lit room in a comfortable chair reading words beautifully written and nicely typeset on real paper—the texture and the feeling of thick sheets of paper between the fingers, the visible thickness of the ink all would be gone. You could see Zimmer shudder behind the podium at the vision of people sitting with small computers on their laps reading poetry.

He argued that not everyone would want to read books on computers, but enough would—because of the potentially lower price—to force up the price of real books to the point where the market might completely vanish. He did not think that the benefits of computer-assisted reading—searching, annotation, cross-referencing—justified the elimination of the university presses and possibly even some commercial publishers. He also worried that the implied elimination of the editor—the selection process—would eventually diminish the quality of writing to a point where people would not want to read anymore.

It seems obvious to me on reflection that publishers should be eager to embrace new technology as long as there is a place in it for them. Certainly I don't look forward to trying to find the few good books among an unselected, unedited morass of self-published trash. We couldn't expect reviewers to take on the task of slogging through such large quantities. Therefore, it would seem that the role of the publisher/editor would reemerge in perhaps a different format, and I, for example, would gladly subscribe to a group of publishers/editors for reading material if that were the alternative—perhaps reviewers would be willing to review material selected and edited in such a form.

So even though I can see that its role is necessary, the publishers and editors are too spooked by the technology to think it through. Maybe if we were able to communicate better the limitations of our technology we could reduce the panic or at least encourage a dialogue with people like Paul Zimmer.

He went on to talk about hypertext. At first I didn't understand what he was getting at: He said that hypertext meant that books and stories would become disjointed incoherent jumbles, barely comprehensible and unrecognizable as literature. From what I knew about the uses of hypertext in documentation and programming environments, this just didn't connect with reality. Then I started to read about hyperfiction in which "text spaces" are linked together in a variety of ways, by the author, by the reader (or both), or by a process, often a random process. This implies that each text is actually a group of texts and that various stories or plots emerge from a single source.

To Zimmer this could very well be a necessary result of the technology—that disconnected texts are what we intended the technology for. Of course this isn't true. Like many accidental media, artists are bound to try to use each new medium as well as he or she can. There are at best only a few writers right now who are capable of putting together any text that can be viewed in multiple ways, and though there may be a curiosity factor today that compels people to read such texts or though there may be a feeling of poking through someone else's life while reading a text in which the hypertext allows the reader to explore (or not explore) different parts of the created world, the art must rise to a level deserving a larger readership.

Right now, as best I can tell, the art is at a stage similar to that of early synthesizers. The emphasis is on playing with the technology and exploring its limits rather than making the technology subservient to the art. At the current stage one can rightly ask, "what art?" Remember those early synthesizer recordings with beeps and sighs and bubbling burps? It was fun and entertaining to hear sounds we had never heard before, but once we had heard them, the novelty wore off. So it is with hypertext.

And Paul Zimmer, how can he really know that this is what is going on? How can he fail to put the two technologies together, seeing the unchallenged shallowness of current hyperfiction, seeing that there would be no useful role for an editor of such work because it is so bad, seeing that the world is being led by the nose by technology to a future with no quality, no literature, only a future with people playing with technology the way some people mindlessly channel or net surf?

I think it is our duty to help people understand our technology and our intentions for its use. Of course, our intentions are only part of what determines how it is used, but unless we get people like Paul Zimmer to see its good uses and to help shape the future, they may resist it and appear foolish in doing so. And perhaps this will help Paul's nightmare scenario come true.

I believe we have more of a duty to represent our technology to the world than we have assumed until now. For example, the public doesn't really know what software is like, what we think about when we do our work. Think of the books on computers. For the most part there are user guides, extravagant books about the promises of artificial intelligence, and books that talk about 1's and 0's and how simple logic drives computers. Does this sound like what you do for a living? Do you push bits? Do you use simple logic? Do you have much to do with the promises of artificial intelligence or user guides? No, we deal with complex programming languages, inheritance, polymorphism, abstractions. Think about how much people know about physics and evolution based on popular books. No one could find out what we do at that level from the books out there today.

For technology visible to the public we should provide exemplars, we should talk about the best uses and clearly explain and illustrate them. We should seek out those professions and industries that are most affected take the time not only to explain what we are doing but also to invite them into the process early on.

At first I thought that Paul Zimmer hadn't taken the time to read up on the technology and his position silly. But then I looked at his evidence, and his conclusions made sense, because we had not given him the facts. Let's think a little bit more about what we do.

~

Writing Broadside

I just came back from a week-long nature poetry workshop at Squaw Valley (California) with the Squaw Valley Community of Writers (1993). At that workshop, Gary Snyder—nature poet, essayist, and former Beat poet—delivered a broadside on nature poetics. In it he encouraged writers to not only push on their writing but to embrace science—get the science right. A number of scientists attended the workshop, most notably geologist Eldridge Moores, the human hero of John McPhee's *Assembling California* (1993). It was fascinating to see poets, fiction writers, and essayists sitting on the edges of their seats listening to scientists, trying to get the science right, trying to learn what to read and what to do to be more science literate.

We could sit back and chuckle, knowing that it is a lifetime's work to get the science right in the sense of becoming a scientist, but I admire the writers who realize that they cannot shut off their left brain while trying to be nature writers. These writers are trying.

Over the years I've tried to push scientists to work on their writing skills, and judging by what I read—or more correctly, judging by what I cannot read—I've not gotten far. As computer scientists we are writers, probably half-time writers. Many computer scientists spend nearly all their time writing, and some of them are pretty good. But a significant number of these decent computer science writers are decent in the same way that someone who picks at a guitar for 5 or 10 years can eventually play something that resembles a tune—they are persistent dilettantes.

If you spend more than 25% of your time writing or a crucial part of your résumé is a list of publications, you are a writer. More than 2,300 years ago Thucydides wrote:

> A *man who has the knowledge but lacks the power clearly to express*
> *it is no better off than if he never had any ideas at all.*
> (Thucydides 1981)

If your writing is unreadable, you will limit the number of people who read and understand your work. It's hard to believe you would choose to limit your readership. Some computer scientists I know tell me people should and will work to understand their results.

This spring I was on the ACM OOPSLA program committee, and I tried to read all the papers—actually I failed and read only about 75% of them. In order for a paper to be considered by the committee as a whole at the face-to-face meeting, each reader had to rate the paper well. Did your paper fail to get into OOPSLA? Could it be because I couldn't read it and gave it a low mark? How many other people have put aside your paper because it was poorly written? How many of those who persevered won't say a good word about you because you write poorly? Sadly, if this is the case, it is likely that you failed to take your career seriously.

Now the broadside. A broadside is a forceful argument or something printed on one side of a single sheet of paper. This is a broadside in both of these senses: I am arguing forcefully that you should take writing seriously, and at the end I will present a short list of things I believe you should do to improve your own writing. You can print those points on one sheet and put it over your desk.

I have a number of familiar suggestions for what to do and one or two very unfamiliar and maybe controversial ones.

First, read a book about how to write. The traditional and expected suggestion is to read Strunk and White's *Elements of Style* (1979). I never found this book to be useful except to inspire me to think about writing. People who read it come away inspired by its most forceful rule:

Omit needless words

I have read almost every book on writing there is. I have studied writing as hard as I've studied anything in my life. And I say to myself, *yes, this is good advice* because after years of study I know what *omit needless words* means.

It is definitely good when people say about your writing that it contains no needless words, but how would you go about eliminating them? How would you know a word is needless? In *Zen and the Art of Motorcycle Maintenance* (Pirsig 1984) we learn that there is a point you reach in tightening a nut where you know that to tighten just a little more might strip the thread but to leave it slightly looser would risk having the nut coming off from vibration. If you've worked with your hands a lot, you know what this means, but the advice itself is meaningless. There is a zen to writing, and, like ordinary zen, its simply stated truths are meaningless unless you already understand them—and often it takes years to do that.

Sure, read *Elements of Style* and every book on writing you can get your hands on, but there really is only one I've seen that tries to teach what it means to omit needless words, to write clearly and simply. That book is *Style: Toward Clarity and Grace* by Joseph M. Williams (1990). Williams seems to know what makes writing clear and graceful and he can explain it. Sometimes he explains where bromides like *avoid passives* come from and tells us how to figure out when to ignore them—for example, when it's a good idea to use passives. He does this by providing a theory of clear writing that we as scientists can use. If you decide to read only one book on writing, this is the one.

You need to learn grammar. There are many ways to do that and many books that can help you. *Chicago Manual of Style* (1982), *Modern English Usage* (Fowler 1987), *Transitive Vampire* (Gordon 1984)—they all do the job. Pay attention to grammar; it's not hard.

Read a lot. And not just science. In 1990 I read an essay in the *New York Times Book Review* that said that to really appreciate good fiction writing and to improve your own writing, you should read poetry. I found this intriguing and started reading the works of the five or so poets mentioned: W. H. Auden, Marianne Moore, Elizabeth Bishop, William Butler Yeats, and Robert Frost. Of these I found Frost the most illustrative and accessible. The point to reading poetry is in several parts.

First, modern and contemporary poetry is about compression: Say as much in as few words as possible. Poets avoid adjectives, adverbs, gerunds, and complicated clausal structure. Their goal is to get the point across as fast as they can, with the fewest words, and generally with the constraint of maintaining an easily spoken verbal rhythm.

Second, poets say old things in new ways. When you read good poetry, you will be amazed at the insights you get by seeing a compressed expression presenting a new way of looking at things.

Third, poets love language and write sentences in ways you could never imagine. I don't mean that their sentences are absurd or unusual—rather, the sentences demonstrate the poet's keen interest in minimally stating a complex image or point. I've seen sentences that state in five words something it would have taken me 20 words or more to say.

Fourth, the best poets balance left- and right-brain thinking. This might come as a surprise to some, but the best poetry is not new-age sentimentality. Moreover, contemporary poetry rarely requires a knowledge of Greek mythology or obscure tribal myths and traditions.

After I had read poetry for a year or so, my technical and scientific writing got much better. I would say that nothing improved it more than did reading poetry.

Since then I have developed a keen interest in contemporary poetry, and my writing skills have continued to improve (I think) ever since.

The best writers in computer science have a strongly developed knowledge of writing. The best writers include Guy Steele Jr., Don Knuth, and Stanley Lippman. Lippman studied creative writing as an undergraduate. All three scientists write technical material that is a joy to read. It is easy to find examples of bad writing. One of the most influential computer scientists in my field (programming languages) wrote a crucial paper that I have never been able to read.

Next, practice writing. Document the last program you wrote. Use a real typesetting system—Tex or Framemaker—and produce real documentation. Describe something in a paper you just read. Spend an hour or two a week just writing—anything. Answer your e-mail carefully—edit it, revise it. Writing takes practice. Do you think a violinist listens to music and reads a book and then steps onto stage to perform? Professional writers are always writing, so it's no wonder they are good.

The best way to understand a subject or idea is to write about it. A good way to practice writing is to write about something you don't understand. If you don't understand inheritance or encapsulation, write about it. You will both learn the subject and improve your writing.

My last piece of advice is something I've never heard of in the sciences, and to be honest, I'm not sure how well it would work there. Here goes.

How do you think fiction and poetry writers become good? Naturally it includes a lot of writing practice and studying good writing and working with a teacher, but established writers also use workshops.

A workshop is a group of people who periodically get together and read and critique manuscripts by fellow workshoppers. Usually the workshop group stays together a long time, although this isn't necessary. But, the longer a workshop group is together, the better their comments will become, and the better each participant will become at knowing which comments to ignore and which to attend to.

Participating in a workshop is better than giving your work to individual people, because a person tends to soften critical comments, particularly if he or she has a long-term relationship with the writer. In a workshop there can be a feeding frenzy when comments are harsh, and, although this might be tough on people with frail egos, it is crucial to producing accurate comments and feedback, and the writing (and the content) can rapidly improve.

I recommend that we all start workshops, particularly around conference-paper submission time. Find people who are in your subfield and also in nearby subfields or even in unrelated ones. Hand out the material a few days in advance, but not too far in advance—real readers rarely take a long time to try to figure out your paper, so neither should the workshoppers. Start the comments by having someone summarize the paper. Then have people state what is new to them, what works about the paper. Finally, let people start saying what they didn't understand, what isn't clear. Talk not only about the contents of the paper but also about the writing. Make specific suggestions—for example, propose rewrites of specific passages.

If the paper contains a major result, be harder on the writing: An important result deserves to be widely read, and wide readership implies less knowledgeable readers. You can provide a lot of background material if you know how to compress—remember, poetry teaches you compression.

Start a workshop in graduate school, particularly at dissertation time. Learn to write while you're in school. It is your profession; act like a professional.

This year's OOPSLA program committee chairman, Ralph Johnson, proposed that the call for papers require people who submitted papers to show them to someone else, preferably an OOPSLA-published writer. This proposal was rejected, and so were 91% of the submitted papers.

Work on your basic skills.

RPG's Writing Broadside

- Your profession includes writing, so learn how to write. No one is naturally talented enough to get by on instinct alone.

- Study writing by reading books on writing. I suggest *Style: Toward Clarity and Grace* by Joseph M. Williams.

- Study writing by reading good writers, and not just science writers. Read Knuth but also John McPhee and Rick Bass. Try to understand how they do it. Think about the good writing you read.

- Learn proper grammar; there are zillions of books on grammar.

- Get a couple of good dictionaries and use them. I have about a half dozen I use routinely. Some poets look up every single word in their poems to make sure they are using language accurately.

- Learn to revise and edit; there are books on this, but I suggest workshops.

- Read poetry. Nothing teaches you better the power of good writing and the skills to write compressed sentences. Poetry workshops are full of fiction and essay writers who are there to learn language skills.

- Practice writing. Write every day. If you are a top-notch computer scientist, you probably read technical papers nearly every day. You are a writer too, so practice.

- Workshop your writing. Writers learn by workshopping. Every night across the country writers sit in groups of 3 to 20, reading and critiquing each other's work. Not only are these professional writers but amateurs who simply want to improve their diaries.

PART IV

~

LIFE OF THE CRITIC

~

A Personal Narrative: Journey to Stanford

Some of my essays have been about software, architecture, productivity, and things technical or concerned with our profession; other essays have been about writing and our day-to-day activities as computer professionals. My goal in all these essays is to spark your thinking—perhaps you'll think new thoughts or look at things differently. This essay is different—it is a personal narrative of part of the journey I took to get where I am today in my profession. I want to give you, my dear reader, a better idea of where my views come from and why I take pleasure in goring sacred cows. And I think it's easier to enjoy essays written by a person who is more than a picture and words on the page. It took me a long time to decide to write this essay, and a longer time to decide to publish it.

Throughout my life I have known people who were born with silver spoons in their mouths. You know the ones: grew up in a strong community, went to good public or private schools, were able to attend a top undergraduate school like Harvard or Caltech, and then were admitted to the best graduate schools. Their success was assured, and it seemed to come easy for them. These are the people—in many, but certainly not all cases—who end up telling the rest of us how to go about our business in computing. They figure out the theories of computation and the semantics of our languages; they define the software methodologies we must use. It's good to have their perspective, but it's only a perspective, one not necessarily gained by working in the trenches or watching the struggles of people grappling with strange concepts.

Worse, watching their careers can discourage the rest of us, because things don't come easy for us, and we lose as often or more often than we win. And discouragement is the beginning of failure.

Sometimes people who have not had to struggle are smug and infuriating. This is my attempt to fight back. Theirs is a proud story of privilege and success. Mine is a story of disappointment and failure; I ought to be ashamed of it, and I should try to hide it. But I learned from it, and maybe you can, too.

Along my odd path I learned a valuable lesson: Good friends and hard work—in that order—pay off. And you don't need to be born a winner to become one at least in small ways.

Just a few days ago I sat in my old friend John's living room in Denver. He was my best high school buddy, and we hadn't seen each other since a smoke-filled and uncomfortably noisy high school reunion a year before. I sat with him and told him this story. He had forgotten the parts that overlapped with our friendship. He's now a psychologist, and he told me I should write it down, maybe for people to see. Here is that story.

I grew up on a dairy farm in northeastern Massachusetts, just north of the Merrimack River in the town of Merrimac. I was born in 1949, and at that time this region was remote. Our farm was several miles from anyone else, and I was an only child growing up on a farm where there was always work and chores to do. The Merrimack Valley back then was depressed by the shutdown of many of the shoe factories along the river. While I was in elementary school and high school, a lot of people were out of work or changed jobs frequently. Because the tax base was poor, the schools were not very well funded by property taxes, and they were pretty lousy. I remember at one point hearing that my high school was the worst in Massachusetts in terms of the percentage of people going on to college and that you had to look to places like rural Mississippi to find worse schools (no offense intended, Mississippi).

My parents never sent me to kindergarten, so when I went to first grade I was put in the class for "slow" children. There was a class for "normal" children, but none for "fast" children. After six months or so they moved me to the normal class.

Whatever happened in elementary school doesn't matter much except to say it made me a wise guy—as people who bent the rules and made a lot of jokes were called—and by high school I was a first-class wise guy. My ambition was to become a writer. Schoolwork was generally pretty easy, but mostly that was because the curriculum was so backward that there was not much most kids had to do to keep up. My parents thought that writing—especially poetry and fiction—wasn't a realistic alternative, so they pushed me into mathematics. Their thought was that I could always write if I had a real job, but I couldn't always have a real job if I wrote. Because my father was laid off several times and had to takes jobs like apple-picking, he was concerned that I would not have even the advantages he did. So when it came time to apply for college, I applied to schools where I could study mathematics: Harvard, MIT, and Northeastern University.

Northeastern was my safety-net school. I was ranked first or second in my school—which was ranked last in Massachusetts—and there was some hope of getting into Harvard or MIT given my SAT scores, which were OK, but I and my parents considered me a long shot for them.

My senior year in high school was the beginning of a long and painful journey which ended nine years later when I got into Stanford as a graduate student. Everyone in senior class was required to take a course called Contemporary Civilization, which was a civics class. This class was taught by a an ex-Marine named Joe Sherry. He was Irish and his temper was a little short, and he was the first teacher we had who treated us roughly. He insulted people and made fun of them, but not—we thought—in a malicious way. He singled out a small group of us whom he thought were a little uppity or snotty and he ragged us. I was one of the ones he felt would always get in trouble by wising off.

We had to write a term paper first semester—jointly supervised and graded by the ConCiv teacher and the English teacher, Ronald Fenerty. They taught us how to choose a topic, make an outline, do the research (using index cards), write a draft, and write the final paper. We had until the beginning of the second semester, which gave us over Christmas break. I chose for my topic the megalopolis, the giant city. In 1966 the concept of a giant city stretching from Washington, D.C., to Boston or from LA to San Francisco was new. I had read something about it at MIT when I was there visiting, and it seemed fashionably obscure and sociological.

Through the fall I worked on it, but it was a background activity for me—the pace of deadlines was slow enough to make sure the average student could keep up. In November I was accepted at Northeastern as part of its early acceptance program to try to attract good students. Northeastern back then was almost exactly in the middle of overall college rankings in the United States.

In December I got what I thought was great news. A Harvard committee to assess students' scholarship potential sent someone to visit me and my family. The discussion revolved around which scholarships I could qualify for—based on national origin, family income, and special qualifications for privately funded scholarships. When we asked the guy whether this meant I had been accepted he said it was almost certain because the committee did not want to spend time with families whose children were not going to be accepted. He said that the committee told him that I would be accepted unless something unusual happened when my application was completed but that I had been screened into a pool of students almost certain to be accepted and with financial difficulties.

Feeling my oats, I decided to press quickly ahead with the term paper and I finished it in mid-December. With time on my hands I thought it would be nice to indulge my writing desire and planned to write a preface that would make concrete the abstract things my paper said about the megalopolis—the isolation, the dependence on TV instead of on live entertainment, the long commutes. I asked the teachers if I could do this and they said I could not, but I could write a one sentence dedication.

It's hard to understand why a teacher would reject a proposal from a student to do extra work and to write a more interesting paper. I suppose it's because real essays or research papers needed to have a specific form to be acceptable.

What is a wise guy? A wise guy is a person who when told that he could write only a one-sentence dedication when he had planned a long preface would simply turn the preface into a dedication—one, very long sentence.

So, I wrote a 3,000-word, one-sentence dedication. I dedicated the piece to a typical resident of the megalopolis who is battered by shallow culture, poor jobs, fast pace, and low reward, someone whose life is barely worth living and whose creative and living juices are throttled by the routine of surviving in a place that is crowded to near-death—he is a man unfortunately trapped by the horrors on contemporary civilization and made less a man, less a person by his circumstances.

Proud, I submitted it just before Christmas break instead of just after.

A few days after the break ended, the English teacher, Mr. Fenerty, called me into a private office after school to talk to me about my paper. He held it as we sat down and told me that he was very impressed with it and had given me the highest grade the principal had allowed. It seems silly now but I remember counting the seven plus signs after the A: A+++++++. This seemed fair and just to me—I had worked very hard on the paper and had tried to make it something worthy of a future Harvard student.

Mr. Fenerty said he wanted to ask me about the paper before we talked about the grade some more; he asked me to explain what the paper was about, and I did; then he asked me to explain the dedication. I told him in the unsophisticated way that a senior in high school can that it was a concrete realization of the abstract discussion in the paper—that the paper started with generalizations and abstraction and moved through implication to the personal and that the dedication started with the concrete—a story—and proceeded to the abstract by generalization: two approaches to the theme. He agreed that that made sense to him but maybe we should go over the dedication phrase by phrase. I read each phrase and explained it, and he nodded each time.

Then he asked me if I thought someone could have taken it personally. No, I answered. Then let's go over it again, he said. When we got to the phrase about contemporary civilization, he asked whether I could see how Mr. Sherry might have locked onto that phrase and so felt that the description was of him—that he was that low brow person. It might seem strange to anyone hearing this story now, but it all dawned on me right then that he could take it that way, even though it wasn't what I had intended.

Mr. Fenerty knew I really wanted to write and that I had done show-off things in writing before and that a sentence that long—the longest sentence I or he knew of in published English—was just showboating. Because I fixed the moment in my mind that day, I can still remember the thought I had when I wrote "contemporary civilization"—what a neat hack!

He told me he had given me the ridiculous grade to balance the one that Mr. Sherry had given me: an F. I was shocked for a moment and then told him that if Sherry had taken it that way, I was glad I wrote it that way. The average of the two grades was a C–.

I thought it was a pity but felt no danger in the situation, and Mr. Fenerty said I should talk to Mr. Sherry. I went to him and explained that I hadn't meant it the way he took it, but he told me this: He felt I had been out to make him look the fool in his class and now he had the chance to get me for it. He said that he had been asked by the Harvard admissions committee to write an evaluation of me, that they always asked the civics teacher to assess how aware students were of the world and that it was a way to get a statement from someone not selected by the student. Furthermore, because every high school senior at that time was required to take civics, they could get a recommendation for every applicant from the same type of teacher.

He let me look at a copy of the letter he had written to them. It said that I had no ethics or morals and that he and other teachers suspected that I had cheated in school on many occasions—my destructive attitude would not only damage my likelihood of success at Harvard but would also hurt other students. He explained to me that his goal was to prevent me from going to Harvard and to destroy my future as much as he could.

Harvard did not accept me, and neither did MIT.

If this happened today, I would own him: My family would have sued and his financial situation would have been ruined. But in 1967 you didn't sue—it just never occurred to anyone in the Merrimack Valley. We appealed to the principal, to the school board, and to Harvard and MIT, but they turned away. I was to go to Northeastern.

I called Northeastern and asked what the real requirements were for me to be admitted; for example, did I need to graduate with a high grade-point average? No, just a diploma was all I needed. I asked the principal of my high school what would happen if I flunked all my courses for the second semester, and he thought I might get C's for the them for the year but that I would still end up with one of the top averages for the four years.

So I decided to go on strike: I told each teacher that because the law required I attend classes every day that I would do that but that I would bring a book, sit in back of class (or in my assigned seat) and not disturb anyone but that I would not participate in the class. Some teachers had trouble understanding it and they would call on me in class to answer a question; I would answer that I was not paying attention and that I did not know the answer. After a while they caught on that I was serious and gave up.

I failed each course that semester and I also quit the debating club and the math club and so did some of my friends, and those clubs lost all the competitions they were in for the rest of the year. I started to grow my hair long in protest, but the school board decided to let it go.

I don't know now whether this rebellious streak was already implanted or was caused by this incident, but it certainly became a strong aspect of my personality and approach to life—I became the cynical and caustic critic, and whatever was expected, I did the opposite.

Some teachers didn't want me to graduate, but the principal pointed out that I had the second highest average in the class and that there was no basis for it. They pressed him not to allow me to march on graduation day, but I didn't care about it so I didn't fight. However, I was to get some awards and the teachers giving them out protested that it was a tradition to make a big deal of these awards at graduation, and so I was finally allowed to march through graduation with my class.

Northeastern is a five-year cooperative school, which means that you alternate school with work in order to build a track record for getting a job. Going on to graduate school from Northeastern was generally not expected. The school was not great at the time, but I was not really prepared to worry about the future beyond undergraduate school, with five years of it ahead of me. I slogged my way through and had an interesting cooperative job in which I learned to program computers—something I had never considered before.

I studied pure mathematics, and all I cared about was proving theorems. My interest in writing faded after the first year. Math students got programming co-op jobs at Northeastern. My programming job was at a little company in Carlisle, Massachusetts, called Parke Mathematical Laboratories—what a weird name and place. There were about five mathematicians, physicists, and acousticians who took contracts, usually subcontracts from local government-funded labs. When I first saw a computer, I was completely blown away. I was helping a young woman programmer run some simulations on an IBM 1130; she showed me the problem they were trying to solve, the simulator setup, and how to watch what was happening to make sure nothing went awry. It seemed like a miracle: You put in your problem and through a process you didn't have to think about, the right answer came out. I was floored by the apparent power of the thought process in this wide, low, blue-and-gray box—its flashing panel an artificial furrowed brow. I wondered how to apply the brain power in the box to my personal problems.

So I started taking philosophy of mind courses to try to unravel what the mind could be that this machine could be like one. By the time I graduated from

Northeastern I was a so-so mathematician, an OK FORTRAN and assembly language programmer, and I had no clear idea about the rest of my life except that I wanted to try for grad school. I had applied to the usual places for someone who thinks he has half a chance—MIT, Harvard, Berkeley, Wisconsin, and Minnesota. All of these were in the top 20 in mathematics back then, and predictably, I was rejected by MIT, Harvard, and Berkeley. The other two took me and offered teaching fellowships. This seemed like a step up from where I had been, but it didn't seem optimal to me. I had girlfriend for the first time and it looked serious, and she was going to go to school in Boston. I had to figure a way to stay in Boston.

Some friends on the Northeastern mathematics faculty talked to me about my interest in the philosophy of mind and programming, and one of them said, "Oh, I see, you're into AI!" After revealing I had no idea what she meant, she told me to go talk to her old friend Patrick Winston, who was the associate director of the MIT Artificial Intelligence Lab. He suggested that I take courses at MIT and see what happened. So I applied for and was accepted as a "special student," which meant I was someone whose money they were willing to take and who they expected would not detract from the education of the real graduate students.

I was "admitted" into the mathematics department, which gave me the feeling that I might be able to get into a better graduate school later. I took a normal load for a first-year math grad student, but weighted slightly toward artificial intelligence and computability. You see, my idea of AI was that it was intertwined with computability and decidability.

I learned something about competition at MIT. A couple of times I was sick and could not attend classes, and when I asked some of the students if I could borrow their notes they told me no. So I learned to not get sick.

I lived at home then and all during my undergraduate years. My parents left me alone in general and I usually ate in Boston, so it was almost like being on my own, but not quite. The commute was 50 miles each way, and in all I did that for six years.

I noticed another thing about competition at MIT. Classes generally started out with 20 to 30 students, and if the course was tough people dropped it rather than take a bad grade. I stuck with every class and achieved an OK B+ average. One course—Algebraic Topology—taught by a category theorist, started with 26 students and ended up with six. I got a B, which I thought a real triumph. The teaching assistant told me he never saw anyone prove theorems the way I did, convoluted but clearly original and certainly not copied out of a book. Left-handed, no doubt, but I took it as a compliment.

The summer after that year I was given an office (shared by three) at the MIT AI Lab on the strength of a highly philosophical and mathematical essay I wrote that year on computer vision. I worked very hard on that essay, and it was 100 pages of single-spaced type and lots of odd mathematical content and theorems. That summer I met several people who would make a difference in years to come. Among them were Patrick Winston, Guy L. Steele Jr., JonL White, and Scott Fahlman. I also met Dave Waltz, with whom I would make my next move.

Patrick Winston took me aside one day in mid-summer and told me that it looked like the Lab would not be funded well the next few years, and though he might be able to get me into MIT on a permanent basis, it was unlikely I would be funded. He also hinted that his being able to get me in would be hampered by the fact that he couldn't fund me. He made a suggestion, though: Dave Waltz was headed for the University of Illinois to start an AI lab—I could get in on the ground floor at what could be a major new lab with good funding. I applied late to the Illinois math department. But Patrick talked me up to Dave, who talked me up to the head of the larger lab within which the AI lab would be built, who talked the university and the math department into letting me in. I visited the Coordinated Science Lab (CSL) late that summer, and my girlfriend, to whom I had proposed that summer as well, agreed to move there with me.

We tried to start the lab but ultimately failed. In the meantime I worked toward a Ph.D. in mathematics. I took a fair number of AI courses, but mostly mathematics. I had better luck than at MIT and achieved something closer to an A average, but as time went on I became less interested in mathematics and more interested in computers. I wrote a lot of programming environment code to try to duplicate the environment we had at MIT, but it was hard to do single-handed, and we weren't on the net and ran a different operating system, and thus it was frequently not practical to get the code from MIT. After the first year it became clear that we weren't going to be funded the way we needed to be to get the new lab started— ARPA (*Advanced Research Projects Agency*) was having its own funding problems, and people were not that enthusiastic about AI at Illinois. Dave and I tried to start up a multidisciplinary curriculum for those of us interested in AI, and it turned out we would need funding and approval from the departments, the schools, the deans, the president, the trustees, and the state legislature. We gave up on the idea.

At the start of the second year I started to worry about getting my own degree more than about setting up programs and labs. I went to the math department and asked them how I could get a Ph.D. in AI from them. After some thought they came up with an idea—an idea like I've never heard before or since.

Their proposal was that I finish all the course and examination requirements for a Ph.D. in math (from the department rated fifth in the United States and upset they weren't first), and then I'd have to write a dissertation that satisfied them as to its mathematics. It would, of course, have to be approved as an AI thesis by my advisor and his department (electrical engineering, EE). And because who at Illinois really is a senior person in AI, why not have the thesis approved by MIT, say by Minsky and Papert?

This sounded pretty hard to me, so I was depressed about what to do.

Dave and one of the full professors of EE in CSL came up with another plan. I should get my Ph.D. in EE! I asked some other grad students about this and learned that I would need to pass a qualifying exam that had big sections on antenna theory and physics. I mentioned to Dave and the other professor that I didn't think I could pass the test. The professor told me that the way the test worked was this: You take the test. Then it's graded and the grades are read at a faculty meeting. If two professors, including a full professor, proposes you pass, you pass. So, the plan would be that I would take the test, get some low grade like 0, then Dave would propose I pass and the other professor would second it, and I would pass.

This didn't sound to me like it was going to work, and I was concerned that someday I might get a teaching job based on a Ph.D. in EE and wouldn't really have a good idea what a resistor was, except that you stuck them in odd places to make a computer work and were quite colorful.

At the same time my wife decided she wanted to go back to school in physical therapy, and the only two graduate programs available were at Boston University and Stanford. So I applied to MIT and Stanford.

My adviser and friend Dave Waltz felt he had let me down a little by bringing me to Illinois, so he mentioned that he had a friend at Stanford in the computer science department from whom he would ask the favor of trying to get me in there.

Around the same time I proved a very difficult result in group decidability as a take-home examination for a decidability course. My proof was novel and cast into doubt the only other existing proof of the theorem. The professor for the course—a well-known mathematician—was notorious for giving very tough oral exams, and given my history of not getting into the schools I wanted, I had no confidence and was scared to take it. He offered the alternative of proving this tough theorem.

I spent several weeks on it trying what turned out to be the approach used by the Russian mathematician who originally proved the conjecture. After a lecture at which a visiting mathematician sat in I heard the professor telling the visitor he had given this particular theorem as an alternative to his oral exam, and they both walked out of the room laughing. I became discouraged.

Then I hit on using a new technique, which I called a simulation technique. I wrote up the proof and gave it to the professor; the proof was 30 pages long. The professor called me into his office to explain the proof, which took me two six-hour sessions because the technique I used was unknown to him. At the end he asked me why I hadn't tried the approach originally used to prove the theorem, and I showed him the counterexample that proved that technique flawed.

The upshot was that this professor really wanted me to stay at Illinois, but he wrote me a strong letter for MIT and Stanford.

This taught me something: An isolated good success can be better than a string of mediocre successes. When I was first at MIT, the long-winded essay got me a shot at the AI Lab, and that essay also proved important when Winston talked to Waltz about taking me to Illinois. It was a combination of the right acquaintances and a single noteworthy achievement that made the difference for me, both back at MIT and at Illinois where it got me a strong letter from a well known mathematician.

I was rejected again at MIT, but someone at Stanford whiteballed me in. A whiteball is an absolute vote in favor: A faculty member selects a candidate and announces he or she will support the student financially, and the admissions committee admits the student. Each senior faculty member gets at most one whiteball. I never learned for certain who whiteballed me because I was too ashamed to ask, and sometimes assignments to projects are changed at the last minute, so I couldn't be certain the project I was originally assigned to was run by the professor who whiteballed me.

Nevertheless, Don Knuth called me up in my office and said I was accepted, and would I please come to Stanford? My wife got into Stanford too, so we went. My career through Stanford was splotchy, but I finally got my degree. One of the troubling things about my Stanford experience was my that adviser calling me up on the eve of my oral exams to tell me that he intended to vote against me. But I had worked for four months straight on my oral presentation, with the help of 10 to 20 other grad students, and the strength of my presentation made it too hard for him to vote against me.

I got my degree in January 1981.

⁂ ⁂ ⁂

Later that spring I traveled back to the Merrimack River Valley to visit my friends, and I brought my hard-won Stanford Ph.D. diploma. I took it to my high school one day after classes were out, and I looked up some of my teachers. I found only one—Joe Sherry. He acted as if he had forgotten about the things that sent me down the hard path. I reminded him and handed him my degree. I told him what a bastard I thought he was and how he had diverted my education by four or five years, but that I had finally achieved something he never could have. He smiled, thinking he had helped me by increasing my persistence and resilience.

There are a couple of things I learned along the way. One is that once you get a bad break in your education—or career, for that matter—you will have a tough time getting back on track. Harvard, I'm sure, originally felt they were giving an underdog a chance or maybe even filling a quota of disadvantaged students. When that break was taken away and I was looking for a graduate school years later, I faced difficult odds—I had gone to a lousy high school, had gotten only OK grades (B+) there, had gone to a lousy university, and had gotten only OK grades (B+) there. Furthermore, the people writing my recommendations were generally unknown to the people making the admissions decisions. So the best I could hope for was a medium boost up in school quality at each step.

The second thing I learned is very important: Being smart is largely *learned behavior*. When I went to Northeastern—mediocre as it was then—I had a tough time adjusting to the way people talked and how smart they were. Keep in mind that every year only a handful of students in my high school went on to a real college, and so there was no pressure at all to be smart. I learned how my peers at Northeastern thought and what I had to know to be like them. After a year I was pretty comfortable there. When I went to MIT for that year, I never quite caught up to the students, but I came pretty close—and I had an A– average, which was respectable. At Illinois I took another step up, and, though it took me a couple of years, I finally moved onto the same playing field as most of my fellow students at Stanford. I feel as though I learned to be smart rather than having been born that way. Maybe this belief is all wet, but I feel strongly that it is true, and I think it should encourage people.

The third thing I learned is a little discouraging: The people you know matters along with your relationship with them. I made friends at Northeastern who helped me make friends at MIT, who helped me get to Illinois, who helped me get whiteballed into Stanford. I think I had some talent and smarts, but those alone didn't help me as much as those relationships did. Now at Stanford I sit almost every year on the Ph.D. admissions committee, and I see that unless you went to perfect schools the whole time, got perfect grades, got walk-on-water letters of recommendation from people whom the committee members know *personally*, you don't get in. Some of the friendships I made at MIT made a big difference to me later, for example, Guy Steele, with whom I have worked on projects on and off for the last 15 years and from whom part of my reputation descends.

The fourth thing is that every now and then you need to do something that grabs attention. For me it was the long essay on vision, the new proof of a tough result, and the well-rehearsed oral exam.

I recall when I got to Stanford, just about all the students there had gone to top high schools (frequently university high schools) or private schools; had gone to excellent universities like MIT, Harvard, and Caltech; and had breezed into Stanford. Some of them failed, as I did, the early exams, and they had a hard time recovering from those failures because they had never had to work hard before from a position of weakness.

My message in this essay is that you don't need to have a silver spoon in your mouth at birth to make it. Even tough breaks can be overcome. If you have half a brain you can learn to be smarter, and if you work collegially, your friendships could pay off. So hang in there.

A Personal Narrative: Stanford

While I was moving a few years ago from the trunk of my car—out of which I had
been living for the previous year—to a rental house on the Peninsula in northern
California, I found a copy of the literary magazine my high school put out while I
was a junior: *Tergiversations*. It's a real word: *tergiversate* means "to change repeat-
edly one's attitude or opinions with respect to a subject or cause." It comes from a
Latin word that means "to turn one's back." What I noticed as much as the bad
writing was that I wrote about half the poems in it; some under my name, some
under a pseudonym, and the rest anonymously. One of the things I did when I
was on strike at my high school was to write a story, which I still have and which
isn't really very good, that caught the eye of the man who wrote the preface to
Carl Sandburg's biography of Lincoln.

Yet between 1967 and 1991 I wrote only two or three very short stories and no
poems at all. For some reason I turned my back on writing, even though I admired
writers in the meantime and I often fantasized about writing books or scientific
papers, even popular books on philosophy. Now I am back to writing in a big way:
I write essays like these as well as stories and poems (my passion). I am currently
enrolled in a master of fine arts (MFA) program at Warren Wilson College and
hope to become a real writer, a poet, some day.

1967–1991: that's a quarter of a century—around a third of a person's life.

The previous essay about my life started in the middle of my passion for writing and told a story in which this passion led me to start off my technical career
on the wrong foot. Looking back I feel that I could fold my life like origami into
three parts in which 1967 butts up against 1991, and it would be a continuous
picture of an aspiring writer trying to make it—and when I unfold it, the middle
24 years look almost like someone else's life. I found I asked myself whether that
long detour—that lengthy turn of my back—was there just to prove that I could

159

recover from the error I made, from Sherry's wrath, from the switch from Harvard to Northeastern and the slow uphill.

When I arrived in California from Illinois to attend Stanford in late summer 1975 to look for a house, I was pretty amazed. For one thing, the sun was always shining, and there was never a cloud in the sky. It was August when the East and Midwest are stifling with heated wet air, but California was dry, dusty, and smelled of exotic medicinal trees and rich herbs. For another thing, there was no such thing as a two-bedroom cottage for $90 a month, which is what my wife, dog, and I had been renting in Urbana, Illinois. As a grad student I was making $650 a month at the University of Illinois; at Stanford I would make $330, and the housing was easily three to four times more expensive. I was able to find a house for $285 a month in south Palo Alto, and a few weeks later my troops and I got in our red, 1973 Volkswagen Beetle and headed across country. We had spent part of the summer in New England, so it was a true cross-country trip. We stopped in Champaign-Urbana and visited friends for a week and then headed west. It was the second cross-country trip I had taken, and there would be many more.

We weren't interested in seeing the sights, so we drove with as few stops as possible—remember, we had a restless, 80-pound dog in the back of an un-air-conditioned small car. It took us only three days to get across from Illinois to California. We pushed very hard the last day to get there rather than stopping in Reno. I had arranged with some friends to stay at their apartment in Sunnyvale (California) when we arrived and we had called them a few days before, but when we drove up at 11:30 P.M., we found a note on their door that they had gone to Yosemite; next to their note was the key to our house, which they had picked up. We drove there and slept on the floor our first night—an unrefreshing start to our new life after 20 straight hours of driving.

Stanford proved to be a little more than I expected. Back then the computer science department admitted only 18 people (out of 600 applicants), and because I was a whiteball, I wasn't in their league, at least not at first. There weren't many undergraduate computer science programs, so almost everyone was from some other discipline: mathematics, physics, music, psychology, chemistry, for example. Four of the students were from the University of New Mexico, including two brothers—it seemed odd that so many from one place would make it through Stanford's fine net.

I was firmly—obviously—at the bottom of the barrel.

I was assigned to a project directed by Ed Feigenbaum—every grad student was guaranteed a research assistantship. I had hoped for an assignment at SAIL, the renowned Stanford AI Lab. Disappointed by being assigned on campus, I went up there to visit one day and talked John McCarthy into supporting me if I agreed to TA his Lisp course that fall. I informed Feigenbaum, and he survived.

The computer science department was located in "temporary" buildings which still exist just west of the quadrangle. The AI Lab, on the other hand, was located about five miles southwest down Arastradero Road, a eucalyptus-lined two-lane that winds through the low foothills behind the main bulk of Stanford. Eucalyptus are very tall, shag-bark Australian trees imported as windbreaks. The bark tends to shed from the trunk leaving smooth bald dull-rainbow patches sometimes covering half of the surface area of the trunk. The leaves are long, dark green—aromatic, used as a medicine. On either side of the road beyond the eucalyptus were dusted gold-brown hills, a kicked-rug thrown back from the Bay with a high fold between the Bay and the ocean.

At a curve in the road, a driveway forked right up a steep driveway to the Donald C. Powers Laboratory—the Stanford AI Lab. The driveway flowed up the best gradient line and then circled the Lab, a partial redwood annulus with an asphalt volleyball court in its center. From the ridge north just beyond the parking lot you could see the Bay and San Francisco 35 miles to the north. Looking left from this view were the hills, a high redwood-topped ridge running south from just south of San Francisco to Santa Cruz and beyond. Mornings and afternoons the fog would push up on the ocean side and droop down on ours.

The air held the scent of eucalyptus and tarweed—tarweed is an oily, short, thin-stalked gray-green plant that grows plentifully only after wet winters; it has a strong sweet smell. The combination of eucalyptus and tarweed on the wind makes the smell of northern California unforgettable.

The Lab sat high above the thicket of suburbia that the Pennisula was quick becoming. In only a few years from the ridge above the Lab you would be able to see the brown edge of the top of the smog layer that would dominate hillside views for the next 15 years. The Lab is where I wanted to be from my first sight, and in a rare outburst of boldness after eight years of hiding in the shadows I approached John and got not only his promise of support but also an office in the annex, behind the main part of the Lab. At the top of the next page is what the Lab looked like. I say "looked like" because around 1989 it was torn down and the land leased for stables.

Originally the building was to be a complete annulus with a bridge linking it to another, smaller one on the hill just to the upper left of the diagram. The driveway went all the way around the building, and the main parking lot was to the right in the diagram.

The Lab was away from the rest of Stanford, and a lot of the grad students—there were no computer science undergrads at the time—envied those who "lived on the hill." John McCarthy is the father of Lisp, the only language I had used in years, and all my AI work was done in it. I used a dialect of MacLisp, and my job after being a TA for John was to port MacLisp from ITS (*I*ncompatible *T*imesharing *S*ystem) to WAITS (we called it the *W*est-Coast *A*lternative to *ITS*). Actually,

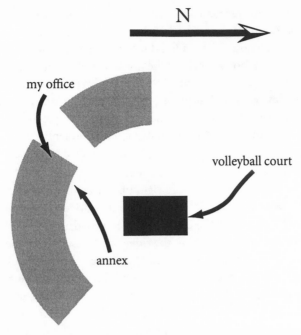

the operating system was just a variant of TOPS-10, the operating system that DEC provided with its PDP-10s and KL-10s. SAIL had a PDP-10, which would be upgraded to a KL-10 in the mid-1970s, a few years after I arrived. The KL-10 was the DEC adaptation of the Super-Foonly, a computer designed at SAIL just before I arrived. All these computers were timesharing computers, and we were on the ARPANET, which was the precursor of today's Internet.

Among the unexpected things I found at SAIL were these: There was a large sauna and showers in the basement of the annex; the terminal system was based on a video display system in which the computer executed display programs that deposited video on a large disk which was then directed to green-phosphor monitors, providing amazing capabilities; there was a volleyball game just about every day throughout the year; there was a computer-controlled vending machine called the Prancing Pony. When the people and machines at the Lab moved onto campus, the KL-10 was kept running until the late 1980s to continue supporting the Prancing Pony because no one had time to build the custom hardware needed to interface it to a UNIX machine or to write the software.

The display system deserves more mention. Remember, I am talking about 1975, and this system had been in place for five years. The video rate was 19.2kb and you could display green-scale on it; there was a video switch which enabled a single person to "own" up to 32 channels or separate screens; this video switch allowed people to observe other people's screens, which helped people work cooperatively without walking from office to office and helped new people learn the system by quietly observing; three TV stations were piped into the video switch so you could watch TV while things compiled or ran; six radio stations were piped into an audio switch so you could listen either to the radio or the TV sound channels while you needed to view the screen.

It looked like my dreams might be coming true.

You see, not only did this seem an ideal place to work, but I had worked fairly hard on my research directions, and my goal—which turned out to be unrealistic—was to blow through Stanford as fast as I could. I felt I could do this because I knew my topic (I thought) and had been in grad school for three years already, though in mathematics. I planned to get through in record time.

To do that required passing two tests, writing a dissertation, and defending it. One of the tests was a comprehensive exam which tested one's breadth of CS knowledge. This test was broken up into several parts: numeric analysis, hardware, analysis of algorithms, theory of computation, artificial intelligence, and a programming problem. This test had to be passed within two years and could be taken only three times.

The other test was the qualifying exam in your area of expertise. It was an oral exam that tested depth of knowledge—whether you knew enough to do research in the area. This test had to be passed within a year of passing the comprehensive. Once you passed the qual, another clock started ticking on how long you had to complete your degree.

I planned to take both tests the first year, and I did.

Meanwhile, there were finances to worry about. My wife was enrolled in the master of physical therapy program and was a full-time student. We lived in a two-bedroom house that consumed all but $45 of our monthly income, so we started looking for housemates. The first one we found was Bill Scherlis, who remained my friend for many years until a scandal split us apart. Bill was one of the silver-spoon guys. I'm not sure he went to a private school, but he went to Harvard and had been admitted the previous year to Stanford, but had deferred one year to spend that year at the University of Edinburgh, a well-known computer science and artificial intelligence school. His family was rich—his father was a physician at Johns Hopkins, they had a summer home on Martha's Vineyard, and Bill had traveled extensively in Europe and Africa. His tastes were impeccable and expensive. He took the second bedroom.

Kathy, my then-wife, found another housemate, Nancy, who moved into our living room, using a curtain across the living-room/dining-room boundary for privacy. This way, and with the help of my parents, we were able to eat.

The qual that year was unique: Ed Feigenbaum was working on a handbook of AI which would present short introductory essays on AI topics. He also chaired the qual committee for AI. He decided that people taking the qual that year would write 13 short essays for the handbook—some selected by the individual and some selected by the committee—and the essays would be judged to determine whether you passed. Because I preferred written to oral tests, I signed up.

The comprehensive had a long reading list, which I started going through—remember, I had no real CS background. Course work was not very demanding because the rule was that to get a Ph.D. you needed a certain number of units or course hours, and those units had to be spread among at least four different professors. One of the popular courses was Reading and Research, and which was really supervised thesis research.

The comprehensive exam was to be held in late spring, and the qual was during that same spring quarter, which was 13 weeks long. This meant writing more than one essay per week for the qual, because the comprehensive exam took a week.

The reason it took a week was the programming problem, a week-long take-home. The problem was gauged to take more than a normal week's effort, so you had to plan on spending 18 hours a day on it—sort of a rite of passage.

During spring quarter my wife's stepfather died, and we went back to New England for the funeral. This interrupted both my essay writing and studying for the comp. When we returned I finished the essays and took the comp.

The test was open book, so I brought a trunk of books—you were limited by how many books you could carry: one load. The test was hard. After it was over, we had a free night before the programming problem.

I was a good programmer, but for some reason I had a lot of trouble with the problem we were given. It was to write a program that would invert a very large sparse matrix. I figured out a good approach and went at it up at the Lab. People working there were warned we'd be using the timesharing system, and so preventive maintenance was suspended for the week. Because of my relative unfamiliarity with the implementation and dialect of Lisp used there and a deep panic, I thrashed for several days on some simple bugs. To catch up I stayed up all night for several nights.

Part of the problem was to provide documentation and a description of the algorithm and some analysis of it. I managed to finish but had slept only about 15 hours for the whole week.

Grading the qual took most of the summer, and I believe that no one actually looked closely at the essays. The pressure was on to publish the handbook which had dragged on for several years—the reason Ed gave essays for the qual was to make some progress. Eventually three months later he declared that everyone who had taken the qual had passed. I know that one of the students who took the test and passed wrote all the essays within a one-week span, so I suspect he simply passed everyone rather than try to find people to read them carefully.

I found out about the comp much faster: I failed. Bill, who took the test at the same time, passed. I went into a deep depression. I knew by then that I was not up to the level of the other grad students, and it seemed like my dream of finishing was over. Bill moved out later that summer, partly because I was too embarrassed to talk to him much and he felt that I was upset with him for some reason.

It took me most of the summer to recover, and in the fall I started reading again: 8, 12 hours a day in preparation to take the comp again in the winter. Another classmate, Ron Goldman, moved into Bill's old room, and Nancy left as well. Ron had failed the comp, too, and so we studied together a bit. We retrieved all the old comprehensives from the department and worked them; we quizzed each other on arcana.

The test was in January, and it seemed pretty easy. One of our other classmates had taken it twice already and failed, so he had to pass or he might be removed from the program. The programming problem was a lot easier too, and I managed to finish in four days. Our classmate had not quite passed the written part, so he needed a high pass on the programming problem; he spent 20 hours a day writing a knockout program, one that used natural language input.

We all three passed, but I can't remember if I got a pass or a high pass—regular pass, I think.

But my case came up with the faculty: The normal course of events was that a student passed the comp then the qual; I had done it the other way around. Because they couldn't think of a reason that it was a problem—and anyhow it wasn't forbidden—they ruled I was OK. Except, of course, that the clock was ticking on other deadlines according to the date I passed the qual, which meant I had lost nine months.

I switched from (robot) vision to natural-language generation and Terry Winograd agreed to be my adviser. I hooked up with Cordell Green's research group which needed a simple natural language-generation system. I did some reading in the area and found that almost no one had done any work, so I set off on my own.

Terry had been the wonderboy of the MIT AI Lab. At a time when AI was languishing and money for AI research was tight, MIT needed a charismatic figure. Terry was the answer. Handsome, well spoken, smooth and compelling as a speaker—Terry wrote the famous SHRDLU program, a natural-language understanding system hooked up to a simulated robot that would move cubes, pyramids, and spheres of various color around according to written questions and commands. They made a film of it and it is sometimes still shown on PBS.

After MIT, Terry became a scholar more than a researcher, though he still did some research, it never amounted to as much as SHRDLU had.

I turned my attention to writing my thesis program, and I took a large dose of Advanced Volleyball to fulfill my courseload requirement. Life was grand.

Then some things started to happen.

Kathy graduated from her program. She and I and a classmate had jointly written a computer-aided gait diagnosis program for her thesis, and then she started working. She wanted to start a family soon, and I had told her I would be done with my Ph.D. after three years. That meant I had one year to go. I, of course, didn't meet that deadline—it had taken me almost two years to pass the tests.

My friends back east at MIT told me that my marriage was the ideal of the CS world—well, they meant the AI lab world of MIT, Carnegie-Mellon University (CMU), Stanford: Most married couples they had known had broken up, and Kathy and I seemed such a pair, what with our eccentric ways and our two Siberian Huskies that gave all our visitors fleas.

After another year Kathy got pregnant and I panicked—we had the pregnancy terminated. Kathy never seemed to recover from that experience, and my delays in finishing just pushed her further and further away. My parents felt doubts based on my inability to finish quickly, and they started telling their friends that I had dropped out of Stanford and become a plumber. They said they did this because it became too embarrassing to them to explain to their friends why it was taking me more than the three years I told them it would. To those friends and to my parents grad school was like any other school: You were on a schedule of classes (and other stuff), and if you didn't graduate when you were supposed to, it meant you were being held back, like being held back in second grade.

Soon my whole family was recommending that I simply give up and get a job.

In 1979 our son was born. Because I had flexible hours and Kathy worked fixed hours, I worked from home over a phone line and took care of the baby that first year while trying desperately to finish. Later, Kathy would say she left because I did not want our child and would not "happily" take care of him.

I had started at Stanford in the fall of 1975 and in 1980 was ready to prepare my orals. To do this I wrote a draft of my dissertation. The system I wrote as the topic of my thesis was able to generate English descriptions of an internal representation of an automatically generated program. My system was part of a larger system that accepted English input concerning what a program should do and produced that program, including doing somewhat sophisticated complexity analysis. My part of the system was to take as input the program that was developed and describe it in order to convince the user that the program generated corresponded to what was desired. I guess the general idea of the research project was to fulfill John McCarthy's advice-taker goal: If a program is to be able to do something by figuring out what to do, it should be able to be told what to do.

I thought the thesis was about natural-language generation—after all, that's what the program did. However, like many AI folks—Winograd included—I designed and wrote a complete programming language and execution environment that made the actual programming easier—today we would say I wrote a framework and a sample system using it. Two of the things I was particularly interested in were being able to have the style of writing vary and to have the competence of the system increase by adding relatively small pieces of knowledge. Given that I spent most of my time working on the language and execution substructure, the actual work on generation was not very interesting and at best represented a simple demonstration of the power of the framework.

It took me a while to understand this, however. I wrote a draft and put together a presentation. The orals are an examination in which the candidate presents his or her thesis to the public including a four-person orals committee. The presentation is followed by public questioning. After that, the orals committee meets in private with the candidate and questions him or her extensively. Finally, the committee gets together and decides whether the candidate should pass. All this happens in the space of a morning or afternoon.

So the presentation I put together was my orals dry run. I presented it at SRI International in Menlo Park to their AI group and it bombed—it bombed badly. I gave it a couple of other places, and it had the same effect. I got together a group of my friends—other grad students—and presented it to them, and it bombed. Fortunately for me, Ron Goldman was one of them.

We sat down, and he asked questions that tried to get at what I was saying, what were the ideas, how should the material be presented, what did I really do. It was during this process that I realized that the bulk of work was on system building not natural-language generation. We refined the presentation and I gave it to the group again. And again and again and again.

I think we iterated on the presentation 20 times over the summer.

Meanwhile, Terry was reading my draft. I was in a tough position because this was around the time he was trying to get tenure and I was the first of his real students to graduate. There had been another, earlier student, but Terry became the chairman of his thesis committee during the quarter the student graduated and Terry arrived at Stanford from MIT. The way we all thought of this first student was that Terry had stepped down the aircraft stairway and signed the thesis as he reached the tarmac.

So I was to be the first of his actual advisees to graduate, and I was graduating some six or seven years after Terry arrived. This was not good for either of us. My draft emphasized natural language, even though the bulk of it was about the way the system and framework were put together. After reading it he told me he thought it stank and he recommended I not do my orals in September.

One of my traits is that I cannot accept praise, because I fear rejection. If there are no high highs, then the lows will be less low. When I failed the comprehensive exam, I was down for six months; I was unable to socialize or even really be with people. I would sit in my living room and just listen to music all day, dreaming about what I would do with my life given my most recent failure.

My favorite was to picture myself living in rural western Kansas, farming a small spread with a wife who would have come from some mysterious place from which she was running. I had been through Kansas twice, and the images of Truman Capote's *In Cold Blood*, which is about a murder in southwestern Kansas in 1959, had stuck in my mind since 1965 when I read the book. I would picture my wife and me holding hands looking westward toward our small farmhouse, tall cottonwoods in a line in front of it, the sun dipping behind and the sky smeared red. She would have very long blonde hair, and we wouldn't be so much in love as we would care for each other in our deep unvoiced sorrow. Our old, separate friends would be wondering where we were—were we still alive? A suicide dream of sorts.

Dreams like this one were how I dealt with most of my failures. After a rejection I would dream sad and tragic dreams like this and eventually they would turn into triumphs. For example, after Joe Sherry cast me out of Harvard Heaven, I dreamt of sublime obscurity until the dreams turned into me walking across a prestigious university as a revered professor. A dream like this is dangerous, though.

Because, when you think about doing something, you tend to do it. For example, if you think about getting better at grammar, you will get better even if you don't study it at all. This happens because you—partly consciously—try to steer away from sentences you're not sure about and toward ones that you're certain are grammatical. You pay more attention to edited writing like newspapers for models. Just thinking about it makes it true.

I wanted to be a writer, but the dream of walking across campus took over, and I made my goal academic success. In a lot of ways this is a good trait: I fail at something, I dream, I get better at it both through the effect I just described and by studying, practicing, whatever. But sometimes you fail at things you don't really care about. I suspect I tried to become an academic because I happened to fail at an attempt to become one that was really half- or quarter-hearted. Then I dreamt, then I acted.

Terry's comments sent me down, but Ron picked me up. We continued the practice. I told Terry that the thesis was going to be more about systems than language, and in fact, language would be just one of several examples of the use of the framework. This calmed him down a bit.

Undoubtedly Terry heard of the failed presentations at SRI and other places, and he continued to phone me as I worked at home to tell me I was on the road to failure. But every time he said no, Ron said yes.

An orals committee is made up of one's thesis committee, someone outside your area within the department, and an outsider in the university who is the chairman of the orals committee. The three people on my thesis committee were Terry, Cordell Green, and Dave Waltz (my adviser and friend from the University of Illinois). As September grew closer, Terry's warnings increased in degree and frequency. I began to panic.

I asked a woman friend of mine who once had had difficulty with anxiety to let me have a couple of Valium pills just in case, and she agreed. My wife and parents had long since given up me. Perhaps they had heard enough of my extreme worst-case scenarios. When I went into my rejection-reaction mood, I always painted the worst picture possible. Of course, that picture never came true, which was part of how I survived—I knew rationally the worst-case scenario could never happen, though emotionally I believed it must, so when it didn't I was bolstered emotionally. When I told my family that my adviser was not confident, they thought it was one of my pessimistic scenarios.

The day before my orals arrived. I had given my talk five times in a row with only minor corrections needed. It was a two-projector presentation in which one projector carried the breadth of what I had done while the other provided depth. Dave would arrive the next morning on the red-eye from Japan. That afternoon Terry called me up and told me he intended to vote against my passing. Ron said not to believe him, but Ron was not on my committee.

I can't remember whether I slept that night, but I know I could not have without artificial help. The orals were at 1:00 P.M. At noon I took the Valium, perhaps twice the normal dosage. I arrived at the classroom and prepared the projectors. I paced the room and made it familiar, a ritual I still follow when I give talks. Ten years after my orals I gave the keynote address at a conference held at Cambridge University—this happened to be one of the dreams I had had at the end of my Northeastern days—and as the audience walked into the hall and seated themselves they saw me pace at the foot of the theater, up on the stage; they saw me sit and dream in the front of the room, stage left.

At 12:45 the audience arrived and 10 minutes later my committee. Refreshments were served as a matter of convention—chocolate chips prepared by the woman with the Valium, a woman with very long blonde hair.

The chairman of the orals committee—the outside guy—started things off.

I started in, oddly calm, induced probably by the Valium. Dave Waltz seemed to be dozing. The blonde woman, who went to school in Berkeley, sat and smiled. Somehow I was confident—how Ron accomplished this I don't know. I still feel this confidence when I speak. I am always panicked, nearly to tears, before I speak, but once I start I am fluent and cogent as at no other times except sometimes when I write and the material just takes off on its own.

The two-projector idea worked great. Most students practiced their orals talks three or four times, so it was unusual to see a talk practiced and refined as many times as I had. It went very smoothly. When the questions started coming, each one had been answered five to ten times already in practice sessions. The effect was that it seemed I was invulnerable. In many cases I had slides already prepared with the answers. I used humor and engaged the questioners.

The public and I were dismissed while the committee discussed my presentation and the strategy for the private session. This was the part I dreaded most. I had heard stories about such private sessions at MIT in which people were asked such things as to compute the gravitational constant from whatever general physics knowledge they had (this was for computer science orals).

I sat outside while people in the audience filed past and congratulated me. I told them the real test was about to start.

I sat there for 15 minutes, still calm but that calmness evaporating. I was alone in the hall. The door opened and Terry stepped out—had he voted no already?

He said, "Congratulations, you passed. That was the best presentation I have ever seen." He walked away. The rest of the committee stopped to congratulate me. I never stood up.

As I recall, the orals were on my wife's birthday: September 12, 1980. I had told her I would drive up to the Lab for a while before coming home.

It was a day just like the first day I visited the Lab: dusty, with the sharp fragrance of tarweed splattered on a background of eucalyptus; hot and dry; hazy and dusty, a few wands of fog wandering behind the hills. I stood on the rise across the parking lot to the north of the Lab and just sat and stared. The nights 'til 2:00 A.M. sitting in the annex listening to music piped in over the terminal system, walking between the back building and the front to the Pony to get drinks, snacks. Afternoons filled with volleyball announced "Now hear this: Bounce! Bounce!"

I spent an hour and drove home.

I never learned what happened in the room after my public session. No one before or since has escaped the private orals session. I still imagine they talked about the stress I was under and Terry talking about how he didn't think my thesis was good but it was good enough and how he had tortured me with threats of failing so why not just spare me the humiliation and pass me without further torment since they would eventually pass me anyway? I waited 13 years to ask them what happened, and they didn't remember except vague recollections of thinking I had done an impressive job. But 13 years later I have a name and what's the point of bringing up old opinions?

I handed in my dissertation three months later and started my marginalized career believing I had sneaked out with a degree. It didn't feel the way I thought it would—there was no victory, no sense even of having been successful. More like I had stolen something and that I had no allies but Ron and the woman with very long hair, that the committee would just as soon forget what happened. Perhaps they felt I would amount to nothing, and so their mistake would not be devastating.

Sometimes when you read a résumé, it seems that there is a constant upward motion of one success after another, one grand title followed by one even more grand. What you don't see is that the steps are sometimes achieved with difficulty or only barely—that the toll is high and the sacrifices almost too much to bear.

But also you don't see the résumé for the other parts of a person's life: We can see the professional climb, but how did he handle his mother's death, she her failed marriage?

Climbing is hard and rarely is the trail constantly upward.

PART V

INTO THE GROUND

~

Into the Ground: Lisp

When you leave school, you face the treat promised for perhaps decades: the real world. This is the place where what you've learned not only can be applied but is supposed to make sense. But think about it: How much like the real world you met was the world of school? I started in 1955 in the first grade, spent six years at Merrimac Elementary School, six years at Pentucket Regional High School (including seventh and eighth grades), five years at Northeastern University, one year at MIT, two years at the University of Illinois, and five years at Stanford, and when I finished it was 1981, I had been married and was on the way to divorce; and I had a two-year-old son. I started with Eisenhower, ended with Reagan, and passed through Kennedy, Johnson, Nixon, Ford, and Carter; I started with the Korean War just ended, witnessed Vietnam, the protests, the humiliation of Nixon, the rise and fall of liberalism, the fall and rise of conservatism; we had decided to go to the moon, done it, and all but abandoned the space program; I started a young boy and ended near middle age.

When I was but a few years into this trek, they told me that I was part of the future and whatever I needed to be a productive member of society was the most important thing of all. And when I finished about to realize that all-important productivity, my son's future became most important and I was secondary. When was my time? I'd spent 25 years preparing, only to turn to prepare the next generation. No one told me that what I was preparing to do was to prepare someone else.

School is a world where failure is hard but not fatal—money can be lost, but for me it was the furtive money of scholarships and cooperative earnings, fellowships, soft money. People's careers could be damaged or even ruined, but rarely did they die, did they shuffle off in shame; everything could renew next quarter, restart in a semester or next fall—you could retake a course, change advisers, transfer to another school, reapply in the winter, hire a tutor, even cheat.

So after school and after my wife drove off to New York with my son and my red '73 Beetle, I stayed for three years in academia because it seemed so easy and familiar. Later, after an exhilarating ride starting and running my own company, I would try my hand at failure.

ᔕ   ᔕ   ᔕ

After I graduated from Stanford in 1981, I spent a couple of years working for John McCarthy on the Advice Taker project and for Lawrence Livermore National Laboratories (LLNL) on implementing a dialect of Lisp for a supercomputer they were building. The Advice Taker was an artificial intelligence project based on the premise that it is not possible to program a computer to figure out how to do something unless you could program it to be told how to do it.

I worked with a philosopher named Lew Creary who was a jazz guitar aficionado and would talk for hours about jazz greats, strange fingerings, unusual chords and voicings, and his particular brand of philosophy of knowledge, based on the work of Frége. He thought up the ideas, and I implemented them in what I thought was a simple and effective arrangement that minimized the need for a heavy intellectual investment from me. My experience getting my degree had not been very wonderful, and McCarthy's remark after he read my thesis before he hired me was, "it's not very good." Nevertheless, he needed a hacker, and I was certainly more of that than he had had in a long time if ever.

I socialized with Lew a bit, and though his wasn't a world-beating personality, he had enough quirks and texture, enough raw stuff, to make for a good companion. He seemed like he was wired into the late '40s or '50s—he looked pretty straight and even a little worn round the edges, though he wasn't much older than me.

Lew was always making a clever, very small joke and laughing silently while watching your face for any sign that you got it. He eventually went off to Hewlett-Packard (HP) Labs and I lost track of him after a few years.

The group at LLNL actually was a group of ex-Stanford and ex-Berkeley students out to build the world's most outrageous multiprocessor, the S1 Mark IIA. I was hired to implement a version of Lisp called NIL (New Implementation of Lisp) which was designed by Jonl White and Guy L. Steele Jr.

The Livermore group that I worked for was a spin-off from the O Group, which was the special projects group in physics, and was led by Lowell Wood, the bad-boy physicist. Lowell did things like charter jets when he missed the scheduled flight to the Nevada Test Site or pick jetway locks when he missed the flight to DC where he would meet with White House officials to convince them of the need for Star Wars.

The O Group was filled with tremendous young physicists who were convinced that all that stood between peace and war with the Soviet Union was their brains, which were locked in battle with their corresponding numbers in bomb labs in the USSR and China.

One of the guys at the Lab had two pictures—a geographic map of the Soviet Union and a geographic map of the moon, labeled "before" and "after". Some of them carried arms in their cars for protection against the KGB and terrorists. One carried a .357 and once was up at Lowell's giant log house showing it off—11,000 square feet on 100 acres on top of a hill above the Lab. A group was standing around in a quarter circle when he shouted, "look, a rabbit!" He pointed the gun, apparently at the rabbit, and tracked it as it ran behind the group, and it didn't require a lot of thought to realize that the gun pointed at one knee followed by a thigh or a waist. When the rabbit emerged from behind the group and started to head down the hill, a shot ripped out—"damn it, I missed."

Out of the LLNL experience I would start a company in 1984 that folded in 1994—Lucid, Incorporated. This experience was unlike anything in my life before and perhaps unlike anything that could ever happen again—I raised nearly $16 million of venture capital, I signed OEM deals with IBM, DEC (now Digital), Sun, HP, and almost all the other major computer manufacturers of the 1980s, I hired dozens of top-notch developers—the company grew to 75 at its peak—I was the president of it for four years, I was the *de rigueur* charismatic leader of the company, I hired and fired CEOs.

There was nothing like it: I worked 60- to 90-hour weeks—because I loved it. We hired fabulous people who were the most talented I've seen, who loved working together toward a goal we felt worthy. We had three or four rock bands, we had parties at work and away, we had an extended family which, two years after the death of Lucid, still has picnics and potlucks, and still has an active mailing list.

A company, though, is like a working gold mine: A prospector, a man with a vision, finds a vein of gold in a desolate area; a company of men smart in the ways of building sluices, constructing extraction facilities, and minding books and deliveries uses the man's vision to create wealth, a part of which is shared with the visionary. The man who puts up the grubstake takes more gold than the finder does. It is not enough to build a mine that employs 90 men well, it also must provide wealth for a handful.

Because of that, all I have to show for the work are two extra-large tee shirts with white lettering on black that says:

> *I founded a Silicon Valley startup in the 1980's, and all I got was this lousy tee shirt.*

When the board of directors decided to close down the company, it employed 60 people and had a yearly revenue of $5 million to $6 million. If you consider that each employee takes about $100,000 per year to support, this revenue figure is close to breakeven, meaning that the company was not that far off from being healthy enough to continue, perhaps indefinitely. The previous quarter was a record in the primary product line, and sales for that product were growing by nearly 30% per quarter. Deals were being made, and the company was nine months away from AT&T adopting one of its products as its official product. The primary product had just won the Jolt Cola Programmer Productivity Award from *Computer Language*, a computer magazine, and things, except the bottom line, were looking good.

One day in late June 1994, at 4:00 P.M., Bill Goerke, the interim CEO, called all the employees onto the second-story porch where most of the company meetings were held. It was a few days before payday, and he told them, "don't bother coming to work tomorrow, we can't pay you."

Robert J. Hoder, the designated representative of the Credit Manager's Association of California, the official liquidator, stood at the front of the Menlo Park council chambers and told the gathered creditors: "In the 20 years I've been doing this job, I have never seen a meeting where there was even a single employee. Every other company was savvy enough to know two weeks in advance of when it was about to run out of money and would let the employees go after their last paycheck."

In 1985 when Brentwood Associates was wooing Lucid, Brad Jones pulled his BMW 700 series over to the side of the road and told Tony Slocum—Lucid's CEO—and me that Brentwood was the kind of firm that stuck with its companies. "Once we had to shut down a company, and Mr. Warren personally made sure that each employee got a full month's pay. We will take care of you through success or failure."

The company kept a couple of people to answer the phone in case customers called support and to ship product if that was required and to collect receivables. But to customers who had recently bought one of the company's products and to the employees, the company simply disappeared for no reason at all.

I think this is a story of business incompetence built on top of technical excellence—I don't assume any credit for that excellence, except that I happened to have hired extremely talented people. Perhaps there are lessons to be learned for the '90s from this story.

I forgot to mention, when the company was about nine months away from folding, the then-current CEO read *Crossing the Chasm* by Geoffrey Moore (1991) and learned one thing: When a company is trying to move beyond the early adopters to mainstream customers, sometimes the technical founder must go, so I went. After Lucid's demise I read editorials about how the company could never grow out from my shadow (Binstock 1994) and how the company was "blinded by science" (Deger 1995).

Since then, as VP of Development at ParcPlace Systems, Inc., I learned that the general belief, at least among executives and venture capitalists (VCs) is that Lucid failed because I did. Perhaps I did fail, and it certainly felt like it. Blame is not something worth ascribing in most cases, and in this one blame can get passed around like a flu. I learned, though, a lot about business practices in the United States, and it seems to me that the "blame" for Lucid's failure lies squarely at the feet of American business education, exemplified by Lucid's next-to-last CEO: Bob Kadarauch.

٭   ٭   ٭

The story started when some of the guys I worked with at LLNL had the idea that we could start a company by spinning out the technology we had developed at LLNL for the S1 project. The original project was to construct a CISC (Complex Instruction Set Computer) multiprocessor, and the uniprocessor for it was successfully constructed by a small team in a short time (the S1 Mark IIA). However, the lesson of CISC was quickly learned: It is hard to write a compiler that takes advantage of the complex instructions and addressing modes, because that requires the compiler to recognize that these complex operations apply while looking at a number of program statements, and it is hard to make devices to go fast when you have to fetch and execute a lot of simple operations along with the complex ones. Hence, RISC (Reduced Instruction Set Computer) was revalidated and the next version of the S1—the S1 Mark IIB—was a RISC processor; this was the one we wanted to spin out.

On top of this was laser pantography. The idea was that the chemical process that deposited semiconductor subparts on a silicon wafer could be activated by a laser. In effect, rather than a photographic process we could use a drawing process. With laser pantography we could build and test a wafer-sized chip in a chamber and, to some extent, repair it. The idea was to combine the RISC design, this technology advantage, and our superior talent—cough, cough—into a supercomputer company.

At the time I was consulting occasionally for a venture capital group in New York headed by Bill Scherlis's Uncle Sid—remember, Bill was the guy who rented a room from me the first year at Stanford. Sid and his assistant Victoria would send me a business plan for a company in the Bay Area, and I would read it, visit the group, and assess the technical likelihood for its success. Of course, I knew nothing about business, so I could really assess only the technology.

For example, the first company I looked at had developed a simple ethernet local area network (LAN) for fast food joints. Each cash register would be a node on the network, which would download its transactions to a backroom computer every few minutes, thereby making it less likely for one of the poorly paid hamburger salespeople to rip off the franchise. In fact, the design of the register itself made it almost impossible to steal from—the keyboard was bulletproof!

This sounded good to me, but I was concerned that their very slow communications software and hardware coupled by the slow backroom computer would bog down during peak periods like lunchtime in large food emporia. I dutifully and diligently visited potential customers (franchise managers) and asked about peak traffic and did calculations based on the technical specs of the proposed products. I also quizzed the hackers about what happened when there were too many collisions on the ethernet and consulted my networking friends at Stanford.

I reported all this on a conference call. Sid and Vic listened carefully and asked probing questions. Then Victoria said, "Well, this is all very interesting, but it is clear these people have no business sense." This didn't seem clear to me because the business plan was thorough, they had researched their market and interviewed many potential customers. She continued, "Everyone knows that the way kids working in hamburger joints make money—given they're paid the same or less than waiters but without tips—is by stealing from the cash register, and management plans for the amount, which they expect to be around $20 per day per employee."

Gleep, no, Victoria, not everyone knows that. How foolish these people were to design a theftproof cash register and to log transactions almost as soon as they were made. No venture capital for these naïve souls.

Armed with this newly found business acumen, I called up Victoria and talked about our plan. She came out to visit, and we explored the idea. I wrote a series of business plans for the Livermore group. It turned out that when faced with the potential of getting a few million bucks to get started and to commit to actually trying the venture outside the comforting chain-link fences at the Lab, away from the full weight and authority of not only the University of California but also the U.S. government as well, my colleagues declined.

But along the way, constructing the business plan, I had made the case that the rise of artificial intelligence (AI) in the marketplace, coupled with the need for commercial implementations of Common Lisp—the de facto Lisp standard I had initiated and politically led—on standard hardware was significant enough that it was a focus of the full-spectrum computer company we proposed. Victoria suggested that that part of the business plan was interesting to her and Sid.

I was surprised, but I looked around for additional folks for the venture and lined up 10 founders, two of which would be silent. One was Bill Scherlis and the other Scott Fahlman, who led the Common Lisp group—during the definition of the standard I did the backroom politicking with research and government groups.

Sid and Vic coached me on how to be a founder and what would happen. One of the disturbing things was that Victoria said that regardless of how things went, one of the key founders would leave the company in a bad way within a year or two—forced out, shamed into quitting, or in a huff over a disagreement. I looked at the founders and only one wasn't a friend, and I wondered who it would be who would leave in disgrace.

Tony Slocum would be the CEO. He had been the CEO at Intellicorp who took it public and then he was forced out. His strengths were building a company from nothing to about $20 million a year, finding a reason to go on when things were bad, and offering wise counsel. Although a weak visionary, he could sell vision like crazy. He corralled almost all the large hardware companies as OEM's for the company. He was a terrific negotiator and had a very smooth delivery that was sincere and adapted well to the level of the listener.

Slocum came from New England, and one of his relatives was the Slocum who was the first person to sail around the world alone. Tony was always smiling and putting the best face on things, but he was ready to help solve a crisis. I would have to replace Tony after a few years for not being able to work through a crisis with the marketplace. I replaced him with Bob.

Jussi Ketonen would be vice president of engineering. He had been my office-mate at Stanford and worked with John McCarthy. We had become friends over the years, and he was interested in making money at some point, and perhaps this was it. He was dogged in researching the business plan, spending days in the business school library. He was a mathematician and logician from Finland. His father was in the government, and Jussi was a child prodigy, receiving his Ph.D. in mathematics from the University of Wisconsin—an excellent math school at the time—at age 19. He was a celebrity in Finland, and he was often interviewed at the airport when he went home to visit his parents. His only weakness was that he tended to play by the book or by rules of honor; because of this he could come off as cold or impersonal when in fact he was neither.

Eric Benson was the main technical guy—he made things work. He was from the University of Utah where he worked on Portable Standard Lisp (PSL), which at least doesn't sound far off from Portable Common Lisp, which was what our company would do. He had worked at HP commercializing PSL and was working at the Palo Alto office of Symbolics, a hardware-based Lisp company. Before we decided to try starting a company, he and I tried to get the Portable Common Lisp project funded within Symbolics, but it didn't work and he quit to become a founder. Eric could do brilliant prototypes and could press ahead toward a commercial product when required, though it wasn't his first choice. Every now and then he came down with the "bright, shiny object syndrome": When working on one thing in the boring stage of getting the details right, he would get distracted by the next exciting project. Even so, he was our go-to guy for most of Lucid's years.

Rod Brooks was another main technical guy, but he couldn't join the company full time. He wrote the compiler for us while getting tenure at MIT as a celebrated roboticist. His idea was to create artificial life by layering intelligence on top of instinct, kind of a series of meta levels each modifying or operating on the one below. Rod needed to become famous, and he wanted to become rich. To accomplish both, he took many jobs: At one point he was teaching at MIT, consulting 40 hours a week for me, and consulting some number of hours a week with someone else. He was at Stanford when I was a student there but he entered two years after me—he and I graduated the same time. Rod, Guy Steele, and I worked together on the S1 NIL project—Rod at MIT, Steele at CMU, and I at Stanford.

Rod got himself into a divorce situation in which his ex-wife and three children got all of his MIT salary and all the money I paid him, and he lived off the other consulting he did. Hard as it is to believe, Rod pulled off achieving his need and became famous and worked four jobs and got tenure.

Erik Gilbert was in the same Stanford class with me—we entered in 1975. He took a little longer than I did but had a much more solid thesis and ended up working with me at LLNL. He turned out to be the most loyal person at the company and the one who had the most common sense. He knew computer science cold, and I turned more to him than anyone else for advice on anything from technology to personal matters. His weakness was not wanting to take risks at all. We called him "Galloping Gilbert" because the last thing we could imagine was him galloping off to wage a hasty war.

Jim McDonald was at Stanford and a close friend of Jussi's. I didn't know him all that well when we started the company, but he was responsible for the Lisp stuff in Pat Suppes's group. He was very thorough at debugging things and wrote elaborate code that aspired to handle all the obscure cases. His only problem was that he overdesigned and overengineered his programs, and so although it was tough to get them to work completely, they had the right architecture. He couldn't accept doing the minimal amount of work to get things to work well. The balancing benefit was that his code would usually anticipate cases and situations that the simpler solutions would not, and it was a matter of getting the code for those obscure cases to work rather than redesigning the program from scratch. We typically gave him the thorniest problems to solve.

Then there were the silent founders, Bill Scherlis and Scott Fahlman.

Bill we already know—it was his uncle who was the venture capitalist who initially funded us. He and I were in the same class at Stanford, and we graduated at the same time. He was on the faculty at CMU, and he contributed the *reader* for the interpreter. The reader tokenized and parsed Common Lisp expressions for execution. He delivered it late, but I think we found only one bug in it in the 10 years of its use.

Scott Fahlman was the leader of the Quinquevirate, which was the group of five who pushed the Common Lisp specification to completion in 1983. He was recognized as the leader of Common Lisp, and he spoke and consulted extensively on Common Lisp. It seemed important to get another Common Lisp big name in addition to me, especially when I was unable to get Guy Steele, the author of *Common Lisp the Language* (CLtL) (1984), the authoritative specification for Common Lisp. Steele and I were close friends, but at that time, he didn't want to live in California, and he was unsure of the company's viability. Scott provided one or two words of advice and help with a major contract.

We put together a business plan that had basically these points:

- AI was taking off and used Lisp as its language.

- Lisp machine companies were doing great.

- There was a new standard for Lisp—Common Lisp.

- Two of the designers of Common Lisp were founders of the company.

- Workstations were fast enough to run Lisp as well as Lisp machines did and at a fraction of the cost.

- We had the best team.

- We were friends with DARPA (*D*efense *A*dvanced *P*rojects *A*gency, formerly ARPA), which was planning to buy a lot of Lisp over the next few years.

This plan got us $600,000 in seed capital and a commitment of three computers from Sun Microsystems, the local up-and-coming workstation company. We had one year to deliver a beta of Common Lisp written from scratch on the Sun 2, which was a Motorola 68010 workstation. DARPA provided (to me) three Symbolics Lisp machines—a 3670 and two 3640s. And we found a building, a law firm, a bank, a business card firm, a used furniture place, and off we went, incorporated in July 1984 in Palo Alto, California.

In that first year we hired around 15 people, including all three employees of a very small Lisp company in San Diego. We established ourselves as competitors of Symbolics, Lisp Machine, Inc. (LMI), and Franz, Inc., a small company based in Berkeley that was selling a Lisp dialect called Franz Lisp (get it?).

Many of the people we hired were either brothers or married—not only was the company like a family, it employed parts of families. There were Eric and Peter Benson (brothers), Jim and Bill McDonald (brothers), Leonard and Jan Zubkoff (spouses), and Harlan and Carol Sexton (spouses).

We used what many people thought was an unusual development methodology. We spent the first months planning our attack on the problem. Common Lisp is very large: The informal specification is 600 pages long and contains almost 800 functions. We needed to start from scratch so that there would be clear ownership of the code—the venture capitalists demanded this.

Each of us had written at least one Lisp system before, so there was no doubt we could do it. We decided to write a Lisp in Lisp, which meant that the bulk of code was written in the language being implemented—a bootstrapping issue. We used Franz Lisp with a Common Lisp compatibility package as the implementation dialect. We used a similar compatibility package for the Lisp machines.

The underlying system understood how to manipulate raw data using special operators, so we could code essentially at the assembly language level for almost everything. This meant that the memory manager and all sorts of low-level parts of the system could be easily written and debugged.

The compiler turned these operations into specific machine code that we understood.

We used inlining as the basis for coding those parts of the system available from the interpreter. For example, there is an operation on binary trees called car, which takes a binary tree and returns the left-hand branch. This function must be available from the interpreter, and the compiler must compile it efficiently. So the interpreter's version of the function is written like this:

```
(defun car (x) (car x))
```

It looks a little puzzling, but the compiler open codes the call to car into a series of machine instructions, and the effect of the defun is to register the existence of a function accessing that series of instructions.

We divided up the system into modules and assigned them to various people. The modules were carved out of an architecture and initial design for the system based on brainstorming meetings about how to implement the system and finally on the detailed low-level design done by Eric Benson.

Each module was assigned to a developer and a buddy. The buddy would participate in the detailed design of the module, design reviews, code reviews, test plan reviews, and test code reviews. The buddy was someone to talk to and also someone who could step in if the main developer was incapacitated.

No coding could start until a design document was created and reviewed by the buddy and a group of developers. Code was reviewed by the buddy and a review committee, as was the test plan and the test code. We used a simple configuration management system and formal ways of checking in and testing parts of the system.

Within six months of turning on the computers after a month of design, we had a basic Common Lisp system running. In that first year we managed to raise roughly $3.5 million of venture capital from SRK Management, Pacific Venture Partners, Bechtel Investments, and Crown (the venture arm of a Canadian insurance company). We also signed up as OEMs Sun, Apollo, and Prime. In all the years of trying to sign OEMs, we failed to sign only Tektronics, which signed with Franz and then disappeared as a Lisp vendor.

In the summer of 1985 we showed our early version of Lucid Common Lisp (LCL) at IJCAI, the big AI conference in Los Angeles. At that time we had the OEMs mentioned and a relationship with Symbolics to provide a development environment for Lucid Common Lisp on Symbolics computers based on the one we used for developing LCL. Recall that before starting Lucid, we had pitched the idea of a stock hardware Lisp to Symbolics, but they did not show interest. It turns out they had estimated that on the next generation of Sun workstations— the Motorola 68020-based Sun 3—Common Lisp could run no faster than 17 times slower than on the Symbolics 3600, which was a custom microcoded Lisp machine.

At that time HP was just getting seriously into the workstation market and had decided to base their Common Lisp offering on Portable Standard Lisp, which was developed at the University of Utah by Martin Griss and his students, including Eric Benson. HP made its debut at IJCAI.

We had around 25 employees by then, and nearly all of them made it down to LA—it was only an hour away by a $70 round-trip ticket. One of our employees, Rob Poor, had a friend who made movie jackets for Hollywood production crews—she made the *Raiders of the Lost Ark* movie jackets. Rob commissioned her to design and make enough movie jackets for every employee. They were black satin with a white *Lucid* across the back and the person's name in the inside pocket. There was a little bit of blue trim around *Lucid*.

We were to pick up the jackets in Hollywood when we got there. The day before the conference started, we had to set up. The exhibit hall was UCLA's gym, and this was the first year of big AI. The big companies—Sun, Apollo, Intellicorp, Inference, Symbolics, Texas Instruments (a Lisp machine company), Xerox (another Lisp machine company), HP, DEC (now Digital), Gold Hill (a small Massachusetts Common Lisp company)—had enormous booths, some 50 feet tall, covering in some cases hundreds of square feet. We sat right next to Symbolics, which had a two-story booth made of black metal, curved at the front with monitors arrayed from the upper deck around the front for easy demonstration access. Some called it the Deathstar, others the Battlestar Symbolica.

The day before the conference started, the booths started to show up. Ours was modest but required a day of setup coordinated with the teamsters manning the loading docks. There were perhaps 50 exhibitors, and the floor was a mess. The jackets arrived and we tried them on. They were fabulous. We wore them around the floor chatting with our friends at other companies as they set up. The next day before the doors opened we decided to walk around the floor with our jackets on.

The show started, we left them on.

One of our people was a break-dancer. To gather a crowd in front of our small booth, Zach would put down a piece of cardboard, turn on a boom box, and start spinning on the floor. Then he would get up and put on his black Lucid jacket and give a demo.

We talked about benchmarks—the standard Lisp benchmarks were called the Gabriel Benchmarks, which I had published in a book that year (Gabriel 1985). The results presented in that book, gathered in confidence over the previous year from the Lisp vendors and providers, was presented at the 1984 AAAI conference (the US-only sister conference of IJCAI) in front of a crowd of 3,000. We had to move from the 500-person hall to the theater to accommodate the way larger-than-that group that showed up.

I knew our benchmarks were better than almost anyone else's, and within shouting distance of Symbolics, too. We tried to pry out the newest numbers from other vendors, but they wouldn't budge. We displayed my benchmark book and the Common Lisp book, of which I was one of the five front-cover-listed contributors, and told the story of how I was the father of Common Lisp—more or less true—the father of benchmarks, and the architect of Lucid, the only company deserving of black movie jackets.

We made an impression that day but not an entirely good one. We became the bad boys of the marketplace, out, apparently, to bring down not only the Lisp machine companies but any company that dared to enter the Lisp arena.

It was a good show.

≈ ≈ ≈

Later in 1985 we moved into the old Intellicorp offices which occupied part of the basement and the entire second floor of Menlo Park city hall. The joke about this was based on expert-system technology in which simple logical rules like if-then statements are strung together along with observed facts to make simple inferences. The joke was that Lucid decided where to move using an expert system with two rules: You can't fight city hall; if you can't beat 'em, join 'em.

That year we came up against a force far stronger than city hall: IBM. IBM was developing a RISC computer. Of course, this was a rumored project, but IBM's practice was to keep such things officially secret. We knew, though, that Scott Fahlman's Lisp group at CMU was porting their Lisp system, Spice Lisp, to the RT-PC (RISC Technology Personal Computer).

Scott, a Lucid founder, finally steered IBM to talk to us about doing the commercial version of Common Lisp. There were some problems.

One was that because Spice Lisp was designed to be the basis of a Lisp machine, it had a full environment—an editor, debugging and development tools, and a window system—and IBM would expect the same for the commercial version, and we had decided not to provide such an a extensive product to our other OEMs.

The other was that Scott was a Lucid founder and IBM would not want any taint on any of their business deals.

IBM had a release date in mind of approximately 18 months to two years out from when they decided to approach Lucid. However, the legal department wanted to make sure Fahlman's connection and actions were above board. It took until 12 months before the deadline for the OK to come down, and then IBM approached us. They perhaps had carefully thought about how much work needed to be done and thus chose with deliberation when to make the approach, but the 6 to 12 month legal delay messed up their timing; the end date did not change. Nor did the requirements: a full Lisp system, equivalent to Symbolics's.

We could not pass up the deal because the RT would perhaps be the fastest workstation and would rival Symbolics for dominance in the AI market. We took the contract and ramped up with 13 people—all but a couple of our developers—on the project. We tried to reuse the Spice code and succeeded with some of it. But what they say about university code is true: It is not developed to a commercial standard, and certainly not to IBM's standard. And the fact that Lucid had an extensive test suite was part of the attraction to IBM. We needed to bring the CMU code up to snuff, and in some cases it was easier to just adapt our own or write from scratch.

The practical aspects of the deal were difficult. We got two machines which had to be locked in inaccessible rooms in the basement, chained to the concrete floor by a sort of digital chastity belt, with motion detectors for when no one was working with them. Also, it was secret who was working on other software and what that software was. One particular secret piece of code was a symbolic assembly language debugger. This program looks at machine-language instructions and displays them in mnemonic form, places breakpoints, and things like that. We knew through the grapevine that another independent software company had developed this for the RT, but we could not get it because then we would know who they were. So we had to develop our own. Same story with the window system. IBM was planning a window system, but it would not be available in time for us to use, so we needed to do our own. This meant, for example, that we had to track the mouse ourselves!

Another oddity was the documentation requirements. IBM had their own standard format, and all documentation had to conform to it. If the product was a language product, that had to conform as well. The format required one page per "function". It didn't matter that there was a commercial book—Steele's book—that defined the language and was suitable even as a user's guide. We had to do our own—the same information, in our words, in IBM's format.

There is a story by the Argentinian writer Jorge Luis Borges entitled "Pierre Menard, Author of Don Quixote" (1962) about a writer who wanted to write *Don Quixote*. But, because Borges was fascinated with hermeneutics, he made this writer want to reproduce *Don Quixote* word for word, but not as a transcription. The writer's name was Pierre Menard. Menard wanted to get into a context in the mid-twentieth century in which he would happen to write the same book as Miguel Cervantes had. The story talks about other projects Menard did and how he was able to write Chapter 15 word for word, and Borges talks about the different meanings that the same words had when written on one hand by the seventeenth century Cervantes and on the other by the twentieth century Menard. I quote a bit of it because it's so much fun:

> *It is a revelation to compare the* Don Quixote *of Menard with that of Cervantes. The latter, for instance, wrote (*Don Quixote, Part One Chapter Nine*):*
>
>> [... truth, whose mother is history, who is
>> the rival of time, depository of deeds, witness
>> of the past, example and lesson to the
>> present, and warning to the future.]
>
> *Written in the seventeenth century, written by the "ingenious layman" Cervantes, this enumeration is a mere rhetorical eulogy of history. Menard, on the other hand, writes:*
>
>> [... truth, whose mother is history, who is
>> the rival of time, depository of deeds, witness
>> of the past, example and lesson to the
>> present, and warning to the future.]
>
> *History,* mother *of truth; the idea is astounding. Menard, a contemporary of William James, does not define history as an investigation of reality, but as its origin. Historical truth, for him, is not what took place; it is what we think took place. The final clauses—*example and lesson to the present, and warning to the future—*are shamelessly pragmatic.*
>
> *Equally vivid is the contrast in styles. The archaic style of Menard—in the last analysis a foreigner—suffers from a certain affectation. Not so that of his precursor, who handles easily the ordinary Spanish of his time.* (Borges 1962)

We hired someone to write the book, which we called the Pierre Menard Edition of CLtL.

This project damaged Lucid, maybe irrecoverably. We had about one year to do two to three years of work. Because we were then on many platforms, there was a push to get all this on all the platforms at about the same time, and some of the contracts with the other vendors required it.

A development organization cannot produce that much quality software in so short a time even with plenty of manpower. Some of it was reworked university software that we didn't really understand all that well. We had strapped ourselves with an albatross.

What's worse, IBM's requirements forced us in the direction of duplicating the Lisp machine environments rather than trying to interoperate with standard OS and development environments. Lucid bet early-on that standard platforms, including software, would win out over customized ones, that the value of Lisp lay in the language and its incremental development paradigm, which could be supported with more standard components like text editors. Rapid prototyping could have been a perfectly fine niche for us. But our relationship with IBM, which paid well and led to further agreements with IBM on their other platforms, forced us to abandon part of this philosophy.

What's worse was that the RT-PC sold poorly—it was actually a flop. It was an eviscerated cousin of the fast 801 RISC processor attached to a PC chassis, which meant that it was underpowered and underfeatured. A lot of the software provided for it was green. It was too expensive and too slow by a wide margin. IBM made a fast recovery, for them, releasing the RS6000 less than five years later, but it was already too late for Lisp and Lucid.

❧   ❧   ❧

Lucid was run well by Tony Slocum (and me) during these years, in the sense that we largely followed our business plan and achieved all our goals. The employees of the company found the environment invigorating, and it seemed like success was just around the corner. We raised an additional million or two, adding the prestigious venture firms Dillon Read Venture Capital, Brentwood Associates, and Trinity Ventures (which took over the Bechtel investment). We attracted talent that frankly, I have rarely before or since seen at a software company.

It might seem odd today that artificial intelligence and Lisp were hot items in the mid-1980s. AI promised to eliminate the drudgery of using computers, to bring human-level intelligence to computers and hence to companies. Take, for example, Schlumberger, one of the largest, if not *the* largest, oil exploration companies. Schlumberger faced a real problem in that it made a lot of money by helping oil companies decide where to find oil and how to drill down to it. Often wells would need to be several miles deep, and the details of how to get to the oil often could not be determined by external tests—rather, you had to drill a bit, look at what the rock was like on the way down, and make adjustments. When you drill an oil well, you don't go straight down, you curve and bend—maybe later when you find the reservoir, you will drill straight down, but not during exploration.

The way to figure out where to go is to pull out the drill and drop down an instrument called a *dip meter*, which records the slant of the strata and, to some extent, their contents. The result is a long strip readout that an expert would analyze.

Here are the problems: It can cost millions of dollars to get a dip meter reading: You have to pull up maybe five miles of drill rig, drop down five miles of dip meter rig, pull that up, and then put down the drill again. Schlumberger had only one truly effective dip meter reader, and he was nearing retirement. AI and expert systems in particular seemed to be a solution. An expert system is a way to capture (the simplest) parts of expertise. It can work remarkably well, but it can be hard to tune for accuracy because people use all sorts of common sense and judgment along with strictly codifiable rules.

It was the realization that expertise was precious and aging or expensive and slow (compared with a computer) or hard to clone that helped lead to the popularity of AI in the 1980s. Compounding this was the hype put out by the AI company founders.

The AI companies were founded almost exclusively by AI faculty from universities—MIT, Stanford, CMU, USC, for example. Academics have an interesting view of business: They equate business with war. A company wins because other companies lose—a classic misunderstanding of evolution (see my later essay "Money Through Innovation Reconsidered"). A company keeps everything a secret. A company tries to spy on other companies. A company cannot trust anyone not part of themselves.

Because of these beliefs, AI companies rarely made strategic partnerships. A partner, learning of your plans, could move into your business, couldn't it? That partner could steal your ideas, right?

AI academics didn't have a good idea of how AI technology would spread to the mainstream. They made the mistake of assuming the technology was in the mainstream when a company that is considered mainstream was using it for something. Companies serving Wall Street were considered the most mainstream companies around, even though every company has an advanced development group or groups dedicated to exploring the effectiveness of new technologies. So just because Morgan Stanley has an AI project does not mean that AI is being used in Morgan Stanley's day-to-day operations.

In addition, Wall Street companies—the ones that serve stock markets—are the most radical companies around, willing to spend a fair amount of money on new technologies that might have an impact on their results, which are as leveraged as anything can be. That is, a 1% performance advantage when multiplied by all the trades made per year can mean many millions of dollars in profit.

The AI companies had no realistic plan to move their expert systems into the mainstream. They were using a large standard language (the smallest Common Lisp system requires several megabytes for its implementation); they had large tools (KEE, Intellicorp's primary product required another four to eight megabytes of implementation code); and the systems built were large because the ambition level of the early adopters was high (remember, early adopters are trying to hit a home run with new technology to make the career moves or corporate improvements they crave).

Most of the development was done on Lisp machines, special-purpose hardware costing around $100,000 per machine. The Lisp machine companies expected people to deploy on these workstations. In fact, they expected people to use these workstations instead of Sun's, Apollo's, or whatever. Part of Lucid's business strategy was to recognize that people would need to deliver on standard platforms, namely, the ones they already had. So our goal was to provide a path from the Lisp machine to the standard workstation.

What we understood intellectually but not viscerally was that customers were not willing to purchase additional RAM to run these large Lisp-based applications. When Sun told the customer that the four-megabyte Sun 3/50 diskless node was plenty computer, that was that. No one bothered to mention that the operating system and window system for that platform required 3.5 megabytes and that paging over the network was something that worked best in the abstract.

Many of the companies that could have warned us of these requirements decided not to, some through neglect, others through explicit decisions. For example, the CEO of one of the AI companies told me that they would not tell us their customers' requirements because they didn't want us in touch with them should we decide to move into the AI market at some point. Besides, business was a Darwinian affair, after all, and if we were to survive, we would discover or understand those requirements ourselves. Help was not part of the equation.

By the way, this company was a close partner of Lucid's. You can see that the concept of working together or partnership was alien to the academic AI companies. Naturally, these companies were disappointed that the stock-hardware Lisp companies didn't provide exactly the product they wanted.

Let's review the plan before we examine how it went wrong. This was the context:

- AI was coming out of academia; that software was written in Lisp.

- The Lisp machine companies were doing great.

- AI was grabbing all the headlines; AI companies were using Lisp.

- Lisp machines were not a cost-effective way to deliver

- Essentially all the computer companies wanted to get on the AI bandwagon.

- There was a new standard dialect of Lisp, called Common Lisp.

- DARPA, the Department of Defense research arm, seemed ready to use Common Lisp for a lot of its AI work and was planning to support a large group purchase.

The strategy follows from this:

- Become the Common Lisp provider through OEM relationships with as many standard platform companies as possible.

- Provide a path from Lisp machines to these platforms.

- Provide the most faithful-to-the-standard, reliable, high-performance implementation we could within budgetary constraints.

We achieved all these business goals with OEM relationships with Apollo, Sun, HP, Digital (Ultrix, VMS, VAX, MIPS), IBM (all platforms), Prime, NCR, Intel, and Bull in Europe, with a full development environment and with the fastest Lisp system in the industry and the reputation for reliability as the "Maytag of Lisp." We also had a few dozen value-added resellers (VARs) like Thinking Machines, Inc.

What didn't happen was the marketplace. In 1986 it became evident to me that the AI companies were overpromising and underdelivering and that the early adopters were not succeeding as well as they had hoped and therefore there was little movement toward the mainstream. About this same time Lucid's revenues were approximately $6 million per year and growing at a modest rate, but not nearly so fast as we had hoped and planned for. The company was up to 75 people, almost all technical—we did almost all our sales through OEM royalties and development contracts, so we didn't really need much marketing or sales. In fact, we considered ourselves the OEMs' development arm.

It was nearly impossible to talk to customers directly because the OEM handled all the sales, marketing, and first-line support. The VARs similarly guarded their customer lists, and so many of our activities like newsletters and booths at trade shows were designed to find out who they were so we could talk to them. Some companies, like Sun, explicit expressed their dislike of these practices.

Therefore, it was not easy to determine what we needed to do to the product to make customers successful. The OEMs were perfectly happy to put together their "AI configuration," which was heavy on RAM and disk.

When we were able to talk to our customers, an ugly picture emerged. Lisp was too big and too slow for real applications. Applications needed to comprise a mixture of Lisp and other code, and the membrane between the two languages had to be thin—they wanted to manipulate Lisp data directly from C, for example.

The AI companies, facing their own serious problems from overhyping their technological potential, were quick to blame the Lisp companies for not understanding customer requirements, and when that didn't work, they blamed Lisp itself. Never mind that we had been pleading for customer contact and that any discussions of using a subset of Common Lisp or a smaller dialect were met with cries concerning the workload to port to another Lisp.

Soon some of the AI companies started to move toward C as a way to show a commitment to the mainstream, and those lovable C programmers were easier to find and cheaper than pesky Lisp guys.

We also had our ups and downs with some of the OEMs. For example, the technical people at Sun were fonder of the Franz developers than of us—we were arrogant. A key problem was the environment that IBM paid us to implement and which we tried to palm off on our OEMs. Sun was creating their own environment with a large development staff, and they seemed to want to use the environment-less Franz Common Lisp (called Allegro Common Lisp).

Sun would give to Franz alphas and betas of our releases to Sun, thereby providing Franz with early access to our technology. Whenever we tried to buy a Franz product or get a report from a customer, Franz refused to sell and threatened to sue.

In 1986, Sun decided to switch to Franz, but in 1987, Bob Kadarauch acted to reverse the decision as his first duty as new CEO.

ว่า   ว่า   ว่า

Tony Slocum was puzzled about why AI and Lisp were not taking off. He had been careful with our money, had worked well with the investors, was a brilliant negotiator, and was just about the most decent guy you could imagine. He was very good at solving people's problems. But the market wasn't happening—I had coined the phrase "AI winter"—and he simply didn't know what to do. He told me, "I just come into work and sit there and I feel powerless. I don't know what to do. I don' think I can do this job anymore; you have to help me get out of it."

We had several offsite meetings to try to figure out a strategy, but the enthusiasm around the table was for making Lisp win somehow. But the market was telling us that our implementation approach couldn't work for them and that perhaps Lisp was the wrong answer anyway, with the Lisp machine companies on the decline and the AI companies flocking to C. That enthusiasm came from the investors, and we came up with no real new strategies for either Lisp or anything else.

Tony's depression continued, so in early 1987 I contacted the board, all of whom were investors except Tony and me, and told them the situation. The investors immediately removed Tony as the CEO and started a search. Rigdon Curry, one of the investors on the board, took over as temporary CEO. Tony stayed on as the Chairman of the Board.

This period was full of upheaval as developers and other employees looked for someone to blame. Many of the key developers started to blame Jussi, who was a firm taskmaster but who relished the organizational details. He got all our many coordinated releases out on time with the budgeted staff. But he had favorites and wasn't very adept at keeping that to himself.

I came under criticism for my lasséz-faire role, and people talked to Rig about it. One day I became paranoid about it and asked Jussi if he had been speaking ill of me to Rig, and he said he hadn't been. But even the suggestion of dishonor was enough, and Jussi left in disgrace, just as Victoria had predicted, though he was the last one I would have picked.

8a   8a   8a

What would have happened had Lucid been a typical start-up? It might have tried to make some changes to its products to increase their saleability, and the revenues would have peaked and then declined or maybe stayed flat, and the venture capitalists would have sold out to the employees or asked the company to check back with them in a couple of years.

We didn't do that—instead, we came up with a new product line and did a restart, something that a start-up almost never gets to do.

Into the Ground: C++

When we saw the candidates for new CEO, all of them were boring except one, Bob Kadarauch. I met Bob at Buck's, a restaurant in Woodside, California, which fashions itself as a horse town of the mostly English variety, smack center on the Peninsula whose tip is San Francisco. Horsefolk can ride to Buck's and rein their mounts to a hitching rail, they can ride the horse paths all through town and chat with Joan (Baez), Shirley (Temple Black), or Billie Jean (King). If you ride down to the flats, you can meet Joe and Jennifer (Montana), and up the hill to La Honda there's Neil (Young).

I was living in Portola Valley up on a hill overlooking Atherton and the Bay with a far view of The City. It was my dream at last of owning land and a home, which I hadn't before, and growing up on a farm lends warmth to the idea of land that's yours.

It was a Sunday brunch in the spring. Bob smoked heavily—no one else at Lucid did—and he seemed to never stop talking. He spoke of his 18 years at HP and how he transferred here and there taking this or that assignment, finally ending up on John Young's staff as a marketing specialist. He went to Stanford in the MBA program and built up a business unit in the UK, Pinewood. We talked for four hours and I gave the board a favorable report.

Bob seemed to have done a lot of things and knew a lot about software development organizations and had a lot of valuable knowledge of HP, which was our favorite OEM because of its professionalism.

I was left a little puzzled by the meeting, however, because there were times when Bob's monologue wasn't particularly focused, and I had a hard time following what he was saying. But I laid it at the feet of my trying to evaluate and appreciate him at first and his nervousness.

We checked his references at HP who said things like he was a great technologist. Tony liked him and so we hired him.

Bob immediately set up appointments with every employee to find out what was up.

While all this was going on, we had been having a series of all-hands meetings—mostly developers—to try to find a new product direction. I asked everyone to come up with as many ideas as they felt were good and we listed them on one of the all-wall whiteboards. Then the proponents of each would make a small presentation of the product idea, their feelings about the market, and a quick take on how well our expertise matched up. We started with about 150 items on the board, and after three weeks we had worked through them all.

What we knew about were low-level implementation, languages, and development environments. What we thought the market was up to was a shift toward object-oriented development and C++ in particular. We identified two potential products: one was a development environment for C++ that was based on a version of Emacs, a text editor, customized for the job, and the other was a development environment for C++ that was based on more of the features we knew about in the Lisp world. We called these the *Hitchhiker* and *Cadillac* products.

After a fair amount of discussion, we decided to try to pursue the Cadillac version, but not to try to go too far in the high-tech direction. Bob allowed us to put together a small investigatory team from some folks less busy than others—I put together a three-person team to look at the issues.

This group designed a simple transcription of a Lisp-like environment ported to C++, including the facility to put information about the program into a database. The environment would provide incremental development, certain types of safety nets, browsing capabilities, and team tools. We tried to peddle it to some potential partners, because Bob's philosophy was to try to raise money from partners rather than from VCs.

Meanwhile, Bob was trying to save the Sun relationship, lower expenses, and get Lisp back on track. We did a layoff in January of 1991, which was one of the hardest things I've done. Maybe I should have taken the hint, but the day of the layoff, Bob got sick and didn't come in to work. So the first-line managers and I told those who had to leave.

When we were about to make Bob his offer, I noticed that the board was talking about his being CEO and president. This raised an interesting problem—all development groups reported to me in my role as president. This meant that the minute Bob took over as president, these groups would have no managerial join point. The board never discussed any reorganization or any particular role for me, yet I was reviewing the letter that threw all that into question. I wrote the following letter and delivered it at the board meeting in which we were to decide to hire Bob:

> *This letter is being sent to inform you that I am resigning as President of Lucid, Inc., effective September 29, 1987. It is my desire, however,*

*to retain the title of Chief Technical Officer. Although this resignation
has the effect of forfeiting my managerial responsibilities and authority, I will provide direction for those groups and individuals assigned
to me at the time of this resignation until the Chief Executive Officer
has either reassigned me within the organization or has designated a
successor or successors to manage those groups and individuals.*

The board was taken aback by this letter and asked me why I was sending it. I replied without emotion or surprise that the board's next action was to authorize an offer letter hiring someone right on top of my position. Still puzzled by it, the board pressed on. My conclusion was that though I had the title of president, it had meant actually nothing to them. Perhaps I was not being taken as seriously as I thought.

Even though some of us were operating under the assumption that Lisp reve-
nues would decline at some point, actually they were merely growing more slowly than we had hoped. Almost all the investors believed that Lisp would recover with only some more perseverance, and Bob was acting that way too. It made sense to try to maximize the return and not only keep the revenues up as long as possible but also to position us to take advantage of any possibility of an upturn.

But it was clear that we had built the wrong product. In the end, Franz would claim that because they had to struggle to stay alive, they simply did whatever a customer wanted and therefore they built a friendlier product. However, the differences actually were that they could not afford to do as much as we could, and in particular they did not build a Lisp-machine-like environment but a low-
tech one like the Hitchhiker environment we considered for C++.

With a reduced staff and a slight upturn in the Lisp market, we were profit-
able in the fourth quarter of fiscal year 1988, and we all got black tee-shirts that said *In The Black*.

The next year saw the first leveling off and decline in the Lisp market. During the summer of 1988 Bob let me hire a couple of people for Cadillac: Patrick Dus-
sud and Matthieu Devin, both French though Patrick was born in the United States and was a citizen. This lent a European flavor to the group: We had "French lunches" every month or so and occasionally indulged in Parisian café squatting during design sessions. Having a group identity helps form a working team.

I was surprised to be able to hire Patrick who was the primary architect of the Texas Instruments (TI) Explorer Lisp machine and an incredible designer. It turned out that he had been interested in building a C++ environment and that this sounded like a good opportunity.

We met at an X3J13 meeting in Boston. X3J13 was the ANSI standard commit-
tee for Common Lisp. I quizzed him about TI, which appeared on the decline in the Lisp market and his interest in Lucid, and he said he wasn't interested. I then

started talking about Cadillac, and he said he was ready to hire on for that—he had not expected we were doing something like that.

He worked for TI in Austin, Texas, so we flew him out for a week to interview, and we made him an offer right away.

Patrick is about 5 feet, 6 inches with dirty blond hair and a low, French drenched voice—some people had trouble understanding the combination of bass and accent, and at first so did I. He wanted to come out to Lucid to work for a month or so while his family—Veronique and his kids Stephanie and twins Cedric and Fabrice—was vacationing in France. He wanted to have his car, a 1984 Corvette, available, so he decided to drive out, and I volunteered to drive with him.

Patrick's thing was fast cars. He did some racing with his Corvette, and the surprising thing was that his wife kind of liked the idea of fast cars. Later, after he had been at Lucid for a few years, she got her own 1964 'Vette.

I flew to Austin, we grabbed a hamburger at McDonalds, and away we went.

The 'Vette had a radar detector and Patrick drove it hard the first two to three hours, from early evening until 10:00 P.M. or so. I took over. I had never driven a car quite like it. Around 270 horsepower, but my experience with other cars since indicates that the 'Vette had high torque so that acceleration was sharp. We drove through the night talking alternately about cars and Cadillac. I learned about the Corvette's advanced design and engineering and steering neutrality, its victories, and how it was banned in some races because it was too powerful or handled too well.

Through the night through west Texas across New Mexico we explored different ways to present program information in Cadillac, and we focused on hypertext. Incremental compilation through a semi-interpreted implementation, a database of information, a multiuser version all were part of it.

Near dawn I dozed a little and I recall the orange haze along the dark base of mountains as we neared Roswell, the first moment when I saw clearly the low creosote and thistles, saltbush, fluffgrass.

Through Roswell past the two UFO museums and toward Ruidoso Downs—but we turned just past Tinnie through Lincoln, where Billy the Kid hung out, through Carrizozo to San Pedro where we stopped at the Owl Café at 8 in the morning to get a couple of green chili cheeseburgers, which one of the writers at Lucid had recommended. We took this odd route between Austin and San Francisco just to get these cheeseburgers. Both Molly, the writer, and Erik Gilbert had strong ties to New Mexico—Erik grew up there and Molly went to school there. There is something about the hard dry desert, the dark distant mountains, the rock formations and the spirituality, the danger of Billy the Kid riding through the low scrub pine, the Native Americans at every turn. It's the fresh but olden cast of the sun on the sand, and sun-cleaved separateness of the rock, your life in context.

Years later I wrote a poem about Lincoln and Billy the Kid, using language of the 1880s. In the 1980s we were only 100 years away from the kind of land where death and escape were commonplace. American law enforcement comes from this background where we have the bullies who prey on us and the bullies who save us by catching, sometimes killing, those other ones. In the West of the 1880s it wasn't apparent from the color of a man's hat whether he would save you, rib you, buffalo you to the ground, or tip his hat. Our system of justice may descend from England, but our system of capture is our own. American business, does it derive from the same roots? Perhaps, and perhaps that's why there is no Lucid today.

A few years later when we were previewing Energize, the marketing name for Cadillac, at OOPSLA in Phoenix, we drove Dussud's 1990 Corvette from Menlo Park to Phoenix, and we visited Tombstone on a day trip. Although Tombstone is more of a tourist attraction than Lincoln is—Lincoln is a little more of a historical museum—Tombstone still has that same feeling of a land that could nurture you toward imagination or toward hate and violence. On the way to Tombstone from Tucson we passed through St. David, which is an oasis of New England oaks, elms, tall green grass and cool air, and Tombstone to the south rests on a high rocky bluff, feels a continent and a century away.

Patrick adopted some of my new-found love of the Southwest during his years at Lucid, and this was just one of the many curious things about his stay. He seemed a devoted friend and adviser, and maybe even an admirer. He sat and stood close to me whenever we were together. And through the years we repeated the essence of our Austin-to-San Francisco death ride as we called it with drives from Hollister to San Miguel on Highway 25 near Salinas, through a narrow valley. Part of the road is about 1.5 lanes and paved beautifully with nice banked curves and a few one to two mile straightaways. On one we got his new 'Vette up to about 150 mph. Once we spun out on a curve and ended up going backward around the curve at 70 mph with no injuries or even excessive dust on the cream white car.

Coming from Austin that first trip, we headed toward U.S. 40 and the direct way to San Francisco—or at least the main road. But because the traffic was so heavy and the pace so slow after our 100 mph run from Austin, we decided to head up through Nevada and across the Sierras. We played tag with a Berreta and got a speeding ticket (only 95 mph because even with instant-on radar our detector gave us enough time to drop from 125 between the first and second readings). We were on a long descent into town when we were hit, and we were the victims of local fundraising.

In Nevada we stopped to sleep for the night, 24 hours away from Austin.

The next day we crossed through the southern basin and range of Nevada across to Bishop and Tioga Pass and into the San Joachim Valley, the Central Valley of California, an ancient inland sea now cropland growing wheat and corn and rice, nuts, fruits, and berries in more abundance than almost any other place. A hot place and dry. The promised land for me and Patrick who longed to make a difference acting on his love of good design and attention to detail.

From Livermore to Portola Valley we were under constant k-band illumination though the California Highway Patrol was supposedly not allowed to use radar, so we set the cruise to 65 and acted just like any other grandma on her way to Thanksgiving while lesser cars sped past.

By the time we got back we had a good idea of the starting point for Cadillac. The team would change quite a bit over the next few years as those members who did not come up with a compelling architecture and design fell away to other projects, and the core team anchored by Patrick grew.

Being an OEM company, Lucid didn't have a true marketing department, though the few marketing people we did have were good marcom (marketing communications) people and good executors. We had neither the resources nor they the interest in finding out about the marketplace for C++ (forgive the misnomer).

We needed requirements because we were not C or C++ people ourselves. Many of the criticisms of Lucid as a technology-happy company stem from the belief that Cadillac was a purely engineering-driven product. It was, in the sense that all the marketing research, product strategy, product marketing, product management, as well as the architecture, design, and implementation were done by engineering.

I had recently written and presented my paper known as "Worse Is Better" (1990) in which the problems with over engineering and over designing were played out, and we therefore adopted the "stubby pencil" approach, which was to be as low tech as we could in both our approach to the problem and our solution—the simplest way, the fewest features, the most straightforward implementation. We moved the group downstairs into the basement to have the worst office space, taking over the old RT-PC area which had no windows—there were four walls between us and a small window. My desk was extended to form a larger flat area with a scrap of outdoor plywood duct-taped between two desks. Whenever one of us would start talking about a new feature or an advanced technique, one of the others would toss him or her (there was a woman on the project) a stubby pencil sharpened with a knife.

The way we gathered requirements was this: We put together a foil-based presentation of the product with details of the architecture and hand-drawn screen shots to show what people would see, what they would get at different points during development.

What we were trying to build was a development environment that would provide tools for the construction and long-term maintenance of object-oriented C++ systems. C++ is a rudimentary object-oriented language descended from C and designed more or less single-handedly by Bjarne Stroustrup, a Dane with a Cambridge University Ph.D. who was working at Bell Labs in New Jersey. In the MIT style of off-naming things (like *You Despair* for *USAir*), we called him "Barney," which, when we accidentally let it slip during one of his visits, was met with a smile and perhaps a hint of camaraderie-based approval.

We took our presentation to potential customers, approaching them by saying that we thought OO was the coming thing, that C++ was the coming OO language, and that the complexity of the language made a development environment necessary. We told them that our philosophy was to do things in the open rather than under nondisclosure; that we would be talking about the outside view of the product, its design to any level of detail, the technology to any level of detail, that we would leave copies of the slides; they could take any notes; they could use any of the ideas; they could tell anyone about it; and that all this would be in exchange for an honest critique from their C or C++ developers and a presentation of how they did development in their shop with emphasis on how Cadillac could better fit in.

We visited hardware companies, software companies, embedded software shops, consumer-oriented programmers, scientific computing shops, compiler companies, Fortune 500 companies, big ones, tiny ones, garages. We visited two to four a week for around nine months. After each visit we tried to absorb what we had learned, and every week we updated the presentation with ideas and refinements. I think we visited over 100 potential customers, and in the end, the presentation was almost completely unlike what we started with, and the architecture was sleek and simple.

We played to enthusiastic audiences because they were ordinary developers surprised by our open approach to them. Not only weren't they getting a marketing pitch about a planned product—take it or leave it—they were getting a hacker-to-hacker discussion that seemed designed to take into account what they said, no promises of use required, no nasty lawyer things to deal with, just a discussion among developers. We were frequently praised for our unusual and commonsense philosophy. And this helped us get the comments we needed. When you go in with *your ideas*, ideas so valuable legal steps were being taken to present them, the natural reaction from the audience is to fight back and criticize not critique. We got brainstorming instead.

The interesting effect was that because of NIH (*Not Invented Here*) the companies we visited that were in markets similar to those we were headed toward never used our ideas—ours were clearly inferior to theirs. Our philosophy was that if other people adopted our approach to environments, it would be easier for us to thrive because the environment—our marketplace—would be predisposed to our way of doing things.

But the critics of Lucid were right: We did not do marketing the traditional way, and it was just an engineering-driven project.

⌘   ⌘   ⌘

Cadillac was an attempt to build an environment with same the degree of integration as the single-address-space Lisp and Smalltalk environments had in the 1970s and 1980s while separating the tools from the application.

The idea was to reduce the number of physical tools as much as possible and to layer information onto those few tools. Basically we had a text editor and a grapher. These tools were able to handle descriptions of the sorts of things they can display along with descriptions of *annotations*. Annotations are a generalization of hypertext. An annotation is an object along with an associated set or sequence of other objects. An annotation acts as a link among those other objects. Each annotation is an instance of a class to which methods can be attached. An example annotation is the simple link associated with a sequence of two objects. When both objects are text, the annotation is merely hypertext.

Annotations and other information about the program under development are kept in a database and managed by a *kernel*. The kernel and database act as the single address space where everything is known. The tools know nothing.

An annotation is *active*: Methods are attached to annotations by being associated with a class. When someone clicks on an annotation, the tool asks the connected kernel to look up what actions are available, which are passed back for the tool for display and selection.

With annotations you can take an ordinary textual display of a program and decorate it with error messages, with breakpoints, with connections to related code, to classes, to methods, and so forth. Instead of a number of browsers there is only one textual browser and one graphical browser. These tools display the same objects, and all action takes place in the kernel. The objects in the kernel are in a persistent object store, so information lasts over multiple sessions.

When you click on the textual representation of any object, you get a pop-up menu with a list of actions. This is nice because it makes you feel that you are interacting with objects directly instead of through the intermediary of a tool.

The kernel learns about the programs by listening to a stream of data about the program sent by the compiler which annotates the source with *language elements*, a sort of generalization of programming language constructs. This implies that the environment is language independent.

The whole user interface was aimed at exhibiting a characteristic called *ready-to-hand*. A tool is ready-to-hand when its use submerges below consciousness. A hammer is the best example: You use a hammer as if it were an extension of your arm—you don't think about how to use the hammer, just as you never think about using your hand, you simply use it.

We described Cadillac in more detail in "Foundation for a C++ Programming Environment" (Gabriel et al. 1990).

&a   &a   &a

In 1989 we got enough money in venture capital to hire some more people. Matthieu Devin, a Frenchman from Paris, came by apparently to demo some of his software. He had been working for one of Lucid's Lisp competitors, and it wasn't clear why he was coming by. We watched his demos and talked to him, and around 3:30 in the afternoon he mentioned he was visiting to get a job—he had heard about Cadillac and wanted to join up. This was fine but he was leaving at 4:30 for a 6:00 P.M. flight back to Paris. Erik Gilbert and I huddled, chatted with Bob, and wrote out an offer letter on the spot. Matthieu became the other key with Patrick on the design team. His specialty was user interfaces.

In 1990 and 1991 we ramped up development with $5.4 million in venture capital based on a prototype (actually the fourth prototype of the kernel) and a business plan. By then Lisp revenues had started to level off, and the board was intrigued that we could have put together another product prototype on a shoestring. Bob had told one of the developers that he "would be damned" if he was going to be the CEO of a company growing at 15% per year. At that stage, 15% growth in Lisp looked pretty good.

One of the things that Bob did was to *cash cow* the Lisp business. I don't know whether cash cow is a standard term the way we used it, but to us a cash cow was a product that made a lot of profit at the expense of moving it forward. To do this, we stopped all development on our main products and kept only the smallest support crew including a handful of developers—at the peak 40 developers were working on Lisp, but at that point it was down to eight or so. This meant that the product was very profitable, and those profits were poured into Cadillac.

I had argued that Cadillac would have the best chance if it were spun off with new management. But the board wanted to make sure that its share of the company would be such that its loss on Lisp could be recouped.

The people in Lisp who were no longer needed were offered positions in the Cadillac group. This was good because they kept their jobs, but it wasn't good because most of the people in the Cadillac group were Lisp people to begin with, and it was tough to see people half-forced into a project and language they didn't care for while the language and projects they loved were being bled dry.

Bob's reasoning was based on assuming that Lisp was a mature market declining away. It certainly isn't large in 1996, but there still are thriving Lisp companies, some of which have grown since then. Bob's interest was partly like the board's: He wanted to win either financially or by being the CEO of a successful company. He actually didn't care what the company did, and he didn't particularly care about the people in it, except to the extent they could help his plans. Or at least this is how it seemed to me and to many others. So. when he started cash-cowing Lisp, people started leaving and grumbling about Bob.

Bob had a lot of bad qualities. He smoked a lot. We had a nice large second floor porch with a roof over about half of it, the middle half. There was a phone out there and Bob spent the whole day—8:00 A.M. to 5:00 P.M.—out there on the phone smoking or meeting with his direct reports. I never knew who he talked to on the phone, but there were few tangible results except for his financings.

It was unusual for me, who had helped raise the first $6 million, to be left out of the fund-raising. This should have been the same situation as the earlier fund-raising activities to which my comments and help were central. But Bob wanted to do it alone, probably so he wouldn't have to share the credit for any success.

I had learned since our first meeting that the reason he talked the way he did was that his speech apparatus was almost always connected to his thought process and what I was hearing was his thinking out loud. This partly explains why I could understand only about half of what he said. Others thought he was pretty smart, and maybe he was, but it was hard for me to tell. I don't think I'm a particularly stupid person, but many conversations with him were mystifying to me—and interminable. He would talk for hours on end, rambling about while he tried to unravel a thread of reasoning or solve a problem. At first I took what he was saying as an explanation or an answer—it was more like a dream.

Bob cared a lot about saving money, and so we called him *Bottom-Line Bob*. Others less kindly called him *Bob Requires a Human Host*, after the evil character in *Twin Peaks*.

೫ ೫ ೫

We needed to have a close connection to a compiler because we had to modify it to annotate source code. We made a no-cost deal with Oregon Software in Portland and with Sun for the Free Software Foundation C++ compiler called G++. In both cases we were able to get a proof of concept going, but not much more.

We tried to get Sun, AT&T, and other compiler companies to go along, but they were rightly not interested in doing a lot of work for a development environment with no obvious (to them) market. So we decided to buy a compiler company, called Peritus. It was a local company that had produced a compiler with very good compiled-code performance. It took six to nine months to get the entire deal done, mostly because the lawyers took so long. The tried and true lawyers we had hired early on who were told to protect us from mistakes with OEMs weren't told anything different about this deal and so tried to protect us. After that Bob fired them and went with one of the Palo Alto–based Silicon Valley–style law firms.

Peritus was a small 12-person company with some OEM revenues and a shoe-string operation. When the deal was done we moved them to our building and placed them at the center, physically, of the Cadillac group. They were highly paid—nearly off our scale—but their knowledge, talent, and work ethic surpassed ours, which surprised me.

On the editor front we tried to work with Free Software Foundation (FSF) to modify Emacs to support our editor protocol. The guy from FSF was a bust. We were also using FSF's GDB as the debugger, and we worked with Cygnus Support on that front.

In the end we had to do all the work ourselves because it simply wasn't getting done or was done so poorly that the results were unusable. We wrote our own grapher, which we handed over to NCR when they became a partner. In all, the work went slowly.

The Lisp guys who were turned into C++ developers suffered about a factor of three decline in productivity for about the first six months to a year, which improved to only about a 30% loss in the steady state.

Tony, who stayed on despite the humiliating demotion, became our primary business partner negotiator. He finally nabbed DEC (now Digital) when their Lisp group folded because it could not compete against our direct-sale product. Although he didn't negotiate the final details, he got them turned around. He patiently negotiated the NCR relationship over an 18-month period. NCR wanted a good C++ environment on their Tower line of 386-/486-based UNIX computers.

I relied on Tony for lots of difficult things. When Bob arrived, he had the habit of using very foul language in meetings. At Lucid we had a fair number of female managers, including the director of marketing, most of the development managers, and the documentation manager. They found his language extremely offensive, and the rest of us merely shifted in our seats when he let one fly.

I asked Tony to speak to him about it, and it stopped.

ॐ   ॐ   ॐ

We had really bitten off a little more than we could chew with the tasks of modifying code that we had not written and which was maintained by volunteers—the FSF stuff.

In October 1990, I asked Carol Sexton to run the Cadillac development group, and she carefully made a detailed schedule which had Cadillac ready for Beta in April 1992. Bob and the marketing director told me "wrong answer, we need it in a year." They didn't like the fact that Carol took into account vacation and sick time. Although we tried to cut back on functionality, there was little to cut. We had not yet experienced the problems with Emacs and GDB.

Bob became more nervous, but when we previewed Energize at OOPSLA in October 1991, it was the runaway hit of the show. People lined up to see demos. We started ramping up a sales force and a support department—we had never before done serious sales ourselves. We had thousands of leads from OOPSLA and things looked rosy. The financial projection of the sales vice president were unbelievably good.

Then troubles with Emacs hit, and we needed to move over more of the Lisp guys to help out. Troubles with GDB and the grapher NCR took over caused more problems. Then there was the bug curve. People took vacations and got sick.

Then there was the Object Design Inc. (ODI) problem. We had selected ODI's ObjectStore as the OODBMS to implement the persistent object store when the simple one we implemented wasn't fast enough. But we were the first customer of ODI's with a commercial product, and installation of the server required root privileges and was just plain hard and dangerous.

We shipped Energize in April 1992, two weeks after the date Carol Sexton had originally planned. We had thousands of leads, but the orders took a long time to get because by that time Centerline (formerly Saber) had a product or people had already started projects with ad hoc tools. Not the least drawback was that AT&T was talking about its own development environment.

Anyhow, the orders did not come in at a rate to keep us afloat according to our plans. We got a $1.3 million bridge loan.

At the end of the summer (1992) I took a partial leave of absence (half time) to work at Stanford, though it was actually mostly at Lucid. I took one of the Cadillac guys with me. We thought this would help save money when we did our second layoff in September. I remember thinking that we needed to adjust our strategy and assess where we were before we could effectively lay people off. Bob didn't think so, so the Lisp marketing guy and I tried to come up with the best idea of what we would do with the now rapidly declining Lisp revenues.

On the Lisp side the OEMs were doing poorly because they had no incentive to push the product, so Bob negotiated back the rights back to almost all the vendor lines. This increased the amount we got per sale, but that was more than offset by the lowered volume because we had no sales force, really, to handle Lisp.

Bob also believed that marketing was not worth building up—perhaps because he was a marketing person himself and thought he could do all we needed. No one really even knew we were still in the Lisp business.

We laid off about 20 people, some of whom were near founders who had lost heart. Included were the vice president of sales and a drunk that Bob hired as CFO. Bob got sick that day and didn't come in.

I went on leave and watched events from afar. Before I left, I negotiated a new position with the company—Lucid Fellow. For a while I had been engaged in mostly marketing activities by writing articles and columns and appearing at shows and as a speaker. Part of my deal was that my activities for a quarter were reviewed and if what I was doing was not what the CEO thought was important, there would be further negotiation and a new plan put in place.

To replace me as effective vice president of engineering we hired one: Warren. Warren was a very well known Lisp guy who had run a large group at a large hardware company, but he had been moved out and went on to a smaller hardware company. His management skills were poor, but I was unable to figure that out from his references and the other checks I made. When I talked to him, he told me the right things about how to run development. Bob was very enthusiastic, and the only negative I heard from Warren's references was that he often sided with the engineers too much. We hired him.

I returned full time to the company when it was in a very bad state. During the previous year the developers had rejected Warren, and I had partially returned to solving problems for them. This was not good for Warren, but his behavior was bad, too. He really didn't like having A players around him, and he got into fights.

In June 1993, just before Bob took off for his two-week golfing vacation in the UK he told me he wanted to measure the developers by their effort alone. I argued that results were the right indicator, but he said, no, he wanted me to identify the top 10 lowest-effort people and warn them that they had until September to straighten out or they would be fired. He told me that effort was equivalent to hours put in per week.

We had a lot of people with digital lines into their homes, and they worked odd hours particularly on weekends, so it was hard to establish how many hours they worked.

It was easy to figure it out for Patrick, though, who was the chief architect and technical director of Energize. He was a strong family man and worked precisely 40 hours per week unless there was a crisis or a release coming up. I found out as best I could how much other people worked, and Patrick topped the list of "slackers."

When Bob returned I showed him the list, and he dropped the issue.

ℬ ℬ ℬ

Bob had an interesting view of developers, one that I think is shared by a lot of CEOs in high-tech companies. Bob felt that developers were lazy and coddled, thought everyone else in the company was stupid or incompetent, never made schedules, and always overengineered or padded their plans. His disdain became apparent when we faced the prospect of Matthieu Devin quitting about a year before Lucid folded. Bob took Matthieu out on the porch and launched into one of his speeches. He told Matthieu that he believed that Matthieu thought he had extraordinary skills as a developer and was therefore indispensable. But in fact— Bob said—he (Bob) would be able to get 200 developers on the porch by nine the next morning to fill Matthieu's position and that each one of those developers would be smarter and more talented than Matthieu.

What Matthieu possessed, Bob argued, was unique in-depth knowledge of Enegerize, and therefore Matthieu should take a sales position where he would earn a handsome commission.

ঞ্চ ঞ্চ ঞ্চ

What happened to Energize? It never took off though it was doing reasonably well when the VCs gave up on Lucid. Energize was, I think, an excellent product that might have done better under different circumstances. In 1993 it won the Jolt Cola Programmer Productivity Award. Here is what kept it on the ground:

- It used too many computing resources. It was a true three-tier architecture with a database server, an application server (the kernel), and the clients (Emacs, the grapher, and so on). Because the database server was essentially performing a virtual memory function, there could be network performance problems at times. The clients were pretty fat, and when you tried to put the kernel and clients and compiler on the same machine, you had paging problems.

- We had problems with quality because we were using public-domain software.

- We had our own compiler on only a few platforms. Until the end we had a product only on the Sun product line.

- C++ had its own problems, being a complex language where interest in OO languages came mostly from COBOL programmers and shops where the level of language competence was not on par with what was needed to conquer C++. C++ itself suffered a strong backlash beginning in 1993 and lasting at least until mid-1995.

- The complexity of the C++ compilation model made incremental compilation difficult when you also tried to use truly compiled code instead of a Lisp-like or Smalltalk-like implementation that could support more runtime-based processing.

- Lucid had a small sales force and no marketing activities, so it was a push sale.

ঞ্চ ঞ্চ ঞ্চ

In 1992 I started to get back to writing—fiction and poetry. I was attending a few local workshops and classes. I applied to some national workshops and got into three, including Bread Loaf. After Bob dropped the effort thing, I went to the workshops, and at Bread Loaf I was taken under the wing by Mark Strand, the 1990 U.S. Poet Laureate. He strongly encouraged me, hinting at potential great-ness. I decided at that point to give it a serious try. Bread Loaf was a heady experi-ence because Strand denigrated just about every poet in his workshop, and I was the exception that caught peoples' attention. I stayed in New England a few days after Bread Loaf to visit friends and haunts. Victoria Hamilton said she was com-ing up to Boston one day and suggested that we get together for lunch.

We met at a place in Cambridge and chatted a bit. The board had asked for Bob to save $500,000 over the next six months, so I knew there would be a layoff.

After we ordered and I talked about Bread Loaf, she told me Bob wanted me to leave, and if I didn't do it gracefully on my own he would lay me off.

I was a little shocked, since I thought our agreement covered exactly this case. Anyhow, it turned out the graceful exit he wanted was a leave of absence. I didn't take the whole thing very well and contacted a lawyer. The lawyer and I worked out a good deal leaving me as chairman of the board. I stayed on the payroll until December and got some other concessions. It took me about three days to find another job when I got back from New England, at ParcPlace Systems, Inc., with a nice bit of stock. ParcPlace went public nine months later.

Bob either was not a very good long-term planner—long term being a few months—or was contemptuous of the board. When you lay off people your expenses go up for the month of the layoff if you offer a severance package. Then the savings start the following month. In September, the layoff month, expenses went up, and in October they went down. But in November Bob started hiring people again, and Warren, in particular, hired some of his favorite B and C players to replace the ones laid off. In November, salary-related expenses were back up to their August levels.

On the day of the layoff Bob got sick and didn't come in. It was either a lung problem or a heart problem, and he went to have an EKG. He asked me to oversee the layoff in his place. I thought about his smoking, and I wasn't sure what I hoped would happen. He had laid off a number of my close friends, the ones he thought were slacking off.

In May 1993, six months earlier, the board had started trying to sell the com-pany, and in December they received a $3 million to $4.5 million offer from Borland. The board rejected it even though, with what I learned about the OO market and the C++ market at ParcPlace (also in the C++ market), my advice was to take it. Later, Lucid got a $1 million offer from Veritas that it then pulled off the table.

At the February 1994 board meeting, I mentioned to the investors that Bob's September layoff hadn't netted anything. At the next board meeting in April they fired him and brought in a shutdown artist, Bill Goerke.

On Bob's last day—oh, they let him quit for show—I told him that ParcPlace had asked me to be vice president of development for a while. He said I should do it and to ask for a corner office with windows facing two directions—and a big couch. That way, he said, when those engineers come in, they'll know right away who the boss is. "Ha, ha, ha," he said.

ɣə   ɣə   ɣə

What was the immediate cause of Lucid's shutting down? Bob had signed some "standard" prepaid royalty contracts with HP, IBM, and Digital. For Lucid a standard prepaid royalty contract was one in which the hardware vendor paid a fee for us to do work and they did the marketing, and if sales went south, well hey, we both took a risk and too bad. Bob's deals had payback clauses. I called them loans.

Bob was not good at negotiating contracts. For one thing, people found him uncouth and obnoxious. Once I set up a negotiating session with ParcPlace's chairman, Adele Goldberg, who was the one who hired me three days after learning my plight at Bob's hands. ParcPlace had a C++ environment. She and her vice president of marketing came prepared to drop their product and pick up Energize as the one they would sell. Bob wouldn't even let her get to the point of proposing the idea. He had decided early on that this competitor had to be shown how resolute we were, and besides they couldn't have anything to offer us anyway. So he talked and talked and smoked and laughed.

Furthermore, once he had the contracts he wasn't good at managing them. In 1992, we got an ARPA contract to modify our C++ compiler and loader to be able to load C++ code into Lucid Common Lisp so that interoperability was inexpensive and automatic, that is, you could subclass C++ within CLOS.

The contract was predicated on cost sharing: ARPA would pay us $250,000, and we would put up $250,000 worth of additional labor. In the spring of 1993 Lucid needed around $180,000 to make its plan. Bob told the developers to charge to ARPA anything that even vaguely could be considered work for them. We were in the process of trying to get our loader to work for Sun—part of a deal with them—and so that work was charged to ARPA. When we had gone through all ARPA's money, the ARPA project was shut down.

We did not deliver on time and didn't plan to. We were lucky ARPA decided they wanted the work done rather than see us in jail or make us pay for one of our competitors to finish the work—both possibilities. They had granted contracts to other parties based on getting the results of this project. This was the last gasp for ARPA to use Lisp for anything. Bob not only killed the Lisp market, but also salted the field, as one developer told me when Lucid was shut down.

Bob told me and others on many occasions during the last years that it didn't matter what the Lisp market did because within a year "either Cadillac would make us rich or else we'd be out of business." He felt that this justified eating up the Lisp market and our position in it. The image I had was that from the *Back to the Future* movies in which the time machine DeLorean was accelerated to moderate speed, at which point the time effect would kick in. For maximum tension the DeLorean would usually be accelerated toward some obstacle like a building or a chasm, and the time effect would kick in right at the last instant. This is how Bob ran the company the last few years. He accelerated Lucid toward bankruptcy because either richness or bankruptcy would kick in. He felt this was the right risk to take.

Bob had accumulated $4.5 million in debt against something like $4 million to $5 million per year in revenue and $4.5 million to $5.5 million in expenses. The board did not want to keep Lucid afloat by paying back the loans, and that's why Lucid folded when it did.

But Bob didn't own exclusive rights to sleaziness. Bill Goerke had his own endearing streak of it. In November 1993 Lucid signed a deal with INS, a Japanese company that wanted to distribute a Japanese version of Energize in Japan. The development would cost $1 million with around $700,000 up front. By the time June rolled around, the work was nearly complete and was staffed by three Lucid developers and two on-site INS developers. The president of INS came to visit on June 8, Bob's last day, which was to be the day that Bob and the INS president finally met and "completed" the agreement by shaking hands and looking each other in the eye. The INS president would be meeting Goerke instead.

Goerke needed the remaining $300,000 from INS to support a reasonable plan for long-term survival, or at least $150,000 to survive until September. Of course, INS knew what was going on because the INS engineers were around, and they knew that a layoff was imminent. One of the INS developers met with the president and Goerke and Warren. The conversation went like this.

The INS president said that he would pay the $300,000 if he knew that the project would be completed on time and that because he had been an engineer (or knew a lot about engineering) he knew that the project would not be completed on time unless the very people on it remained on it until completion. Bill looked him in the eye and said, "I give you my word today that no Lucid engineer on that project will be laid off."

Two or three days later, all three were laid off. Warren didn't like these particular engineers, and one can only speculate on what the motives were and why things were done the way they were. But INS decided not to pay and that was the last straw.

To some American businessmen, one's word means nothing when money is involved. Besides, one's word only signals intention at the moment—it is not a promise like a contract carefully reviewed by lawyers and signed in front of witnesses. Except, in some cultures it is a promise.

In December 1994 in *UNIX Review*, Andrew Binstock wrote:

> *Certainly, many failures within Lucid persisted long past any reason-*
> *ably excusable period: the late delivery of the Energize programming*
> *environment, its daunting installation, the lack of upgrades to the*
> *compiler, and an inability to move out of the shadow of its founder,*
> *Dick Gabriel. By the time Energize shipped and Gabriel was*
> *replaced, the company was already mortally gored. However, these*
> *two factors, while important, were not the primary cause of Lucid's*
> *downfall. The central cause was that Lucid underestimated how dra-*
> *matically the market for UNIX development tools has changed. That*
> *change can be summed up in one word: SunPro.* (Binstock 1994)

This article goes on to point out that capitalism is like evolution, that only the fittest survive, and that SunPro produced the best environment. Objective compari-
sons showed this not to be true, that in evolution a species survives when it has
numbers, not when it is the best.

In March 1995, Renee Deger wrote the following in an article entitled "Blinded
by Science" in *Venture Capital Journal*:

> *The créme de la créme of software engineers had flocked to Lucid and*
> *thrived in its academic, think-tank-like corporate culture. Even when*
> *the company ran into some financial problems, forcing it to lay off*
> *some developers, several of them continued to work for free. . . .*
>
> *An argument could also be made that Lucid management and*
> *their backers were slow to recognize their miscalculations, letting the*
> *company's formidable technical accomplishments blind them it its*
> *market missteps.* (Deger 1995)

This magazine tells the stories of companies from the VC's point of view, and naturally the venture backers were not to blame, even though they had held a majority share of the company since 1985 and a majority on the board the whole time.
They were kept up to date with numbers and research at the board meetings,
which were held every month for the first seven years and every six weeks after
that.

Sure, we made mistakes—lessons from them are in the next essay, "Money
Through Innovation Reconsidered"—but mistakes were made everywhere in
sight. I don' think developers can be blamed for doing what they were asked to do.

৵৹   ৵৹   ৵৹

The day after Bob quit he and his wife moved to England. When Renee Deger
tried to call him for the *Venture Capital Journal* article, "a message left at Mr
Kadarauch's home in England was not returned by press time."

Victoria Hamilton remarked to me a year after Lucid had been shut down that Bob was a tragic character: He seemed so talented and smart, but everything he touched went bad.

Although I have to admit bias because of my hatred of him and what he did to my company, I cannot place all the blame on Bob's faults. More blame, I think, must be ascribed to the American business system and the business education system. Bob learned to run a business as an abstraction. He wasn't able to understand the market we were trying to penetrate; he didn't want to understand the customers' needs except only insofar as it was necessary to make them pay, he didn't care much about the company's employees—what he seemed to care about was his position of getting credit for success and the bottom line. There is nothing wrong with caring about the bottom line, but there is everything wrong with being obsessed with it. These traits were learned at school and in his earlier business career.

Bob always said that blame was for children and dogs.

ɣə   ɣə   ɣə

My daughter was born in 1987, and my second wife divorced me in 1993 after a two-year separation. I lost the house on the hill, and I lived out of the trunk of my car for the first year of our separation. I then hooked up with one of the Lucid technical writers, with whom I now live in Mountain View.

ɣə   ɣə   ɣə

The world sometimes has a long memory, and when you stick out of the crowd a little, it's hard to predict how that will affect you.

After I had been at ParcPlace for a year, I was asked to "reengineer" engineering, which I did for a year as vice president of development. At the tail end of that year ParcPlace decided to merge with one of its competitors, Digitalk. I was not interested in being a vice president of engineering for the merged company especially with a three-site operation on the horizon, and I'm not really into management per se. I was happy to let the Digitalk vice president take over.

As it turned out, however, I would not have had a choice. ParcPlace was eager to merge and needed to make some concessions to Digitalk to cement the deal. One of Digitalk's board members had been one of Lucid's, one of the less important members on the board, representing a venture capital firm. Perhaps from his own knowledge or from reading Renee Deger's piece, he remarked that I had had a bad influence on Lucid and that I was at least a partial cause of its failure from having been too technical and too much opposed to management. When I quizzed ParcPlace's CEO about this, he said that the board member in question was "weak" and so his opinion was not taken seriously.

ℬ   ℬ   ℬ

If he or she is lucky, a developer will work for a company that carries an emotional hold. I cared more about building a company that people would want to work for than a company that would make people rich. I think I built a place where I liked to work and I was hurt to see it fold. I think, also, I built a place—possibly by accident—where some of its employees liked to work

In January 1991 when we had our first layoff, one of the people who had to go, Chris, had been hired about three months earlier. He later married Jan, my administrative assistant, who divorced one of the developers (whom I laid off in September 1993). Chris sent an e-mail message to everyone, which I excerpt here:

> *To: Lucid*
> *Subject: So long*
>   *It probably goes without saying that I'm sorry to be leaving. I'll miss you all. Despite the briefness of my time at Lucid, I'm finding that this is first time that I have become emotional about leaving a job.*
>   *To all of you, who made me welcome when I arrived, thank you. A special thank you to the other 370-ists, to my two office mates, to all who answered my questions and provided advice, to Burton and Robert for their help and patience with my occasional special requests, and to Jan for the much-needed hug therapy after I got the word.*
>   *The bottom-most of all bottom lines is this: If my fairy godmother had appeared an hour before [the hiring manager] was to call with the job offer and told me that I would be laid off in January, but had also given me a preview of what my time at Lucid would be like, I would still have taken the job. It's been a good 3+ months.*
>   *Lucid is a fine company, staffed by as fine a group of people as I could hope to find anywhere. It's been a pleasure to get to know you, and an honor to be of your number for a time. I wish you all, and the firm, the very best of luck.*

~

Money Through Innovation Reconsidered

I would guess that fans of capitalism generally believe that innovation is the critical success factor and that natural evolution derived from competition makes the world better for consumers.

Every word of that belief is true, but the assumed meaning is not. Rather, the assumed meaning is that companies are rewarded for *their* innovation where innovation means invention, that the more innovation the better, and that consumers get a better world by leaps and bounds. Let's look at some evidence. The first is the editorial by Andrew Binstock quoted in "Into the Ground: C++":

> *The net effect shows that the forces of capitalism are much like those of evolution: the fittest survive. And when the fittest leap forward in their abilities, many weak or sick competitors are driven off or eaten. The benefits are clear: consumers such as you and me have better tools.* (Binstock 1994)

No less an authority than the editors of the *Economist* appear to share this belief. In a lead editorial on Bill Gates and Microsoft they wrote the following:

> *Antitrust policy must try to strike a balance between allowing market leaders to profit from their innovations and stopping them from abusing their power.* ("How Dangerous" 1995)

In a backing piece in the same issue they wrote:

> **Innovation.** *Computing, telecoms and the media have all seen rapid technological change. A stream of new ideas and products has sustained vigorous competition in most areas of these industries, driving costs and prices down. Thus, even if the product market were monopolised, trustbusters could afford to be sanguine if producers of new*

> *ideas were still able to make their way to market, or at least to force*
> *dominant companies to keep innovating and cutting prices them-*
> *selves. But if such innovations also became monopolised, antitrust*
> *authorities would be right to worry.* ("Thoroughly Modern Monopoly"
> 1995)

The first problem is thinking that innovation means invention. Innovation means "to change a thing into something new, to renew, or to introduce something for the first time into the marketplace." The *Economist* seems to understand this partly because their lead editorial on Gates says this a few lines above the quoted passage:

> *As a young Harvard drop-out, he gladdened every nerd's heart by*
> *selling IBM a software system [MS-DOS] that his own tiny company,*
> *Microsoft, did not even own.* ("How Dangerous" 1995)

On the other hand, the backing piece refers to innovations as "a stream of new ideas."

But even in innovation there is a degree of improvement implied by "alter" or "make new," which is the root meaning of the word. I'll adopt the term *radical innovation* to mean an innovation based on new ideas rather than on incremental improvements to known ideas.

The second problem is in thinking that innovation causes the world to greatly improve for consumers, as witnessed by Binstock's comment, "when the fittest leap forward in their abilities."

My thesis is simple: Invention, radical innovation, and great leaps forward do not produce revenue commensurate with the required effort in the software industry, and invention usually doesn't work in any industry.

Before we get too general or abstract, let's look at some examples, starting with Microsoft. First, as the *Economist* points out, Microsoft didn't even own DOS when it sold it, so it did not invent it. Moreover, at the time IBM innovated—*introduced to the marketplace*—MS-DOS, its technology was at least 15 years old, perhaps older. Even if we look at Windows 95, which is just coming out as I write this, the newest ideas in it date to the mid-1970s, and the core of it is still rooted in inventions of the 1950s and 1960s. Windows 95 is an innovation in the true sense because it is a renewal of those old ideas in the current context and contains some improvements over them, yet the ideas are the same. It contains no stream of new ideas.

To be precise, the core operating system ideas of multitasking and threading, address space protection, and file system organization were well known by 1965. The idea of window-based user interfaces was well known by 1975, the ideas of hypertext (that's what OLE really is), mouse interaction, and menus were known in the late 1960s. Pop-up menus and drag-and-drop were invented in the early 1970s, I believe.

The artwork is new; the attention to detail in the interface is important; the upgrade to a modern computing platform makes the ideas effective rather than merely amusing; and the documentation and on-line help systems make it all palatable.

In short, there are plenty of reasons that Windows 95 is good for consumers—it moves the technology center of gravity up to the late 1960s from the late 1950s—but few of those reasons have to do with invention or radical innovation.

I believe Microsoft is pursuing the correct strategy for a technology company, but this strategy has nothing to do with invention, radical innovation, creativity, or imagination.

Let's look at UNIX. UNIX is an operating system written as a free alternative to then-existing operating systems with multitasking capabilities, such as Multics, in contrast to whose name the name UNIX derived. UNIX was developed at Bell Labs and later major improvements were made at the University of California at Berkeley. A copy of UNIX went out on basically every tape that was delivered with a PDP-11 and later with every VAX as freeware. Universities used it because it was free and it was good enough and because the sources were included so that local budding wizards could customize it to local use.

From the mid-1970s until nearly the mid-1980s, UNIX was unknown outside the university setting. But around 1981 a group of grad students, graduates, and faculty from Stanford and Berkeley and some others founded Sun Microsystems (SUN was an acronym for *S*tanford *U*niversity *N*etwork, which was the project for which the workstation later known as the Sun 1 was built) and chose to use "standard" or, at any rate, existing components: the Motorola 68010 processor, Berkeley UNIX, and the Stanford networking hardware.

Now UNIX is the default workstation operating system.

When UNIX first came out there was nothing inventive about it; in fact, in some ways, it was poorly engineered. A good example of this is the PC-losering problem we encountered in the essay "The End of History and the Last Programming Language."

The PC-losering problem occurs when a user program invokes a system routine to perform a lengthy operation that might require significant state, such as IO buffers. If an interrupt occurs during the operation, the state of the user program must be saved. Because the invocation of the system routine is usually a single instruction, the program counter (PC) of the user program and the registers do not adequately capture the state of the process. The system routine thus must either back out or press forward. The right thing is to back out and restore the user program PC to the instruction that invoked the system routine so that resumption of the user program after the interrupt, for example, will reenter the system routine. It is called *PC-losering* because the PC is being coerced into "loser mode," where "loser" was the affectionate name for "user'" at MIT when the problem was solved there in ITS, one of the MIT operating systems of the 1960s and 1970s.

ITS has several dozens of pages of assembly language code dedicated to backing out of a system call so that the normal context-saving mechanism of saving the PC and registers will work. The trade-off was made that implementation simplicity was sacrificed so that the interface to the system in the presence of interrupts would be preserved: Programmers need know only that when an interrupt occurs and has been handled, the main computation can be resumed by restoring the registers and jumping to the saved PC.

In UNIX as of the late 1980s the solution is quite different. If an interrupt occurs during a system call, the call will immediately complete and will return an error code. The trade-off was made that the simplicity of the interface to the system would be sacrificed so that implementation simplicity would be preserved, and therefore the implementation could be more easily checked for correctness: Programmers must insert checks for error codes after each system call to see whether the system call actually worked.

It might seem odd that one would write a system call and then have to explicitly check whether it worked—it returned, didn't it? But, UNIX doesn't need that 60 or so pages of complex and probably incorrect assembly language code that backs out of every system call, and therefore it was easier to make UNIX portable—UNIX was simpler and smaller.

UNIX chose implementation simplicity over interface simplicity, whereas while ITS chose interface simplicity. As you might suspect, many UNIX programs were incorrect because after an interrupt they would crash, but UNIX is an operating system still in existence and ITS is not.

Over the years, with so many people adopting UNIX, it was improved so that now it is a fairly good operating system—consider Mach and Solaris. The pattern is to start modest and improve according to the dictates of the users.

There are many examples of this pattern in industry. Japanese automobile manufacturers started by producing low-cost, moderate-quality automobiles for sale in the United States, and as they were accepted the manufacturers upgraded their product lines with improvements. It was well known in the 1970s how to make excellent-quality cars with lots of features—all you had to do was look at European cars—but that approach would have resulted in minimal acceptance. No one wanted to buy a luxury car or even a regular car from a company named Toyota or Nissan. But they might want to buy a minimally equipped, moderate quality car at a low price.

The pattern is to get something of acceptable quality into the largest marketplace you can and then later improve or add a narrower focus with higher-quality, more inventive products. Today many people look first to Japanese automobile manufacturers for luxury cars as well as for cars at all levels of quality and features.

In 1990 I proposed a theory, called *Worse Is Better*, of why software would be more likely to succeed if it was developed with minimal invention (Gabriel 1990). Here are the characteristics of a worse-is-better software design for a new system, listed in order of importance:

- *Simplicity*: The design is simple in implementation. The interface should be simple, but anything adequate will do. Implementation simplicity is the most important consideration in a design.

- *Completeness:* The design covers only necessary situations. Completeness can be sacrificed in favor of any other quality. In fact, completeness must be sacrificed whenever implementation simplicity is jeopardized.

- *Correctness:* The design is correct in all observable aspects.

- *Consistency:* The design is consistent as far as it goes. Consistency is less of a problem because you always choose the smallest scope for the first implementation.

Implementation characteristics are foremost:

- The implementation should be fast.
- It should be small.
- It should interoperate with the programs and tools that the expected users are already using.
- It should be bug-free, and if that requires implementing fewer features, do it.
- It should use parsimonious abstractions as long as they don't get in the way. Abstraction gets in the way when it makes implementation too hard, too slow, or hides information that shouldn't be hidden. (I once heard an interesting comment—sort of a motto—at a scientific computing conference: Abstractions = page-faults.)

It is far better to have an underfeatured product that is rock solid, fast, and small than one that covers what an expert would consider the complete requirements.

These are the benefits of a software system designed and implemented this way:

- It takes less development time, so it is out early and can be adopted as the de facto standard in a new market area.
- It is implementationally and functionally simple, so it can run on the smallest computers. Maybe it can be easily ported as well—if it uses a simple portability model. At any given time the mainstream computer users—whether individuals or corporations—are running hardware at least two generations old.

- If it has some value, it will be ported or adopted and will tend to spread like a virus.

- If it has value and becomes popular, there will be pressure to improve it, and over time it will acquire the quality and feature-richness of systems designed another way, but with the added advantage that the features will be those the customers or users want, not those that the developers think they should want.

The path of acceptance is that the worse-is-better system is placed in a position in which it can act like a virus, spreading from one user to another, by providing a tangible value to the user with minimal acceptance cost. There is little question it can run everywhere, so there are no artificial barriers. The system can be improved by the end users because it is open or openly modifiable, and its implementation is simple and habitable enough that users can do this.

This simple implementation provides a means for the originators to improve the system over time in a way consistent with how it's being used, thereby increasing the magnitude of the most important evaluation factors. Over time, the system will become what lucky developers using a more traditional methodology would achieve.

This may seem counterintuitive—many people believe that being competitive requires doing the absolute best development you can. The following is a characterization of the contrasting design philosophy, which I call *The Right Thing*:

- *Simplicity:* The design is simple, both in implementation and interface. Simplicity of implementation is irrelevant.

- *Completeness:* The design covers as many important situations as possible. All reasonably expected cases must be covered.

- *Correctness:* The design is correct in all observable aspects. Incorrectness is simply not allowed.

- *Consistency:* The design is thoroughly consistent. A design is allowed to be slightly less simple and less complete in order to avoid inconsistency. Consistency is as important as correctness.

There really is only one implementation requirement:

- It should use hard abstraction throughout. Elements must be properly encapsulated in order to achieve information hiding.

The acceptance path for a right-thing system is that it is the right thing off the bat, and even though it came late to the marketplace, it is so wonderful that it is quickly accepted. Of course, it has to be on every necessary platform either right away or quickly. This scenario can happen, it is simply unlikely.

One of the more familiar examples of a right-thing system is the Macintosh and the Macintosh operating system. When the Mac was introduced in 1984 it was arguably the product of largely right-thing design though worse-is-better implementation. It used ideas and technology only 10 years old or so, and it was considerably ahead of its competition. One might say that Apple tried to run up the score on the competition by producing a product so far in advance as to be almost not in the same competitive milieu.

Although one could argue that the Macintosh today—some 10 years later—is a success, it enjoys only about 10% to 15% of the total PC market. It is not used in the mainstream; rather, its strongholds are primarily in desktop publishing, graphic design, and marketing organizations, whereas Microsoft platforms are used throughout the corporation. There are many good reasons for this failure to capture more of the market in addition to the problems of the right-thing philosophy, which we'll look at further. MS-DOS was licensed to all the PC clone manufacturers, so that consumers had a choice of a variety of price and performance characteristics. Of course, IBM, having strong influence among MIS departments, helped seed the PC in mainstream settings.

The popularity of the PC and DOS created the opportunity for a market of software on this platform: A company wishing to write and sell a software product always looked to the PC and DOS first because it had a larger market share to start with because IBM shipped DOS, other manufacturers did too, and they all shipped the same platform.

The difference between what happened to DOS and the Macintosh is an example of what is known as *gambler's ruin*. Suppose two players have equally large piles of pennies—pick a round number like a jillion. If the players have a fair coin and flip it, with one particular player taking a penny from the other if heads, vice versa if tails, what will happen? It would seem that the players would keep their positions of roughly equal amounts of pennies. But in mathematical terms, this is an event of measure 0—it will never happen. The probability is essentially 1 that one player will lose all his or her pennies. But if one of the players starts out with more pennies than the other, the probability that that player will end up with all of them is equal to the proportion of that player's pennies to the total number of pennies.

There is a tendency to think that somehow the free market is fair and that all seemingly fairly matched competitors will survive. If there is some aspect of a business that involves consumable resources used in competition, that business is subject to gambler's ruin.

In the case of PCs versus Macintoshs, the PC/DOS player started with many more pennies and won. However, there is more to it than chance. The Macintosh was clearly superior, yet it lost. Among the reasons for losing was that Apple didn't license its technology until 1995 so that a clone market didn't appear earlier (and one could say that waiting 11 years to do it was a suboptimal strategy).

There are other problems stemming from the difference between the two philosophies. One is that MS-DOS provided a simpler, more malleable base so that the aftermarket could more easily mold MS-DOS into what it needed. Once those characteristics of improvement were known, MS-DOS evolved.

ɣ̇ɜ   ɣ̇ɜ   ɣ̇ɜ

One of the obvious criticisms of worse-is-better is that there is something worse going on, that is, something not good or not right. It seems like the idea is intentionally to put out an inferior product and then hope that things go well. This isn't the case, but even this argument itself can be attacked.

When you say that a system is inferior to what it could be, you are basing that conclusion on an evaluation criterion. Necessarily you are using, perhaps intuitively, a metric based on a projection. That is, no one can evaluate an entire system in all of its use settings, so you are looking at either only part of the system or some of the settings, that is, a projection.

The problems with this are that a projection always loses information and the choice of projection is typically based on bias. For example, Modula-3 is a great programming language that is unsuccessful. Proponents of Modula-3 believe that it is a fabulous language and better, in particular, than C++. Modula-3 is based on a Cfront-like compiler, runs on a lot of computers, and is free. These are characteristics it shares with C++. Unlike C++, Modula-3 is optimized for mathematical and abstractional cleanliness. Moreover, it doesn't have a very good compiler, it lacks an environment, and it has no compelling systems written in it that people want to use and could use in such a way to see and appreciate the advantages of Modula-3. This last point can be understood by thinking about how much more likely it would be for people to use Basic English or Esperanto if there were a compelling piece of literature written in it.

Most important, the evaluation function—mathematical cleanliness—is not valued by the users, and perhaps they can't understand why it would be valuable except in theoretical terms.

The PC-losering example can be viewed this way, too. The characteristic valued by the ITS designer is simplicity of interface, which has led, in this case, to a large, complex system that can run on only a specific computer (the PDP-10) because it is written in assembly language *because* that is the only way to write it so that it's fast enough. UNIX is written in C, which is portable, and UNIX was simple enough early on that even this implementation choice offered acceptable performance.

In the modern era, we have come to favor simplicity over complexity, perfection over imperfection, symmetry over asymmetry, planning over piecemeal growth, and design awards over habitability. Yet if we look at the art we love and the music, the buildings, towns, and houses, the ones we like have the quality without a name, not the deathlike morphology of clean design.

In many cases, the software system that succeeds starts with a kernel of good technology, but it is not committed to fully to realizing that technology. By enabling users to live in the implementation to some extent or to mold the technology to users' needs while dropping hurdles to the use of the technology, that system is able to survive and evolve.

⚘ ⚘ ⚘

The right-thing philosophy is based on letting the experts do their expert thing all the way to the end before users get their hands on it. The thought is that until the whole grand structure is built and perfected, it is unusable, that the technology requires an expansive demonstration to prove its effectiveness, and that people are convinced by understanding the effectiveness of a technology, as if we needed to know that vehicles based on internal combustion engines could carry immense weights—tons and tons—or seat dozens of people before someone would be willing to buy a four-person, 15-horsepower car.

Worse-is-better takes advantage of the natural advantages of incremental development. Incremental improvement satisfies some human needs. When something is an incremental change over something else already learned, learning the new thing is easier and therefore more likely to be adopted than is something with a lot of changes. To some it might seem that there is value to users in adding lots of features, but there is, in fact, more value in adding a simple, small piece of technology with evolvable value.

The goal of a software enterprise is to make it into the mainstream, and being in the mainstream does not mean selling to a particular set of corporations. It means selling to customers with particular characteristics.

One of the key characteristics of the mainstream customer is conservatism. Such a customer does not want to take risks; he (let's say) doesn't want to debug your product; he doesn't want to hit a home run so he can move up the corporate ladder. Rather, he wants known, predictable improvement over what he is doing today with his own practices and products. He wants to talk to other folks like himself and hear a good story. He doesn't want to hear how someone bet it all and won; he wants to hear how someone bought the product expecting 10% improvement and got 11%. This customer is not interested in standing out from the crowd, particularly because of a terrible error in his organization based on a bad buying decision. These aren't the characteristics of someone who would love technology and build an extravagant product based on it; therefore, it is hard for a technologist to understand what this customer values.

The ideal of the free market supports this kind of growth. If you decide to spend a lot of resources developing a radical innovation product, you may be throwing away development money. Why bet millions of dollars all at once on something that could flop when you can spend a fraction, test the ideas, improve the ideas based on customer feedback, and spend the remainder of money on the winning evolution of the technology? If you win, you will win more, and, if you lose, you will lose less. Moreover, you will be out there ahead of competition which is happily making the right-thing mistake.

Microsoft won by putting out junk with a core good idea—and usually not their own idea—and then improved and improved, never putting out something too innovative, too hard to swallow, too risky.

When you put out small incremental releases, you can do it more frequently than you can with large releases, and you can charge money for each of those releases. With careful planning you can charge more for a set of improvements released incrementally than the market would have borne had you released them all at once, taking a risk on their acceptance to boot. Moreover, when you release many small improvements, you have less risk of having a recall, and managing the release process also is easier and cheaper. With incremental improvement, the lifetime of an idea can be stretched out, and so you don't have to keep coming up with new ideas. Besides, who wants to base one's economic success on the ability to come up with new ideas all the time?

The free market means improvement for the consumers, but at the slowest possible rate, and companies that try to go faster than that rate are almost always hammered down or killed. On top of these factors is the feedback loop in the free market. We've seen some reasons that it makes business sense to make small improvements rather than large ones. Because companies use these techniques, the pattern is established that the free market goes slowly. Given that, consumers now act in accordance with the free market. For example, because consumers rarely see radical innovation—it's too expensive, so companies don't do it, and a series of incremental improvements seldom if ever amounts to a radical innovation—they suspects its value. You might say that consumers are conditioned by the free market against radical innovation.

When you add the risk aversion of the mainstream marketplace to the minimal innovation fostered by the free market, it is easy to see that the right-thing is just too risky to try unless you really are sure it will work.

ॐ ॐ ॐ

The key idea is to identify the true value of what you bring to marketplace, to test those ideas in a small context, to improve them in a participatory manner, and then to package that value in the least risky way.

Let's look at the Lisp example. In order for Lisp to succeed as Lucid promoted it, the customer would have had to buy into AI; buy into using an unusual language; buy into the peculiar development environment with its own code construction, debugging, and maintenance tools; and accept the view that the standard computing world was at the other end of a narrow foreign function interface. This is too much to ask someone to accept when the value to the customer is a simple rule-based computing paradigm from AI and incremental development from Lisp. There is no reason not to have presented expert-system technology in more familiar surroundings or to introduce incremental development using a Lisp constructed more like a traditional programming language.

If you decide to go whole hog and produce a right-thing product, you may have made too much of an engineering commitment, certainly in terms of effort put into the product. If the product is not right, it will be too large and complex to modify to be more in line with customers' needs. So the very investment you might have thought was the way to put distance between you and possible competition by making the effort for entry too great is the very impediment to modifying your product to be what customers need.

When you release a modest product first, however, the sheer amount of typing necessary to adapt is small, and therefore can be done quickly, which means that your company is making rapid transitions in the marketplace, transitions your customers may require.

The ideal situation is that your proprietary value is small compared with the total size of your product, which perhaps can be constructed from standard parts by either you or your customers or partners.

There is a saying adapted from something Wade Hennesey said about his own way to making money:

Wade's Maxim: *No one ever made money by typing.*

What this means in our context is that you cannot try to build too large and complex product by yourself—you need to get parts from other places if your product is complex, and you must make your value clear and apparent, and it must be a simple decision for a customer to use your technology.

ⁿ   ⁿ   ⁿ

If you go out with a product without cachet, you might not like the results. *Cachet*—a word whose meaning has changed recently to include the characteristic of having a positive or desirable aura—is what will attract your customers to your product. For example, Netscape has cachet because it is the hip window into the Web.

Cachet is that which makes a system or language attractive over and separate from its objective features and benefits—it's why kids ask for particular toys for Christmas. There is nothing wrong with your customers acting like kids and bugging their parents—their managers—into buying them your toy.

Cachet is how you appeal to your early adopters, whose successes pave the way for acceptance into the mainstream. For many early adopters, technological innovation is enough, but you should make sure that the cachet is technological only and not based on overwhelming mass of technology. I use the term *acceptance group* to refer to people who must accept your product and technology in order for you to be successful—at first they are the early adopters, later the mainstream.

The larger you want your acceptance group to be, the lower technical skill level you have to aim for. This is not a matter of elitism, it's a matter of mathematics. And if you aim for a lower technical talent group, you have to provide a simple habitat—your system—for them to have to learn and inhabit.

Furthermore, the larger the acceptance group, the smaller and lower-power the computer they will be using. The less technologically advanced the target acceptance group, the less likely they will be to upgrade their computers unless there is a specific reason to do so. And it is unlikely your system will be the ultimate reason.

Nevertheless, any acceptance group needs to see that your system has the right mythos, the right cachet. Their first impression must be good in order to generate word of mouth, so it must have visible value right out of the box. If your system has a lot of complex functionality, it will be difficult to make sure the first look turns into a good first impression. The less functionality it has, the more controlled an initial look the users get. If you provide a free or cheap implementation with sources, then you might add a "wizard" component to your acceptance group, adding not only a free development arm but also cachet.

ఞ   ఞ   ఞ

Don't be afraid to find the rhinoceros to pick fleas from. There is nothing wrong with attaching your fortunes to those of a platform manufacturer or other system provider whose star is bright and gaining brightness. For example, it has made sense for the last 10 years to bet your company on Microsoft by writing software for DOS and Windows. Especially smart is being able to use parts of the rhino's products and technology to fill out your product. The less innovation you do, the better. Run just fast enough to win, but don't ruin your chances in the next race.

ఞ   ఞ   ఞ

Recall that Andrew Binstock invoked evolution:

The net effect shows that the forces of capitalism are much like those of evolution: the fittest survive. (Binstock 1994)

The popular idea even today is that evolution operates by making improvements—some large and some small. Darwin himself recognized that the effect of natural selection in making improvements was local at best. Darwin was writing his work when Britain was in the midst of its industrial expansion and its interest in showing that the free market led to improvements. Darwin was also under pressure to show that the press for perfection was inexorable from slime to people vectored through apes.

The theme of this theory is wedging out another species through competition—and this is just what Binstock believes is happening.

To respond to the pressure he was facing, Darwin came up with his wedge theory, which stated that the panorama of life was chock full of species occupying every ecological niche. Each species was like a wedge, and the only way that a new species could find a place in the world was to wedge out another one, and the way that happened was by being better somehow.

Undoubtedly this happens in many cases, but usually only in cases of small local improvements. For example, the human brain has increased in size since the first appearance of *Homo sapiens*, and this happened because a large brain had advantages, and so population dynamics selected for this trait—perhaps early men and women preferred to have intercourse with large-headed members of the opposite sex.

But this cannot explain how a large complex brain came into existence in the first place. Until something like a brain, only smaller, reaches a certain size and complexity, it has no purpose and doesn't really do anything. Therefore no selections are based on it except ones irrelevant to its ultimate use. This means that there was no reason not to grow increasingly larger brains—maybe such a brain simply belonged to someone more attractive. Eventually some environmental change occurred in which the large brain just waiting for something to do had a new purpose—language, for example—and its usefulness started to dominate natural selection.

To get to the point of understanding why brains can't just have grown and grown we need to look at mass extinctions. The best-known extinction was that of the dinosaurs. Dinosaurs and mammals overlapped by 100 million years, plenty of time for any wedge-related competition to have increased the mammals' niche or even forced out the dinosaurs if the mammals were so much better than dinosaurs. However, it took a disaster—currently believed to be a comet or asteroid hitting the earth—to dislodge the dinosaurs. The small mammals were able to survive the cloud-induced winter or the flash-induced heat that resulted but the dinosaurs were not. The mammals had something that enabled them to survive, and almost certainly it was something marginal or irrelevant until the catastrophic event—

otherwise you have to believe that evolution operates by the future influencing the past.

Natural selection is a mechanism to reject changes not to establish them. In fact, natural selection is used to slow down changes in the areas that matter—if a particular wing structure works, you don't want to try changing it. Therefore, those parts of an organism most central to its survival mutate over time the most slowly. In fact, biologists use the rate of mutation to determine whether some puzzling organ or structure has a purpose: The higher the rate, the less important purpose it has.

Only things that are relatively worthless change rapidly and dramatically. These worthless things provide variety, and someday an environmental change can make one of those changes or a related group of them important to survival. Then that one or that group will join the ranks of the natural-selection protected, and perhaps some formerly static parts may no longer be essential and can begin to change.

For example, we use tires for automobiles, but in Africa and India where cars aren't so numerous, people use them to make sandals. If a disaster occurred in which cars and industry disappeared, car tires might thus be used to shoe people. Nothing in the design or intended purpose of tires had anything directly to do with sandals, but quirks of the new environment make them useful for the new purpose. Then perhaps tires could begin to be improved for their new use.

Mass extinctions teach us this when we look at the details, but those details are too extensive to go into in this essay. I recommend *Eight Little Piggies* by Stephen Jay Gould (1993) for those interested.

In other words, natural selection provides very little incremental improvement. Rather, almost all dramatic change occurs because the environment changes and makes the worthless invaluable.

I think that this works in the marketplace as well. The simulation-based mechanisms of Smalltalk still are useful, but Smalltalk's success in the mid-1990s as a business-oriented language stems from the use of those mechanisms to model naturally, not simulate, simple business objects. This was not one of Smalltalk's design goals, yet it has turned out to be the key success factor.

Population dynamics also makes a difference. Dinosaurs coexisted with mammals for 100 million years, with the rat-sized mammals making no headway. And nothing about the mammals forced out the dinosaurs through competition.

ℬ ℬ ℬ

The lesson is to put out your small technology nugget, not typing too much, and wait to see whether the environment changes so it has an interesting new use for your nugget and then change your product to take advantage of it and how it's used. Make a small, simple wing, wait 'til flying takes off, then build a flying machine.

ɣ⟩   ɣ⟩   ɣ⟩

These ideas on innovation might seem odd, but they echo those of prominent economic thinkers. Roland Schmitt and Ralph Gomory wrote:

> [The Japanese company] gets the product out fast, finds out what is wrong with it, and rapidly adjusts; this differs from the U.S. method of having a long development cycle aimed at a carefully researched market that may, in fact, not be there. (Schmitt and Gomory 1988, 1989)

And L. M. Branscombe wrote this:

> After carefully assessing the functional requirements and the permissive cost of a new product for consumer markets, the [Japanese] engineering team will work on a series of designs, incrementally approaching the cost target, testing for consumer acceptance. The initial design will very likely incorporate technical processes of a most sophisticated nature, taken from the best publications in science. But they will be used in an exceedingly conservative application. . . . When the product is introduced it already incorporates leading edge technologies with a high degree of extendability, but with little of the risk associated with pushing the limits of the technology too soon. American engineers faced with the same problem would spend much more time and money pushing the scientific level of the technology to a design point where it is clearly superior to proven alternatives before introducing it. . . . In all likelihood, their costs will be higher and risk of program slippage greater than the Japanese approach. And the technology in the product, when introduced, will be more difficult to extend incrementally. (Branscombe 1987)

Remember: No one ever made money by typing.

Epilogue

People build computers, write programs; a person is harmed when a bug occurs, people form software development teams, people read programs; people write compilers that read programs to create other programs, people write patterns to communicate programming knowledge to other people. Software is elegant or bogus to other people. Software serves a human function or fails to. There is no Plato's heaven where mathematical cleanliness sits supreme, where the correctness of an abstraction is alive.

Clean abstractions help people understand and fix things the way a clearly written sentence can make a hard concept accessible, and it would take just as many books on writing abstractions to help people get how to write good ones as it takes books on writing to explain how to write a clear sentence. And though there are perhaps hundreds of books on writing, none of them nor all together can really turn someone who cannot do it into a writer of clear sentences.

When we talk of architecture, we are talking about art as well as engineering. As Jim Coplien (1995) pointed out, Vitruvius, the classic Roman architect, characterized architecture as the joining of Commodity, Firmness, and Delight (Pollio 1960). In software engineering—if there really be such a thing—we have worked thoroughly on Firmness, some during the last 10 years on Commodity, and none on Delight. To the world of computer *science*, there can be no such thing as Delight because beauty and anything from the arts or the so-called soft part of human activity has nothing to do with science—it is mere contingency.

But to take people out of software development is to leave it empty.

My purpose in writing these essays has been to glorify humanity in its struggle to remain human though the weight of science and management and business leans heavy on that struggle, sees it in opposition to elegance, efficiency, and profit.

231

Engineering is a discipline that fosters creativity to contrive means to a goal, and when we think of engineers, we think of bridge designers or the people who design the physical structures of skyscrapers, or the person who can build a radio out of a box of wires, resistors, transistors, power supplies, and capacitors.

But there are river engineers. The Mississippi River has a broad floodplain, which floods many hundreds of square miles around the main course of the Mississippi every few years; and the course of the Mississippi changes from time to time as erosion and climate-related forces change the river's equilibrium.

The Army Corps of Engineers was asked to harness the river and to control 20-year floods—a 20-year flood is a flood so great that it appears, statistically, only every 20 years—so that the rich floodplain could be planted and harvested, so that homes and towns and cities like St. Louis could be safely built, so that the river would stay in its banks and remain navigable. To do this they built control structures that use the power of riverflow to dig channels deeper, built dams and release points, bulldozed high levees. And it mostly worked, though in the early 1990s a series of heavy rain years caused catastrophic flooding, and the question was whether the river control structures made the floods more destructive than they would have been without them.

The river cannot be tamed because we cannot control everything about the river and the weather; worse, we cannot even model or mimic or understand well enough how the river operates to predict how it will behave, so how can we control it except by applying large control structures and continually repairing them as the river eats and picks away at them?

River engineers are engineers who do their jobs by trying to model small parts of rivers in idealized miniaturized laboratory mockups, by building control structures, and by repairing them when they inevitably fail. This is not the picture we are accustomed to for other engineers.

The river is human nature and human failings, and it runs through software as it does nowhere else in human endeavors. The salt sweet tears, the edgy new love affair, the first birth, the exhaustion falling on exhilaration, frustration and anger, the kicked heart of rejection, and all the world of life finds its way into the lines of code, the designs, the architectures and frameworks we find essential to running our system of life in the political and economic world. We cannot test the river, we cannot model it, we cannot understand even the smallest part of it to the level of science in high school chemistry. And because the river and the warming and cooling of the earth cannot be figured, because the man and woman and the loving and hating cannot be figured, some engineers can only build, hope, and in the end, repair.

References

Alexander, Christopher. 1964. *Notes on the Synthesis of Form.* Cambridge, Mass.: Harvard University Press.

———. 1968. "The Bead Game Conjecture." *Lotus* 5: 151.

———. 1975. *The Oregon Experiment.* New York: Oxford University Press.

———. 1977a. "On Value." *Concrete* 1 (December): 1, 6–7.

———. 1977b. *A Pattern Language.* New York: Oxford University Press.

———. 1979. *The Timeless Way of Building.* New York: Oxford University Press.

———. 1985. *The Production of Houses.* New York: Oxford University Press.

———. 1987. *A New Theory of Urban Design.* New York: Oxford University Press.

———. 1991. "The Perfection of Imperfection." In *Roots and Branches: Contemporary Essays by West Coast Writers,* ed. Howard Junker. San Francisco: ZYZZVA.

———. 1993. *A Foreshadowing of 21st Century Art: The Color and Geometry of Very Early Turkish Carpets.* New York: Oxford University Press.

Alighieri, Dante. 1994. *The Inferno of Dante.* Trans. Robert Pinsky. New York: Farrar, Straus, and Giroux.

Balzer, Robert, Frank Belz, Robert Dewar, David Fisher, Richard Gabriel, John Guttag, Paul Hudak, and Mitchell Wand. 1989. "Draft Report on Requirements for a Common Prototyping System," ed. Richard Gabriel. *SIGPLAN Notices* 24 (March).

Binstock, Andrew. 1994. "Editorial." *UNIX Review,* December.

Borges, Jorge Luis. 1962. *Ficciones.* New York: Grove Press.

Branscomb, L. M. 1987. "*Towards a National Policy on Research and Development.*" Delivered at conference of the Council on Research and Technology (CORE-TECH) and Conference Board, MIT, October 8.

Carroll, Martin D., and John F. Isner. 1992. "The Design of the C++ Standard Components." In *C++ Standard Components Programmer's Guide.* Murray Hill, NJ: AT&T and UNIX Systems Laboratories.

The Chicago Manual of Style. 1993. 14th ed. Chicago: University of Chicago Press.

Clinger, Will, and Jonathon Rees. 1993. *The Revised⁴ Report on Scheme.* IEEE Standard.

Coplien, James O. 1994. "Borland Software Craftsmanship: A New Look at Process, Quality, and Productivity." In *Proceedings of the 5ᵗʰ Annual Borland International Conference.* Orlando, Fla., June 5.

———. 1995. "Software Development as Science, Art, and Engineering," *C++ Report* 7 (July/August).

Dataquest. 1992. *CASE/Software Development Tools.* San Jose, CA: Dataquest. [This study does not give Lisp, PROLOG, and Smalltalk figures; the ones shown were determined by personal communication with one of the authors.]

Deger, Renee. 1995. "Blinded by Science." *Venture Capital Journal,* New York, March.

Dingle, Herbert. 1979. Time in Philosophy and Physics." *Philosophy* 54.

Feyerabend, Paul. 1987. *Farewell to Reason.* London: Verso.

Fowler, H. W. 1987. *A Dictionary of Modern English Usage.* Rev. by Sir Ernest Gowers. Oxford: Oxford University Press.

Gabriel, Richard P. 1985. *Performance and Evaluation of Lisp Systems.* Cambridge, Mass.: MIT Press.

———. 1990. "Lisp: Good News, Bad News, How to Win Big." Keynote address, known as "Worse is Better," presented at the European Conference on the Practical Applications of Lisp, Cambridge University, March. Reprinted in *AI Expert,* June 1991, pp. 31–39. Excerpted in *The UNIX-Haters Handbook,* by Simson Garfinkel, Daniel Weise, and Steven Strassman. San Mateo, CA: IDG.

Gabriel, Richard P., Nickieben Bourbaki, Matthieu Devin, Patrick Dussud, David Gray, and Harlan Sexton. 1990. "Foundation for a C++ Programming Environment." *Proceedings of C++ at Work,* September.

Gabriel, Richard P., and Guy L. Steele Jr. 1990. "The Failure of Abstraction." *Lisp and Symbolic Computation: An International Journal* 3 (January).

Gordon, Karen Elizabeth. 1984. *The Transitive Vampire: A Handbook of Grammar for the Innocent, the Eager, & the Doomed.* New York: Random House.

Gould, Stephen Jay. 1993. *Eight Little Piggies: Reflections in Natural History.* New York: Norton.

Grabow, Stephen. *Christopher Alexander: The Search for a New Paradigm in Architecture.* Stocksfield, UK: Oriel Press.

Haas, Ken. 1993. "How to Go from CFO to CEO (Without Really Trying): On Advancement." *The Red Herring: The Technology Financial & Investment Monthly.* November.

Harbison, Samuel P. 1992. *Modula-3.* Engelwood Cliffs, NJ: Prentice-Hall.

"How Dangerous Is Microsoft?" 1995. *The Economist,* July 8.

Johnson, Samuel. 1816. *The Idler by the Author of "The Rambler."* London: A. Strahan.

Knuth, Donald. 1969. *The Art of Computer Programming.* Reading, Mass.: Addison-Wesley.

McPhee, John. 1993. *Assembling California.* New York: Farrar, Straus & Giroux.

Moore, Geoffrey A. 1991. *Crossing the Chasm: Marketing and Selling Technology Products to Mainstream Customers.* New York: HarperCollins.

Nelson, Greg (ed). 1984. *System Programming with Modula-3.* Engelwood Cliffs, NJ: Prentice-Hall.

Pirsig, Robert M. 1984. *Zen and the Art of Motorcycle Maintenance: An Inquiry into Values.* New York: Bantam.

Pollio, V. 1960. *Vitruvius: The Ten Books of Architecture.* Trans. Morris Hickey Morgan. New York: Dover.

Read, Herbert. 1951. "Preface." In *Aspects of Form*, ed. Whyte Lancelot Law. New York: Pellegrini & Cudahy.

Schmitt, Roland W., and Ralph E. Gomory. 1988/1989. "Competition from Japan." *MIT Report.* December/January.

Steele, Guy L., Jr. 1984. *Common Lisp: the Language.* Maynard Mass.: Digital Press.

Steele, Guy L., Jr., and Richard P. Gabriel. 1993. "The Evolution of Lisp." Paper delivered at ACM Conference on the History of Programming Languages-II. Also in *ACM SIGPLAN Notices* 28 (March). Also in *History of Progamming Languages-II,* Eds. Thomas J. Bergin, Jr. and Richard G. Gibson. 1996. Reading, Mass.: Addison-Wesley.

Stroustrup, Bjarne. 1987. *The C++ Programming Language.* Reading, Mass.: Addison-Wesley.

Strunk Jr., William, and E. B. White. 1979. *The Elements of Style.* New York: Macmillan.

Tennent, R. D. 1981. *Principles of Programming Languages.* Engelwood Cliffs, NJ: Prentice-Hall.

"Thoroughly Modern Monopoly." 1995. *The Economist,* July 8.

Thucydides. 1981. *The Pelopponesian War.* Trans. Richard Crawley. New York: Random House.

Van Fraassen, Bas C. 1980. *The Scientific Image.* Oxford: Clarendon Press.

Varela, Franciso J. 1979. *Principles of Biological Autonomy.* New York: North Holland.

Williams, Joseph M. 1990. *Style: Toward Clarity and Grace.* Chicago: University of Chicago Press.